Date Due

TOWARD
A RATIONAL
POWER POLICY

TOWARD
A RATIONAL
POWER POLICY

ENERGY, POLITICS, AND POLLUTION

A REPORT BY THE ENVIRONMENTAL PROTECTION
ADMINISTRATION OF THE CITY OF NEW YORK
JEROME KRETCHMER, ADMINISTRATOR

PREPARED AND WRITTEN BY
Neil Fabricant
&
Robert Marshall Hallman

George Braziller   *New York*

This Report was originally submitted to the Mayor's
Interdepartmental Committee on Public Utilities in April, 1971.

For information address the publisher:
    George Braziller, Inc.
    One Park Avenue, New York, New York 10016

Standard Book Number:
    0-8076-0623-5, cloth;
    0-8076-0622-7, paper

Library of Congress Catalog Card Number:
    70-163462

First Printing
Printed in the United States of America

PREFACE

This document was prompted by the Environmental Protection Administration's activities as a member of the Mayor's Interdepartmental Committee on Public Utilities, by the controversy over Consolidated Edison's proposed expansion at Astoria, Queens and by a request from the Temporary State Commission on the Environmental Impact of Major Public Utility Facilities for the views of EPA concerning appropriate state procedures for siting electric power facilities. It was prepared and written by Neil Fabricant, Chief Counsel of EPA, and Robert Marshall Hallman, Deputy Counsel. The authors are grateful for the invaluable contributions of Carolyn B. Harris, Staff Economist, and Dr. Sidney Socolar of the Department of Physiology of Columbia University.

TABLE OF CONTENTS

-v-

INTRODUCTION

In the closing days of the 1970 session of the State Legislature, Governor Rockefeller introduced legislation to invest the
Public Service Commission with exclusive power to determine the
need and location of all future transmission lines and electrical
generating plants in this state.

Though legislation on transmission lines was enacted, public
opposition stopped the passage of the power-plant siting legislation and a Temporary State Commission on the Environmental Impact of Major Public Utility Facilities ("Temporary Commission")
was appointed instead, with a mandate to develop a new proposal
for introduction in the 1971 session. We believe that the report
which follows will be of assistance to the Temporary Commission.

The present Environmental Protection Administration of the
City of New York became involved in the issue of power siting in
May of 1970 when the Mayor presented the question of approving
the construction of a 1600 megawatt (MW)*, fossil-fueled plant
by Consolidated Edison Company of New York, Inc. ("Con Ed") at
Astoria, Queens to his Interdepartmental Committee on Public
Utilities. The ensuing controversy, played out against a back-
drop of a serious air pollution alert and an equally serious
power crisis, raised one of the most significant environmental
problems which the nation now faces and has no adequate policy
or mechanism for resolving.

---

*One MW is equal to 1000 kilowatts.

The problem is the conflict which is fast developing between demands for increased electric power and demands to protect the environment and public health.

On the one hand, electric power cannot be generated or supplied without serious adverse effects - air pollution and its attendant effects on health, water pollution, radiation hazards, noise pollution, despoiling of the landscape, depletion of our resources.

On the other hand, demand for electric power is rising at a phenomenal rate, far faster than the population.

There is now no rational and comprehensive policy, on the local, state or national level, to attempt to resolve these conflicting interests. There is hardly even a rational debate, at least on any level that could make a difference.

No existing governmental or private body is equipped to analyze in depth the total societal costs and benefits of continuing or decreasing the growth in demand for electric power. None is capable of determining whether or under what circumstances environmental concerns should outweigh power demands, or vice-versa.

The power companies and the regulatory agencies that are supposed to supervise them have a dominant purpose - to meet all demands raised by the economy and the public for electric power.

Government and the electrical industry, including utilities, have failed to examine or deal with the social costs of the "demand" constantly fostered through advertising and a broad array of promotional practices.

No meaningful effort has been made
to develop methods for eliminating the growing air and
thermal pollution from power plants, to develop more efficient
methods of power production, or to consult the public whose
health and well being are compromised by the prevailing policy
of meeting all demand regardless of social cost.

The public interest clearly requires that a rational
energy policy be developed for this state before the formulation
of standards, procedures, or regulations for the siting of
electric power facilities.

The situation today regarding the potential commitment of
resources to electric power is analagous to the situation in
the early 1950's, regarding the potential commitment then to
automotive transportation. The failure to assess the long-run
costs and benefits of the automobile has locked us into a
technology, subsidized by a massive Federal Highway Trust Fund,
which we are virtually unable to control; it is creating enormous
environmental problems.

Moreover, our commitment to the automobile has prevented
the allocation of adequate resources to the development of
urgently needed mass transit facilities, particularly for large
urban areas such as New York City.

We cannot afford to make a similar thoughtless commitment
to electric power without a complete understanding of its
potential long-range consequences. In this regard, the preamble
to the New York State Environmental Conservation Law (Chapter 140,
Laws of 1970,) enacted last Spring, is instructive:

> "Continued economic, technological and social progress
> is of little benefit if secured at the price of polluted

waters, contaminated skies, a waste of land and a
ravaged national heritage....

"Technological advances, and unwise resource
utilization have too often caused a serious burden
on the quality of our environment, posing a threat to
the life-giving ecological balance upon which man and
his world depend. This trend must be reversed.... New
efforts and new attitudes are required...."

Furthermore, we are concerned with the single-minded
commitment to nuclear power of Governor Rockefeller, his
New York State Atomic and Space Development Authority, and
the utilities in the state without a full and open debate
of the risks and benefits involved.

Following the Con Edison-Astoria debate in August, the
Environmental Protection Administration undertook a study to
begin to analyze the social costs of power generation, and
to make the case for the development of an energy policy that
will provide for essential needs while adequately protecting
the environment and public health, and making the best use
of limited resources.

Our study, which resulted in the following report, was
done over a six-month period with limited manpower and no outside
funding. While we believe that the report raises the questions
which must be answered before the state and the nation commit

themselves to a policy of unlimited expansion of power
generation, we recognize that resolution of the energy-environment
conflict requires the commitment of far greater economic and
human resources than are currently available to this agency.

THE PROBLEM - EMERGING POWER (ENERGY) AND ENVIRONMENT NEEDS IN CONFLICT

Nationally, electric power consumption is now growing by
about 9 per cent a year. The electric utility industry estimates
that demand will double every 10 years, at least for the next
two or three decades. By 1990 -- from a base of 1965 -- this
would mean an increase of 450 per cent in a single generation.

Levels of sulfur oxides, nitrogen oxides and particulates
are already at dangerous levels around the country. New York
City has sulfur oxide levels three times higher than those
deemed safe by the federal government. Despite state and city
requirements for the use of low-sulfur fuels, prospects are dim
for the city to meet federal air quality standards even without
any new construction of power plants. Yet Con Edison Chairman
Charles Luce has declared that a 1000 MW plant will be needed
every two years to meet demand through 1980 in Con Ed's service
area -- an area in which population growth is negligable.

In particulates, New York City air exceeds by 33 per cent
the State air quality standards and in nitrogen oxides, the city's
average daily level has exceeded the point where a recent study by
federal air pollution authorities finds a significant increase
in the frequency of acute respiratory disease.

By 1990, we can expect a dramatic increase in respiratory
diseases, such as emphysema, bronchitis, asthma and pulmonary

fibrosis, as well as common colds, headaches and sore throats.

By the year 2000, the United States Atomic Energy Commission projects an increase from 20 to 900 nuclear power plants in America, the majority of which will be 1000 megawatts or larger. Though nuclear plants eliminate major air pollutants from the combustion of fossil fuels, they create substantial environmental and health problems as a result of radioactivity. Major problems are the management of highly radioactive, liquid wastes which must be isolated from man for centuries; the risk of a power reactor accident, spewing large amounts of radiation into the environment; spills of radiation during transport of nuclear fuels and wastes; emissions from plants and fuel reprocessing facilities. Radiation in large doses can cause acute injury or death within hours; small doses may show delayed effects on human tissues (e.g., cancer) and cause genetic damage, producing mutations.

A drastic increase in thermal pollution is expected to accompany a rapid growth in nuclear plants, which require 50% more water for cooling than fossil-fuel plants. On Long Island Sound alone, projected nuclear plants, together with existing plants, are expected to pour more than 7.2 million gallons of heated water per minute into the Sound by the early 1980's - more than the flow of the U.S. Niagara Falls - with unknown effects on marine ecology.

In the year 2000 projected power plants throughout the country would require half of the average daily natural runoff of water in the continental United States (excluding Alaska) for cooling.

Large amounts of valuable land are also at stake. For example, within 30 years, a total of 11,000 square miles would be devoted to electric transmission lines - an area roughly equal to the states of Massachusetts, Delaware and Rhode Island combined.

At the same time that power companies are projecting enormous increases in demand, and thus in pollution, they are engaged in a number of practices that are already costly in terms of strain on the environment; and the regulatory agencies have done little to curb them.

Funds committed to research and development by the utilities are minimal. One eighth of what is spent for advertising and promotion is spent for all research and development.

There is no meaningful search for more effective pollution control technology, for new supplies or methods of processing of low sulfur fuel or for funding a more efficient system of producing energy. This, in spite of the following facts:

- technology for controlling SO_2 and NO_x emissions from fossil fuel plants is inadequately developed.
- governmental requirements to burn low sulfur fuels or natural gas, compounded by oil import quotas and restrictions in domestic production, are resulting in an increasing shortage of low sulfur fuels.
- the efficiency level of power production from power plants remains at about one third, resulting in the production of large amounts of excess heat and pollution and wasted fuel though at least one promising avenue of increasing efficiency - magnetohydrodynamics - has been in existence since the 1920's and still remains undeveloped.

In spite of decreasing fuel supplies and increasing pollutants from fossil fuel energy production, regulatory agencies continue to permit utilities to create an ever-increasing demand for the use of electricity by permitting industry

- to project future demand -- unquestioned; to charge
  promotional rates, which decrease the unit cost of
  electricity as consumption increases, to engage in
  large scale advertising and promotional activities
  to foster that demand,
- to include advertising costs as operating expenses
  recoverable in the rates they charge customers,
- to practice load-balancing (promoting off-season
  demand to balance high peak-season demand -- which
  results in a new peak season in the off-season, rather
  than attempting to control the original peak season
  demand by, for example, imposition of peak demand
  surcharge.)

Lack of supervision by the Public Service Commission has
encouraged utilities in New York State

- to promote electric heating, though it can result in
  substantially more pollution and waste of valuable
  resources than direct home heating by natural gas and
  oil,
- to buy up valuable land for future use and do so without
  public disclosure,
- to build plants close to urban centers, which is
  cheaper, instead of purchasing power from another
  utility or building away from load centers, which may be
  more environmentally sound,
- to build larger units and power complexes, though this
  can intensify the impact of power generation on the local
  environment, increase the risk of a single breakdown causing a
  massive power shortage and increase reserve requirements, i.e.,

the need to build more plants,

- to omit from the sale price of electricity, the environ-

mental costs of producing and supplying power.

The United States Atomic Energy Commission is the major regulator of nuclear power plants. It is also a major promoter of nuclear power.

The AEC has refused to keep the public fully informed of the
risks and consequences of power reactor accidents. The last report was published in 1957 and dealt with reactors at least <u>six</u>
<u>times</u> smaller than those being put in service now.

The AEC has failed to reduce radiation emission standards
and to allocate a specific level of radiation exposure to nuclear
power facilities, though power plants in operation today appear
to be capable of meeting standards far below the levels permitted.

The AEC budget on nuclear safety research for the large water
cooled reactors to be placed in service at least for the next 15
years has been substantially cut.

The AEC is attempting to develop a safer method than the current one of storing high-level radioactive wastes in boiling, liquid
form in metal containers which must be changed at least every 20
years to protect against corrosion and leakage, but, the AEC's
current estimates are that this new method (solidification and
storage in salt mines) will not be available for large-scale use
for at least 5 to 7 years. Moreover, detailed studies remain to be

carried out regarding chemical, physical and radiological properties
of solidified wastes, as well as safety and environmental implications of storing them in salt mines.

The AEC has supported the federal Price-Anderson Act of 1957
which limits the financial liabilities of utility companies and their
suppliers for radiation damage resulting from major nuclear reactor
accidents to a minute percentage of possible harm to the public.
The industry has testified that they would probably abandon the
nuclear power business if this limitation on liability were dropped.

The AEC's criteria for siting nuclear power plants are extremely vague. Though it has claimed to oppose siting power plants
near population centers, Con Edison's Indian Point Units No. 1, 2
and 3 are located one mile from an area with 25,000 people.

Governor Rockefeller has committed the state to meeting future
power needs by the use of nuclear power. New York State does not
have an Energy Council. It has an Atomic Energy Council (which is
an arm of the State Commerce Department). It does not have an
Energy System Development Authority. It has an Atomic and Space
Development Authority, which, among other things, has the power
to buy land and make it available to utilities to house nuclear
power facilities.

While other states are setting standards for radioactive emissions from nuclear power plants that are more stringent than AEC
regulations, Governor Rockefeller has ceded exclusive regulatory
authority over New York's nuclear facilities to the AEC.

The Governor's Electric Power Committee (which had no environmental representatives) in 1967 advised obtaining all potential sites

for future nuclear plants "in time to prevent their preemption for
other purposes." The full accommodation at such sites of the public interest in health, safety , conservation, esthetics and recreation, according to the Committee, was to be assured at minimum
cost to the electricity-consuming public.

SUMMARY OF RECOMMENDATIONS

Government must take immediate steps to decrease overall demand for energy in general and electric power in particular, as
well as to ensure that essential needs are supplied with the least
possible harm to public health and the environment. If permitted
to continue unchecked, industry's efforts to expand the use of
electricity will inevitably result in irreparable damage to public
health and environment, and in crisis-rationing of power.

The Governor's 1970 power facility siting proposal, to vest
exclusive power to approve power plant sites in the Public Service
Commission, does not address the questions of unchecked demand for
electricity or the adverse environmental results associated with
electric power. In fact, the Commission's ability to override
opposition on the part of local communities affected by power facilities would enable the state-wide body to facilitate rapid expansion of power generating facilities at the expense of environmental considerations and may well eliminate the industry's chief
incentive to put its own house in order.

Accordingly, the Environmental Protection Administration
has developed a number of recommendations which we believe would

more directly readdress the environmental neglect of past energy policies. The recommendations include

- the immediate establishment of a 15-member Temporary State Com-

    mission on Energy Needs, the Public Interest and the Environment

    to formulate a rational, energy policy and environmental action

    plan for the state.

- interim procedures for siting power plants and transmission lines,

    until that policy has been adopted, which would provide for re-

    view and recommendations by a multi-interest, state siting com-

    mittee, with strong representation of environmental, health and

    community interests, and ultimate decisional authority in local

    (for power plants) and county (for transmission facilities)

    governing bodies.

- an immediate prohibition against all activities on the part of

    utilities that serve to promote or encourage the use of electric

    power.

- immediate measures to encourage research and development,

    including:

    - a requirement that utilities commit a fixed percentage of gross
      revenues to research and development and establish a program
      for undergrounding existing and future transmission lines;

    - the establishment of an Environmental Energy Systems and Resour-
      ces Corporation to assist utilities and others in securing more
      efficient and less-polluting energy systems and fuels, together
      with the creation of an Environmental Energy Systems and Resour-
      ces Management Fund.

    - a major increase in federal R & D funding to develop methods for
      increasing the efficiency (to save fuel and reduce pollution) of
      generating electric power; alternative sources of power such as
      solar energy, which appear to offer resource conservation, and
      some environmental, advantages; and technology for controlling
      noxious emission from fossil-fuel plants.

- immediate measures to improve control over the quality of

    utility equipment and meaningful penalties for failure to

    satisfy reasonable quality control standards.

- requirements for advance consultative planning and for the
  development of comprehensive long-range planning programs
  by utility companies, including governmental approval of
  agreements with customers expected to require substantial
  increases in electrical load.
- creation of five-member Citizen Advisory Boards for each
  utility in the state to provide a means for meaningful
  public participation in utility planning.

As regards the projected growth of nuclear power, our judgment is that no proposal to install additional nuclear facilities,
i.e., those that have not received a construction permit from the
AEC, in this state can be responsibly evaluated, or should be
supported, by governmental authorities or the public at least until
valid state standards are established regarding safety and radiation hazards; and federal, as well as state, authorities make public a comprehensive analysis of the risks and possible consequences
of major reactor accidents involving the large units (e.g., 1000 MW,
3000 MW) now being planned for service, as well as spills and leaks
of high-level, radioactive wastes produced by such facilities in
storage and transit. If acted upon in good faith, these conditions
can be met in a relatively short period of time. They are not
intended to and should not interfere with the satisfaction of
power needs in this state.*

*For example, all three nuclear plants scheduled for service between
now and 1975 have received construction permits from the AEC and,
thus, would not be affected. Including these facilities, New York
State utilities' planned power reserves for 1971, 1972 and 1973 are
29 per cent, 25.7 per cent and 37.7 per cent, respectively. Con Ed's
planned reserve for this year is about 30.3 per cent, expected to
rise to 32.6 per cent in 1972 and 38.1 per cent in 1973. These
planned reserves substantially exceed the 20 per cent reserve margin
recommended by the FPC and the PSC. There is, of course, some un-
(footnote continued)

Our other recommendations with respect to nuclear power include:

- abolition of the State Atomic Energy Council.
- repeal of the federal Price-Anderson Act of 1957 which limits
  the liability of utilities and their suppliers for harm
  caused by nuclear accidents and radioactivity.
- transfer of full regulatory authority regarding licensing,
  safety, public health or environmental impact of nuclear
  facilities at the federal level from the AEC to the EPA.
- review by the federal EPA of current radiation exposure
  and emission standards and establishment of new federal standards which set limits for specific nuclear facilities.

Our recommendations are all developed in the body and conclusions of this report.

(continued from previous page)
certainty as to whether all planned capacity will be placed in service on schedule or will operate reliably. Such problems, however,
largely reflect inadequate planning, possible construction delays,
management inefficiencies and inadequate control by utilities over
the quality and delivery of equipment.

II. Health Hazards and Other Environmental Problems Posed by
    Electric Power

  A. Health Hazards Created by Primary Air Pollutants
     Emitted by Fossil-Fueled Power Plants

Steam-electric power plants which burn fossil fuel are major

sources of air pollution nationally, on a statewide basis, and in

many local communities throughout the state. Although the utili-

ty industry is committed to nuclear power as the major source of

electric energy in the future, fossil-fueled plants are expected

to play a significant role at least until the end of the century.

The primary air pollutants emitted by fossil-fuel burning

power plants are sulfur oxides, nitrogen oxides and particulate

matter, i.e., soot, smoke, carbon, fly ash.* Such plants also

emit some trace metals such as vanadium and mercury.

On a national basis, electric power plants discharge about

50 per cent of all sulfur oxides, 25 per cent of all nitrogen

oxides and 25 per cent of all particulate matter. While motor

vehicles discharge about 60 per cent of all air pollutants in the

atmosphere by weight, they are not significant sources of sulfur

oxides or particulates and their relative contribution of nitro-

gen oxides depends on the number of other sources in each locality

involved.

Current estimates are that power plants in the United States

emit about 41.8 billion pounds of sulfur oxides and 9.24 pounds of

nitrogen oxides per year. Some federal officials have recently con-

_____
*Fossil-fuels include coal, oil and natural gas. Nitrogen oxides are
produced by the high temperature combustion of all fossil-fuels. Sulfur oxides are produced by the combustion of sulfur-containing coal
and oil; particulate matter is also produced by burning coal and oil.
The amount of sulfur oxides produced is directly proportional to the
amount of fuel burned and its sulfur content.

cluded that "unless vastly improved control technologies are developed and applied by the year 2000...,"* sulfur oxide emissions will increase 5 times to 209 billion pounds annually, nitrogen oxide emissions will increase 3.5 times to 32.34 billion pounds annually, and emissions of fine particulate matter will increase more than four-fold.

Another perspective regarding air pollution from power plants is gained by considering that an 875 MW plant, burning only 1% sulfur fuel oil, would emit about 55,000,000 pounds per year of sulfur oxides, 19,000,000 pounds per year of nitrogen oxides, and 900,000 pounds per year of particulates.

1. Sulfur Oxides and Particulate Matter

The excess deaths that occurred during periods of higher air pollution in the Meuse Valley, Belgium, in 1930, in Donora, Pennsylvania in 1948, London in 1952 (about 4,000 deaths) 1956, 1959 and 1962, and in New York City in 1953, 1962 and 1966 (about 168 deaths in 1966) were blamed largely on the combination of sulfur oxides and particulates in the air. Those disasters are euphemistically characterized by some, including utilities and their regulators, as air pollution "episodes."

When sulfur oxides are taken into the lungs, a variety of chronic respiratory diseases such as emphysema, bronchitis and

---

*"[o]n the global scale, the total emissions of sulfur by power plants would exceed those produced by biological processes and sea spray (142 million tons), since power plants in the United States alone would contribute about two-thirds of this total. Hence, emissions from power plants not only can dominate the local scene, but could become the primary source of global sulfur contamination." Niemeyer, L.E., McCormick, R.A., & Ludwig, J.H. Environmental Aspects of Power Plants, (Page 3), paper presented at IAEA Symposium on Environmental Aspects of Nuclear Power Stations, August 10-14, United Nations Headquarters, N.Y., N.Y.

bronchial asthma can occur. In 1969, federal air pollution officials issued a report, based on then available scientific information, documenting the levels of sulfur oxides in the air, plus the
lengths of exposure, at which specific adverse effects to health and
welfare are detectable ("air quality criteria"). They found that
adverse health effects result when (i) the level of sulfur oxides
exceeds 0.03 parts per million (ppm) on an annual average, and (ii)
when twenty-four hour averages exceed 0.11 ppm more than 1% of the
time, i.e., more than three days per year.* The Committee on
Public Works of the United States Senate recently cited this, as
well as federal air quality criteria reports relating to other
pollutants, in support of the Clean Air Act Amendments of 1970,
stating:

> "The Committee's concern with direct adverse effects
> upon public health has increased since the publication of
> air quality criteria documents for major pollutants....
> These documents indicate that the air pollution problem is
> more severe, more pervasive, and growing at a more rapid
> rate than was generally believed."(Emphasis added).**

The Division of Health Effects Research of the Air Pollution
Control Office (APCO)***of the federal Environmental Protection
Agency, in connection with the New York City Health Department and Air
Resources Department has undertaken an epidemiologic study of the health
hazards of air pollution exposure among residents of Westchester, the
Bronx and Riverhead, Long Island. According to Dr. Carl Shy, Chief of
the Epidemiology Section of APCO's Division of Health Effects Research,
the study

---

*Air Quality Criteria for Sulfur Oxides (NAPCA Publ. No. AP-50, Jan. 1969)
**Report No. 91-1196 of the Committee on Public Works United States Senate
91st Cong., 2d Sess., p.1 (Sept. 17, 1970).
***APCO was formerly called The National Air Pollution Control Adminis-
tration (NAPCA).

- 17 -

group has already observed:

> "annual average sulfur dioxide concentrations of 0.08
> ppm (i.e., about 3 times the safe level)...in the
> Westchester, Bronx and Astoria, Queens areas. These
> annual averages, and the concommitant short term peak
> levels exceeding 0.15 ppm (24-hour average) SO_2, have
> been shown to produce aggravation of asthma and chronic
> obstructive respiratory symptoms (chronic bronchitis and
> emphysema) in persons suffering from these incapacitating
> diseases. In our preliminary survey, we found that 10
> to 20 per cent of adults who are parents of elementary
> school children in the Westchester area have chronic
> obstructive lung disease. In addition, another 2 to 4
> per cent of the total population have active asthma.
> If another source of SO_2 emissions were added to this
> community, from 10 to 20 per cent of the total popula-
> tion would be subject to an additional health hazard.
>
> We have also found that many elderly subjects, some
> with chronic lung and heart disease, are living in
> apartment complexes located in that area. Previous
> studies...have shown a statistically significant in-
> crease in mortality rate among this segment of the
> population during short-term peak levels of SO_2 ex-
> posure. At lower levels, exceeding 0.04 to 0.12 ppm
> daily, a group of elderly subjects living in Chicago
> and having chronic obstructive lung diseases had a
> significant increase in the frequency of their symp-
> toms.*

Adverse health effects of sulfur oxides are greatest

when accompanied by particulates. Small pieces of particulate

matter e.g., carbon, often reach the lower respiratory

passages and lodge in the tiny air sacs which terminate them.

Sulfur oxides are adsorbed on these particles and brought

into contact with the lungs in concentrated amounts.

Sulfur dioxide may also be oxidized to sulfur trioxide,

which combines with water vapor to form sulfuric acid mists.

The acid mists are not only harmful to humans. e.g., eye

irritations, but   are also highly corrosive

*Report of Dr. Carl Shy, Chief of Epidemiology Section of the Division
of Health effects Research, APCO, accompanying letter from Kenneth
Johnson, Regional Air Pollution Control Director to Jerome Kretchmer,
Administrator, N.Y.C. Environmental Protection Administration,
dated 7/22/70 ("Shy Report").

to building materials, including stone, marble and steel, clothing (e.g., nylon stockings) and injuries to vegetation.

In addition to greatly worsening the health effects of sulfur oxides with which they become associated, particulates may be toxic in themselves and may injure the surfaces of the respiratory system. Moreover, "particles cleared from the respiratory tract by transfer to the lymph, blood or gastrointestinal tract may exert effects elsewhere [in the body]...."*

Air quality criteria for particulates issued by federal authorities in 1969 indicate that adverse health effects occur when the annual mean level of particulate matter exceeds 75 micrograms per cubic meter. They have cautioned, however, that "when promulgating ambient air quality standards, consideration should be given to requirements for margins of safety which take into account long-term effects on health and materials occurring below [this level]...."**

In addition, particulate matter decreases visibility, causes a wide range of damage to vegetation and property (e.g., corrosion of metals), and is a major source of grime and dirt which soils, as well as contributes to the deterioration of, buildings, statuary and textiles (particularly cotton, linen and nylon). Particulates may act "as reservoirs of acids, and thereby sustain a chemical attack..." which will damage even the most resistant kinds of material.***

_____

*Air Quality Criteria for Particulate Matter (NAPCA Pub. AP-49, 1969) p. 182
**Air Quality Criteria for Particulate Matter (NAPCA Pub. No. AP-49, Jan. 1969), p. 189.
***Id., at 186.

While the utilities are fond of pointing out that control devices exist which are capable of removing 98-99% by weight of the particulate matter emitted by power generating facilities, larger particles are more readily captured by control apparatus, than smaller particles. Thus, even though a control device may remove over 90% of particles in terms of mass, it will remove substantially fewer particles in terms of actual number. Yet smaller particles, particularly those in the submicron range, cause the greater biological harm since they much more readily penetrate into the lower respiratory passages.

In addition, particulate matter and carbon dioxide (also produced in sizeable amounts by fossil-fuel plants) may have serious, long-range effects upon the climate. Particulates may contribute to a general cooling of the earth's atmosphere by impending entry of radiation from the sun. On the other hand, carbon dioxide, which is virtually opaque to radiation emitted by the earth's surface, may contribute to overheating. As more carbon dioxide concentrates in the atmosphere, a "greenhouse" effect occurs which reduces heat loss through radiation from the earth's surface. A small rise in the earth's average temperature might start melting of ice caps and lead to flooding of coastal regions.*

---

*Environmental Quality, The First Annual Report of the President's Council on Environmental Quality (Aug. 1970), pp. 95-98; E.K. Peterson, The Atmosphere: A Clouded Horizon; Environment (April, 1970) pp. 32-40.

2. Nitrogen Oxides and Photochemical Smog

Of the nitrogen oxides, nitrogen dioxide presents the most serious health problems. Like sulfur oxides, nitrogen dioxide may cause chronic respiratory diseases such as emphysema, bronchitis and pulmonary fibrosis. Cellular degeneration may result from prolonged exposure and, at short term exposure, nitrogen dioxide causes eye and nasal irritation, pulmonary discomfort and irritation, including tightness in the chest.

The Division of Health Effects Research of APCO recently completed a study on school children and their families in Chattanooga, Tennessee, which documented a significant increase in the frequency of acute respiratory disease, including common colds and sore throats, among residents exposed to a mean 24-hour nitrogen dioxide concentration between 0.062 and 0.109 ppm (measured over a 6-month period).* APCO has also concluded that yearly average nitrogen dioxide concentrations exceed the adverse health effect value of 0.06 ppm in 10 per cent of cities in the United States with populations of less than 50,000, in 54 per cent of cities with populations between 50,000 and 500,000, and in 85 per cent of cities with populations over 500,000.**

Nitrogen dioxide, as well as nitric oxide, also has damaging effects on materials and vegetation. For example, leaf abscission and decreased yield among navel oranges has been observed at exposure to 0.25 ppm for eight months.

*Air Quality Criteria for Nitrogen Oxides (APCO Pub. No. 84, Jan. 1971).
**Id. at 11-8.

In addition to causing direct damage to health, plants and materials, nitrogen oxides react under the influence of sunlight with hydrocarbons (produced in part by power plants)* in the air to form the Los Angeles-type, photochemical smog. This smog mist not only affects visibility, but the oxidants (or smog products) in it can cause adverse health effects, as well as vegetation and property damage.

In general, one or more smog products, either alone or in combination, can cause irritation of the mucous membrane and eye, breathing difficulty, and reduce resistance to respiratory bacterial infection. They have also been implicated as accelerators of the aging process.

In March, 1970, federal air pollution officials issued ambient air quality criteria for photochemical oxidants. They found that adverse health effects, as shown by impairment of performance of student athletes, occur at hourly average concentrations as low as 0.03 ppm; exposure to hourly average concentrations of 0.025 ppm to 0.05 ppm causes eye irritation; exposure to hourly average concentrations of 0.05 to 0.06 results in aggravation of respiratory diseases.**

Specifically, ozone causes irritation of the mucous membrane which in turn may result in coughing, headaches, and pulmonary edema. On long-term exposure, ozone may result in a reduction in breathing capacity and structural changes in the lung. In humans,

*Major sources of hydrocarbons are automobiles, incinerators and industrial processes.
**Air Quality Criteria for Photochemical Oxidants (NAPCA Pub. No. AP-64).

adverse respiratory symptoms and a decrease in arterial capacity have been observed at exposure to concentrations of .3 ppm, and exposure of .6 to .8 ppm for two hours has resulted in impairment of the diffusing capacity of the lung. In animals, exposure to 3 ppm for several hours has caused hemorrhage of the lung.*

Peroxyacl nitrates and the photochemical smog associated with them causes irritation of the eye at low concentration levels. Higher levels aggravate pulmonary conditions, e.g., asthma, emphysema, bronchitis.

In addition, oxidants may directly affect psychomotor performance. One study has found a statistically significant relationship between oxidant levels and automobile accidents.** Oxidant pollution may, thus, impair driver performance by interfering with oxygen transport or by eye irritation and respiratory discomfort.

* * * * * *

Unfortunately, methods for controlling the air pollution hazards associated with fossil-fueled electric generating plants have not been adequatly developed.*** Low-polluting fuels, e.g., natural gas, low-sulfur oil and coal, are currently in short supply and the shortage is likely to continue for some time. Moreover, even if such fuels were available, air pollution attributable to those plants would continue to be a serious problem.

---

*Id., at 10-5, 10-6.
**Ury, H., Photochemical Air Pollution and Automobile Accidents in Los Angeles, Arch. of Environmental Health 17(3), pp. 334-342.
***See Section III. C., infra.

Also, at present, there are no commercially proven processes
for limiting stack emissions of sulfur oxides or nitrogen oxides.
Such processes are unlikely to be developed in the near future unless
government and industry drastically increase current levels of
funding and make a serious commitment in this area.

The lack of low-polluting fuels, as well as control technologies,
is primarily attributable to the failure of the utility industry and
government to allocate substantial time and resources to solving the
air pollution problems created by electric power; and the total lack
- at the federal and state levels - of a coordinated, resource
utilization and environmental protection policy designed to serve
the public interest.

3. Fossil-Fuel Plants Are a Major Source of Air Pollution Throughout New York State

(a) New York State*

On a statewide basis, power plants account for almost 75 per cent
of sulfur oxides (1.6 billion pounds per year), 27 per cent of particulates (196,000,000 pounds per year), 35.4 per cent of nitrogen oxides
(396,000,000 pounds per year) and 9.7 per cent of hydrocarbons. Power
plants are the largest single source of sulfur oxides in the State,
and the second biggest source of particulates** and nitrogen oxides.***

In the Capitol District****power plants contribute about 50 per cent
of sulfur oxides (182,000,000 pounds per year), 20 per cent of nitrogen
oxides (37,400,000 pounds per year) and 11.5 per cent of particulates
(23,000,000 pounds per year).

On the Niagara Frontier, which includes the heavily industrialized
Erie County, power plants produce 33 per cent of sulfur oxides (178,000,000

*This information is based on reports submitted by the New York State
Department of Environmental Conservation to the federal EPA.
**Industrial processes rank first.
***Motor vehicles rank first.
****This includes the following 13 counties: Albany, Schenectady,Schoharie,
Putnam, Ulster, Dutchess, Orange, Saratoga, Renssalaer,Montgomery, Colum-
bia, Rockland and Greene.

-24-

pounds per year), 18 per cent of nitrogen oxides (34,200,000 pounds
per year) and 18 per cent of particulates (30,000,000 pounds per year).

   (b) New York City*

In New York City, Con Ed's eleven power stations account for
approximately 40 per cent of annual sulfur oxide emissions
(314,000,000 pounds per year), 38 per cent of nitrogen oxide
emissions (228,000,000 pounds per year) and about 10 per cent
of particulate emissions (13,000,000 pounds per year). The
only larger source of sulfur oxides and nitrogen oxides is
space heating.

Con Ed's proposed new 800 MW unit at Astoria, Queens, will
emit about 15,000,000 pounds per year of sulfur oxides. This
alone would amount to approximately 5 per cent of all sulfur oxides
emitted in the City in 1975. The new unit will also produce
about 25,000,000 pounds of nitrogen oxides per year - about
4 per cent of all such emissions projected for 1975 - and 1,700,000
pounds of particulates per year. These calculations assume that
the company will be able to obtain adequate supplies of low
sulfur fuel, i.e., 0.37 per cent sulfur content.

   4. Levels of Major Pollutants in New York City Far
       Exceed Acceptable Air Quality Standards and Pre-
       clude Any Additional Power Plants in the City.

New York State's declared policy regarding air pollution
is "to maintain a reasonable degree of purity of the air resources
of the state, which shall be consistent with the public health
and welfare and public enjoyment thereof...."** In an attempt
to carry out this policy, the New York State Department of Environmental
Conservation (DEC) has established four sets of air quality standards
which vary according to the population

---
*The information set forth in the text was compiled by the City's
Department of Air Resources.
**Public Health Law, §1265.

density, industrial development, etc. of specific areas of the state.

Under the recently enacted, federal Clean Air Act Amendments of 1970 (P.L. 91-604) the federal Environmental Protection Agency is required to establish federal air quality standards. Current New York State ambient air standards will remain in effect if they are equal to or more stringent than the national standards.

According to the DEC, ambient air quality standards for the New York Metropolitan Area have been established at the least stringent level, "the one primarily designed to prevent adverse health effects."*

(a) Sulfur Oxides and Particulates

New York City has the dubious distinction of having the worst air in the country in terms of sulfur oxides. The level of sulfur oxides in New York City on an annual average basis is now over 3 times (0.10 ppm) the level regarded as acceptable by federal and state officials. Proposed federal and current state air quality standards for sulfur oxide are that (i) the level of sulfur oxides shall not exceed 0.03 ppm on an annual average and (ii) twenty-four hour averages shall not exceed 0.11 ppm more than three days per year.

The annual mean level of particulates in the City is about 100 micrograms per cubic meter (pcm), which also exceeds the proposed federal and current state air quality standard of 75 pcm designed to avoid adverse health effects. (The proposed

*Letter from Henry L. Diamond, Commissioner of DEC, to Mayor J.V. Lindsay, dated August 18, 1970.

-26-

federal standard for preventing damage to property and vegetation is 60 micrograms pcm).

As federal officials have recently pointed out,

"...great difficulty is being encountered (by New York City)in meeting the sulfur dioxide and particulate standards that have been adopted [by the State].... The sulfur dioxide standards are not even being achieved during the summer when emissions from space heating sources are at a minimum."*

At current levels, there is evidence that the combination of sulfur oxides and particulates present in New York City's air is responsible for the premature deaths of 1,000 - 2,000 New Yorkers per year. The Ralph Nader Study Group Report on Air Pollution reached a similar conclusion.**

This conclusion is supported by a recent study made by Dr. Thomas A. Hodgson, Jr. of the Division of Epidemiologic Research of Cornell Medical College. He found that mortality from respiratory and heart diseases in New York City is significantly related to levels of sulfur dioxide, and the combination of particulate matter with sulfur dioxide, ordinarily occurring in the City's air. The report states that:

"Sulfur dioxide and the combination of sulfur dioxide and particulate matter even more so are considered severe irritants of the respiratory tract, capable of causing sufficient stress upon the body in times of high air pollution to bring about death, the severe irritation of the respiratory tract may cause the heart to labor so hard to circulate oxygen through the body that the heart fails.... Air pollution is an environmental stress which yearly pushes many hundreds prematurely to their death."***

*Report of Donald Walters, Chief of APCO's Division of Abatement attached to letter from Kenneth L. Johnson, Regional Air Pollution Control Director, APCO, to Jerome Kretchmer, Administrator of the City's Environmental Protection Administration, dated July 20, 1970 (Walters Report).
**Vanishing Air, Ralph Nader's Study Group on Air Pollution (Grossman Publishers, New York, 1970) at p.809.
***Hodgson, Short-Term Effects of Air Pollution on Mortality in

Moreover, as noted above, deaths may occur during air pollution crises caused by atmospheric inversions, i.e., stagnating high pressure air masses which trap pollutants and force them down to ground level. On the average, New York City experiences "inversions" at least 5 to 10 days a year. According to the DEC, "During these adverse weather conditions, contaminants in the air frequently build up to alarming proportions.... It has been necessary for official agencies to implement an alert and warning system to curtail the operation of large sources during these (crises) ...."* For example, last summer the City experienced inversions for more than a week, which required the Mayor to declare the first stage of an air pollution alert, requiring 20 per cent cuts in the operation of incinerators and a switch to natural gas by Con Ed.

(b) Nitrogen Oxides and Photochemical Smog

The proposed federal air quality standards for nitrogen oxides are that the twenty-four hour average shall not exceed 0.13 ppm one day per year; and, that the level of nitrogen oxides shall not exceed 0.05 ppm on an annual average.

The proposed federal air quality standard for photochemical oxidants is that the hourly average shall not exceed 0.06 ppm. Current state standards for oxidants in the New York Metropolitan Area are that 24 hour averages should be less than 0.05 ppm and 1 hour averages should be less than 0.15 ppm.

New York City, Environmental Science and Technology, (July, 1970).
*Report on Con Ed - Astoria Proposal by DEC, submitted with a letter from DEC Commissioner H. L. Diamond to Mayor J.V. Lindsay, dated August 18, 1970.

Levels in New York City are Unacceptable

In 1969 and 1970, the maximum daily level of oxides of nitrogen in New York City was 0.25 ppm and the annual average level was 0.09 ppm, which is almost double the proposed federal standard and exceeds the 0.08 ppm levels associated with increased frequency of acute respiratory diseases in APCO's recent Chattanooga Study. It is virtually certain that the projected safe levels will not be met in the City in the foreseeable future.

Photochemical smog is becoming an increasing problem in New York City. The level of photochemical oxidants in New York City has risen substantially during the last three years. For example, the oxidant levels in the months of June and July of last year were six times the oxidant levels for the same months in 1965, 1966, and 1967.

Currently, New York City is experiencing significantly high levels of oxidants. The average daily level (six hour average) of oxidants in June of last year was 0.07 ppm. The maximum hourly average last year was 0.19 ppm, more than three times the proposed federal standard of 0.06 ppm.

Increasing concern over the rising level of oxidants in New York City is evidenced by the inclusion of an oxidant level alert in a proposed agreement between the City and the Federal Government regarding air pollution emergencies. The alert level is 0.15 ppm (one hour average).

B. RADIATION HAZARDS ASSOCIATED WITH NUCLEAR POWER

   1. Introduction

Nuclear power offers certain environmental and resource conservation benefits: it eliminates air pollutants released by the
combustion of fossil fuels; "breeder"reactors(projected for service
in the 1980's) which produce more nuclear fuel than they consume,
offer a possible means for substantially extending the life of
nuclear fuel supplies and conserving fossil-fuels for power, as
well as other useful purposes, e.g., petrochemicals, baterial
conversion to food.*

However, the lightwater, "burner" reactors now in use, and to
be used increasingly during at least the next 15 years, offer no
such resource conservation advantages. Such reactors use only about
0.6 to 1.2% of potential energy in uranium ores, whereas breeders
are expected to use from 60 to 90 per cent of uranium processed
from ore.** According to Joseph C. Swidler, Chairman of the New
York State Public Service Commission, this generation of reactors
is " unfortunately even more wasteful of limited uranium resources
than the conventional power plant is of fossil fuel."*** It has
been estimated that expanded use of current reactors would exhaust
the economically extractable world reserves of uranium -235, the
primary nuclear fuel, within the next 20 to 30 years.**** The fact
that the current generation of reactors will substantially drain,
rather than prolong the life of,fuel resources has led some to call

---

*Dean E. Abrahamson, Electric Power and the Environment, p. 21
(Scientists Institute for Public Information - 1970) ("Abrahamson
Report".)
**AEC Authorizing Legislation, Fiscal Year 1971 (Pt.3), Hearings
Before Joint Committee on Atomic Energy, 91st Cong., 2nd Sess,p.1205
(March 11, 1970) (hereinafter listed as "Fiscal Year 1971, pt. 3")
***Problems of Energy Supply In a Crowded World, address before the
Bar Association of the City of New York (October 15, 1970).
****Abrahamson Report supra at 12;David Rittenhouse Inglis, Nuclear
Energy and the Malthusian Dilemma, Bull. of Atomic Scientists (Feb.1971),
14,16. See also Donald F. Anthrop, Environmental Side Effects of
Energy Production, Bull.of Atomic Scientist (Oct. 1970), 39,41; M.King
Hubbert, Energy Resources for Power Production (publication authorized
by the Director, U.S. Geological Survey), presented at IAEA Symposium

for a termination of their development. According to one authority, "apart from temporarily catering to our craze for power [and serving to promote nuclear power]...reactors of this generation, technically refined though they appear, are too primitive to be worth developing for themselves."* Others, however, including Alvin W. Weinberg, Director of the Oak Ridge National Laboratory in an article in the June 1970 issue of the Bulletin of Atomic Scientists, maintain that useful experience can be obtained from the present generation of reactors in terms of handling radioactive wastes, controlling radioactivity and accident prevention. In view of the operational and safety problems remaining to be solved prior to successful development and acceptance of breeder reactors, however, it is an open question whether experience on current reactors will be able to be put to long-term use, as Mr. Weinberg suggests.

Nuclear plants are also alleged to have certain economic advantages over other types of plants. Although the capital cost of such plants is expected to be considerably higher than the capital cost for fossil-plants, the electrical industry maintains that operating costs(primarily fuel costs) are likely to be cheaper and, thus, the unit cost of power produced by nuclear plants will be cheaper.** The existing utility rate structure and method for calculating returns provide a strong economic incentive for utilities to promote nuclear power. The high capital cost of nuclear plants

on the Environmental Aspects of Nuclear Power Stations, August 10-14, 1970 United Nations Headquarters, New York, New York.
*Inglis, Nuclear Energy and the Malthusian Dilemma, supra at 16.
**Statement of Commissioner of the United States Atomic Energy Commission James T. Ramey in Environmental Effects of Producing Electric Power, Hearings Before the Joint Committee on Atomic Energy, 91st Cong., 1st Session (Pt. 1) p.131-33 (1969)(Hereinafter cited as "Hearings").

is included in the utility's rate base, which increases its allowable revenues.

But nuclear power poses substantial environmental problems,
e.g., current plants contribute 50 per cent more thermal pollution
than fossil-fuel plants,* and presents unique public health problems owing to the production of radioactivity.

2. Health Hazards

There is no good justification for assuming a threshold limit
below which radiation will not cause biological injury. According
to the Federal Radiation Council (FRC), established by Executive
Order in 1959 to advise the President on radiation matters affecting
health and to guide Federal agencies in formulating radiation standards, "...every use of radiation involves the possibility of some
biological risk either to the individual or his descendants." **

Exposure to large doses of radiation, i.e., 100 rem*** total
body exposure and above, poses an immediate and serious hazard to
human health. The potential biological effects of low-level radiation are technically difficult, if not impossible, to measure.
Although at present, there is a lack of data demonstrating substantial adverse effects at very low levels and rates of radiation exposure, the FRC, National Council on Radiological Protection (NCRP)

---

*See discussion of thermal pollution infra at
**Federal Radiation Council Staff Report (1960), p.1. The Internat-
ional Commission on Radiological Protection takes a similar position,
see Hearings,Pt.2(vol.I),supra, as does the National Council on Radiation Protection and Measurements. (See New York Times, Jan.25, 1971).
***The rem, which stands for roentgen equivalent man, is a unit of
measure of the average radiation absorbed per gram of human tissue.
The average absorbed radiation is in turn related to the biological
damage done to such tissue.
****The data supporting the conclusion that serious harm occurs at
this level of exposure has been gathered from persons exposed to atomic
bomb explosions in Hiroshima and Nagasaki, as well as medical patients.

and International Commission on Radiological Protection (ICRP) "have
maintained their basic philosophy - and conservative postulation
- that there would be effects in the low dose range proportional
to those observed at vastly higher dosages."*

The risk from radiation appears in large part to be proportional to the degree of exposure. Large doses of radiation can
cause acute injury or death within hours; small doses show delayed effects. The delay may be many years. According to Dr.
Clarence E. Larsen, Commissioner of the United States Atomic
Energy Commission (AEC), a current major concern involves the
delayed effects produced by relatively low doses of radiation,
accumulated over protracted periods of time.**

Exposure to radiation can have basically two effects on
humans: (1) somatic damage, or direct damage to body tissues
other than reproductive cells, which may cause various forms of
cancer, e.g., leukemia, central nervous system cancer, bone
tumor, thyroid cancer, lung carcinoma, miscarriages, cataracts,
shortening of life span, and damage to unborn children, e.g.,
mongoloidism, microcephally (abnormal smallness of head); and
(2) genetic damage to reproductive cells producing mutations,
e.g., fetal and infant deaths, deformities (physical and mental).***
Damage to human genetic material is one of the most potential

---

*Lauriston S. Taylor, President, NCRP, "What We Do Know About
Low-Level Radiation," (1971).
**Hearings (Pt. 1), supra at 247.
***E.g., Dr. Karl Z. Morgan, Director, Health Physics Division,
Oak Ridge National Laboratory, Never Do Harm, Environment (Jan./
Feb. 1971) p.28; Hearings, (Pt. 1), supra at 247-55.

-33-

effects of low levels of radiation.* Present knowledge of
genetic risks is, however, "very far from complete."**

The direct hazards associated with nuclear power all involve
the large amount of intensely radioactive wastes produced in
fuel assemblies, i.e., rods which contain the nuclear fuel, during
normal operation of nuclear power plants. This radioactivity
is generated   only consequent to operation of the plant.
Although these wastes are almost entirely retained within the
sealed fuel elements, they threaten humans and the environment
in several ways: (1) in the event that an accident in the reactor
should release a substantial part of this material to the external environment, the consequences could be catastrophic, particularly if the plant were in a populous area, resulting in intense radiation doses to many people and substantial contamination of the surroundings,e.g., food and water supplies; (2)
minute, but significant, fractions of the radioactivity in the
reactor are routinely and regularly released to the environment
via air and water; (3) similar but larger environmental releases
occur at nuclear fuel reprocessing plants where, after several
years use, the fuel elements, no longer economically useable,
are sent for recovery of their remaining fuel content and separation of high-level wastes; (4) accidents during transport of the
used fuel elements or radioactive wastes may cause releases of

---

*Environmental Quality, First Annual Report of the President's
Council on Environmental Quality (August 1970), p.141.
**Statement of Dr. William L. Russell, geneticist in Biology
Division of Oak Ridge National Laboratory, in Hearings, supra
at 633.

-34-

radioactivity; (5) at the reprocessing plant, most of the
radioactive matter from the used fuel is sequestered, but this
is such hazardous and long-lived material as to require isolated
storage for many centuries. Management of these boiling, radioactive wastes is a critical problem.

3. High-Level Liquid Wastes

The management of high-level radioactive wastes produced
in large quantities in the reactor fuel elements presents a
serious hazard associated with nuclear power generation.*   In
liquid form, high-level wastes contain several hundred to several
thousand curies of radioactivity per gallon and some of the
radioactive elements will remain hazardous for centuries.**
Strontium -90 (which when dispersed into the environment, enters
the food supply and tends to concentrate in human bones) and
cesium -137 wastes are considered hazardous for 600 years.

These wastes are much more radioactive than any materials
ever before handled by man. For example, about one billion gallons of water are required to dilute one curie of strontium -90
to current guidline levels for drinking water.*** High-level
wastes may contain as much as 50 to 100 curies of strontium -90
per gallon. According to the United States Atomic Energy Commission (AEC), "high-level wastes pose the most severe potential

_____

*The rate of generation of such wastes is roughly proportional
to the rate of power production.
**Charles H. Fox, Radioactive Wastes (1969), p.12, a booklet
distributed by the United States Atomic Energy Commission. A
curie is a standard unit of radioactivity representing the number
of atomic disintegrations taking place per second (37 billion).
***See, AEC regulations regarding allowable concentrations, 10
C.F.R. Pt. 20 (Appendix B), p. 161 (1970).

health hazard and the most complex technical problems in management." *

During the disposal of high-level, radioactive liquid wastes, there is a substantial danger of large amounts of intensely radio- active material escaping into the environment. High-level, radio- active liquid wastes are intensely radioactive and give off vast amounts of heat as the wastes decay - enough heat to keep the mixture boiling for years.

In 1966, a Committee on Geological Aspects of Radioactive Waste Disposal of the National Academy of Sciences advised the AEC that " ... concentrations of radionuclides in waste materials should not be allowed to appear in the earth's biosphere before they have de- cayed to innocous levels."** This concept requires that hazardous wastes remain isolated from the environment for as long as they may be harmful. The Committee noted that, for long-lived wastes, this would require a period of isolation of at least six to ten centuries, longer than any records or human government can be expected to survive. Its basic criteria for evaluating disposal methods are:

> "(1) permanent isolation from the biosphere of all
> hazardous concentrations of radionuclides; (2) pro-
> tection from long-lived radioactivity must extend
> for 600 to 1000 years; (3) where safety is involved,
> cost is secondary."***

The Committee's report was kept from the public until early last year, when Congressional critics of the AEC obtained and published it in the Congressional Record.****

*Fox, Radioactive Wastes, supra at 12.
**National Academy of Sciences - National Research Council report of
The Committee on Geologic Aspects of Radioactive Waste Disposal (May,
1966), reprinted in Underground Uses of Nuclear Energy, Hearings before
Subcommittee on Air and Water Pollution of the Senate Committee
on Public Works, on S.3042, 91st Cong., 1st Sess., p. 461, 472 (1969)
(hereinafter "NAS Waste Study.")
***NAS Waste Study, supra at 501.
****Environmental Action, (October 3, 1970), p. 10.

4. Hazards of Nuclear Fuel Reprocessing and Waste Transport

A 1,000 MW plant contains about 100 tons of uranium as fuel in the form of fuel elements. Annually about one-third of the plant's fuel inventory is removed for reprocessing. When it can no longer be utilized economically, used fuel, which contains a large volume of high-level radioactive wastes as well as recoverable material, is removed from the reactor. Before the fuel elements can be shipped to reprocessing plants, they must be stored at the power plant for about three months to cool. In many power plants, the highly radioactive fuel elements are stored in ordinary industrial buildings where a conventional accident, e.g., gas explosion, or sabotage could disrupt the fuel elements and release large amounts of radioactivity into the environment.

A similar hazard exists during the transport of the used fuel, which is carried by truck or rail in lead shielded, steel casks to fuel reprocessing plants like the one located 30 miles south of Buffalo in West Valley, New York. Spills of radioactivity can and have occurred in transit as a result of impact or exposure to fire. The likelihood that such accidents will involve used reactor fuel is a matter for serious concern as many additional reactors are built, producing more wastes with higher levels of radioactivity, and increasing the amount of wastes transported over public thoroughfares. It has been estimated, for example, that transport of radioactive wastes from the proposed 820 MW nuclear plant at Shoreham, Long Island to the West Valley reprocessing plant would involve at least 100 to 125 trailer-type trucks a year (about 3 trucks every two weeks) to pass through the New York metropolitan area.*

At the reprocessing plant, high-level wastes in the fuel elements must cool for another one-half year and then are separated from the reusable fuel.

The most highly radioactive materials remain in the waste liquids of the fuel recovery process. Reprocessing used fuel from a 1,000 MW nuclear plant yields about 8,000 gallons of high-level wastes per year (about 1,000 cubic feet.)** At this point, the wastes are in a form "which could most easily reach the environment in an accident."***

The hazards present at fuel reprocessing plants were recently acknowledged (albeit mildly) by Congressman Chet Holifield, Chairman of the Joint Congressional Committee on Atomic Energy, when he stated:

> "We are under the impression that probably the reprocessing plants are the key to assessing the impact of nuclear power on the environment.... Because of the actual handling and the separation of this noxious material in the processing plants, it seems to be a more delicate operation and one that might result in some potential risk to the employees at least, if not to the general public nearby."****

Now there is only one commercial reprocessing plant operating in the United States, located about 30 miles south of

---

*Testimony of L. Wolford, Project Engineer for LILCO, in AEC Public Hearing in the Matter of Long Island Lighting Company, Shoreham Nuclear Power Station Unit 1, Dkt. No. 50-322, pp.3132-33.
**AEC Authorizing Legislation Fiscal Year 1969, Hearings Before the Joint Committee on Atomic Energy, pt. 1, 89th Congress, 2nd Sess. p.704 (1969)
***The Economy, Energy and the Environment, A Background Study prepared for the use of the Joint Economic Comm.,Congress of the U.S., by the Environmental Policy Division, Legislative Reference Service, Library of Congress (Sept. 1, 1970), p.113 (hereinafter "Energy Report").
****Hearings (Pt.2., Vol.I), supra at 1728.

Buffalo in West Valley, New York.* Another will be placed in service shortly near Chicago, Illinois (owned by General Electric)
and construction has begun on a third plant in South Carolina.**

5. Solid Wastes

All nuclear facilities create radioactive solid wastes, which
are usually low-level wastes.*** These consist mostly of residues,
e.g., resins, and contaminated equipment and materials, such as
clothing, filter elements, cleaning materials and scrap piping.
Such wastes may amount to 4,000 cubic feet per year for a small 250
MW reactor. They are usually baled and buried in unlined pits or
trenches. In 1970, some 1,500,000 cubic feet of solid radioactive wastes were buried at AEC - supervised sites and about
1,000,000 cubic feet at disposal sites operated by private industry.****
The volume of wastes to be buried on commercial sites is expected
to climb to 3,000,000 cubic feet per year by 1980.*****

6. The Risk of a Power Reactor Accident May be Small But the Consequences Could be Catastrophic

A major risk associated with nuclear plants is the possibility
of a reactor accident. Early accidents (more than ten years ago)
in special purpose and developmental types of nuclear reactors
helped to point up some of the most hazardous features in the designs
of those reactors. In 1957, a plutonium production reactor in
England malfunctioned, all reactor safeguards failed, and radioactive fission products (approximately 20,000 curies of

---

*The operation of the plant is discussed in Section V.B. infra at 240-242.
**Energy Report, supra at 112.
***The AEC has defined low-level wastes as wastes that "have a
radioactive content sufficiently low to permit discharge to the
environment with reasonable dilution or after relatively simple
processing. They have no more than about 1000 times the concentrations considered safe for direct release." Fox, Radioactive Wastes,
supra at 12.
****Commercial burial sites have been established in Nevada, Kentucky,
New York, Illinois and Washington. Fox, Radioactive Wastes, supra at 23.
*****Idem.

iodine -131) went up the stack and were spewed over a 400-mile
area, contaminating milk and vegetables. The reactor used
air cooling, a concept since abandoned, and its fuel elements were
directly exposed to the atmosphere via the stack.

In 1961, three reactor staff members were killed by radiation
and an explosion of steam in an experimental AEC reactor in
Idaho owing to the mismanagement of a single control rod.
Reactors of this type are no longer being built in this country.

An atomic explosion is not possible in current light water
reactors, but a malfunction of the reactor with a simultaneous
failure of safeguards could result in a fuel meltdown releasing
sufficient radioactive material into the environment to endanger
large numbers of people. The fuel in a reactor reaches temperatures of 4,000 degress Fahrenheit and becomes semi-molten (in
the interior of the fuel elements) when operating at maximum
capacity. In light water reactors, water flows continuously
through a primary coolant tube in the reactor core at pressures
up to 2,500 pounds per square inch, drawing off the intense heat
from the surfaces of the fuel rods and carrying it to a heat
exchanger to produce steam. The most probable kind of hazard
"that really worries nuclear experts..."* is a sudden loss of
primary coolant water through the plugging of a cooling duct or
pipe of a primary coolant system, and resultant meltdown of
the fuel rods. Even if the nuclear fission is shut down promptly upon failure of cooling, built-up radioactivity in the fuel
continues to generate heat at a sufficient rate to melt the
fuel.

─────────────
*Dr. Ralph E. Lapp, The Four Big Fears About Nuclear Power, in
the New York Times Magazine (February 7, 1971), p. 22.

This type of fuel meltdown occurred in Detroit in 1966 in the Enrico Fermi Power Plant. The reactor was an advanced type "breeder", which used molten sodium as a reactor coolant. A piece of metal blocked the liquid sodium coolant, causing partial melting of a few fuel assemblies. Some radioactive gas escaped within the plant, although none was detected outside the building. While they analyzed the possibilities, the operating staff hesitated for a month to probe for the source of trouble and scope of damage fearing that an explosion might be triggered because of the distorted fuel configuration that resulted from the meltdown. This explosion hazard is peculiar to such "fast neutron" breeders, which have fuel that is highly enriched with an isotope, e.g., U-235, that is readily fissioned by fast neutrons. The reactor had to be dismantled in large measure before the cause of the accident could be discerned.* Nearly four years have been required to restore operation.

Reactors contain emergency cooling systems, as well as thick steel pressure vessels and containment structures, to safeguard against major core meltdowns and the escape of large amounts of radioactivity. The reactors are also generally equipped to shut down automatically if the coolant water heats up beyond a specified level. But, the reliability of the protective devices cannot be guaranteed. A report entitled "Emergency Core Cooling", prepared by a task force headed by Dr. William K. Ergen of Oak Ridge National Laboratory and issued by the AEC in 1967, concluded

---

*This was in part necessary because sodium in the reactor prevented photographing the interior of the core. See
Sheldon Novick, The Careless Atom (1969)

-41-

that "reliable and practical methods of containing the large molten masses of fuel that would probably result from ... a meltdown (of the reactor core) ...do not exist today.... Accordingly, it is not considered possible to assure the integrity of the containment if meltdown of large portions of the core were to occur." In such an instance, much, if not most, of the radioactive material in the fuel could be released to the environment.

Dr. Edward Teller, a one-time advisor to Governor Rockefeller on atomic energy, has cautioned that: "A gently seeping nuclear reactor can put its radioactive poison under a stable inversion layer and concentrate it onto a few hundred square miles in a truly deadly fashion.... In my mind, nuclear reactors do not belong on the surface of the earth. Nuclear reactors belong underground...."*

The risk of a reactor accident has been estimated by Alvin Weinberg, director of Oak Ridge National Laboratory, as one in 10,000 per large reactor per year, which would amount to one accident per century per 100 reactors operating. As Davis Inglis points out, however,

> "in another man's opinion 1/1000 might seem more realistic, expecting one bad accident per decade of 100-reactor operations. Recent experience is only enough to make the figure 1/100 seem very doubtful insofar as it can be transferred at all to larger reactors making somewhat greater demands on materials."**

*Quoted in Power, Pollution and the Imperiled Environment, by G.D. Friedlander, IEEE Spectrum (November, 1970) p.44.
**Inglis, Nuclear Energy and the Malthusian Dilemma, supra at 17.

While the reactor safety record in the United States reflects a decline in the frequency of serious reactor accidents (i.e., accidents which damage the reactor severely), it is based on performance of only 21 civilian reactors varying size from 40 MW to 800 MW. Current AEC predictions are that up to 900 reactors will be in service by the year 2000 to meet projected demand for electricity, most of which will be 1000 MW or larger. The over forty-fold increase in the number of reactors, their increased size and consequent increase in fission products will increase the risk of a major accident. At least one authority has concluded that in view of the projected growth in the number of large plants, "it would appear a certainty we will have a serious nuclear accident -- and by that time (i.e., 2000)...population, if uncontrolled, will hem in our reactor sites."*

As noted above, many of the reactors projected for service beginning in the mid-1980's are expected to be "breeder" reactors, which produce more fuel than they consume.
They produce heat through a fission reaction in which there are excess neutrons that act to convert non-fissionable atoms into nuclear fuel.**

The potential for a serious reactor accident resulting in wide-spread dispersion of radioactive waste is higher in some types of breeder reactors than in the light water reactors used today: an explosive accident is possible in a breeder. As explained by David Inglis, professor of physics at Massachusetts University:

---

*Dr. Ralph E. Lapp, Safety, in the New Republic (Jan. 23, 1971) p.21.
**Many will use melted sodium for cooling instead of water. Sodium

-43-

> "The greatest danger is that, if a cooling duct should
> be plugged, the uranium in that part of the core could
> melt and become concentrated enough to cause an explosion,
> one that might at first be mild on the nuclear-scale
> -- much less than an A-bomb. But if it happens in a large
> reactor such as those being planned, this explosion could
> possibly compress the rest of the uranium enough to make
> a big nuclear explosion. Such possibilities seem less
> remote after the trouble-plagued record of the two commercial
> prototypes, particularly the meltdown of the one near
> Detroit (i.e., the Enrico Fermi reactor)....*

Another danger is the possibility of the molten sodium or potassium

used in breeder reactors coming into contact with water or steam

as the result of a leak in the part of the system where the liquid

metal is used to heat steam. If this happened, a violent reaction

could occur with catastrophic consequences. Attempts are now being

made to develop reactor designs to protect against such occurrences.**

Dr. Glen T. Seaborg, Chairman of the AEC, recently acknow-

ledged the increased safety hazards associated with "breeder"

reactors:

> "We agree that the use of large quantities of plutonium
> in large fast breeder reactors does involve safety consid-
> erations beyond those associated with the present generation
> of light water reactors.... The important point is that large
> quantitities of radioactive material...constitute a hazard
> only if there is some way in which appreciable quantities
> can escape the protective barriers of fuel cladding,
> primary coolant system and containment. Providing assurance
> that this cannot happen has been one of the important
> objectives of our program...."***

Regardless of the magnitude of risk, the consequences of

a reactor accident could be catastrophic. In a report prepared

in 1957, the AEC estimated the worst that could happen to a 100-

200 MW reactor which had been operating for 180 days, located

---

is capable of absorbing much more heat energy than water before
boiling and is a better conductor of heat.
*Bulletin of Atomic Scientist, p. 50 (Feb. 1970).
**Walter Sullivan, Clean Reactors Delayed In a Drive for Atomic
Power, N. Y. Times (3/8/71), p. 18.
***Hearings (Pt. 1), supra at 93-94.

about 30 miles from a city of 1,000,000, in an accident where all
safeguards failed and residents were unable to be evacuated.
Assuming that 50 per cent of all fission products were released,
became airborne and were dispersed over a wide area, the AEC concluded that about 3,400 people would be killed; 43,000 people would
be injured; property damage would be about $7 billion;* people
would be killed at distances up to 15 miles and injured at distances
up to 45 miles.**

These figures become even more alarming when it is recognized
that the reactor in the AEC study was about 6 times smaller than
those being placed in use today; that breeder reactors are projected
for major use beginning in the 1980's; and that by 1990 most sites
will contain power plants of 1000-4000 MW, with some as large as
6000 MW.***

7. Discharges of Radioactive Gases and Liquids During
    Normal Plant and Fuel Reprocessing Operations

Another basic problem associated with nuclear power development
involves the routine, controlled (as opposed to accidental) discharging of "low-level" radioactive wastes****into the air and water.
at nuclear power plants and nuclear fuel reprocessing facilities.
Such discharges, the levels of which were until very recently
regulated by the AEC,***** can result in radioactive contamination
of the air, water, land and food.

*This figure is largely owing to assumed contamination of land with
fission products.
**WASH-740 (AEC, March, 1957), reprinted in Underground Uses of Nuclear
Power (Part 2), 91st Cong., 2nd Sess. (August, 1970), supra at 1703,
1721-22. The authors' stated purpose was to portray the worst situation that might result from an accident that dispersed to the environment the largest possible proportion of the radioactive contents of a
reactor of the size chosen, without reference to particular causal
factors. In that context, it was deemed not pertinent to consider
reactor containment or other engineering features designed to limit
accidents, which, in practice, are subject to failure.
***Electric Power and the Environment (August, 1970) , a report spon-
sored by The Energy Policy Staff, Office of Science and Technology,
Executive Office of the President, p. 26 (hereinafter "EPE Report").
****"In liquid form low level wastes usually contain less than a micro-
curie of radioactivity per gallon." Fox, Radioactive Wastes, supra at 11.
*****As of October, 1970, the newly created federal Environmental Pro-
tection Agency has the responsibility for establishing radiation
standards and emission limits for radioactivity. AEC retains
authority over enforcement, as well as siting and safety

Radioactive substances, e.g., krypton -85, xenon -133, are discharged as gases via stacks or exhaust ducts at power plants.

Radioactive gases and liquids are also released to the environment at fuel reprocessing plants. Of particular concern are the long-lived radioactive gas, krypton -85 (half-life of 10.76 years) and tritium (half-life of 12.25 years)* which are inevitably released from the fuel elements and to the surrounding area. Neither of these radionuclides are removed from plant effluents by present waste handling techniques.**

Since krypton -85 is long lasting and does not react chemically with other substances, its quantity in the atmosphere is increasing.***While the AEC maintains that exposure to the general public by the year 2000 will not exceed approximately 1 per cent of its radiation protection guides, AEC Commissioner James T. Ramey has acknowledged that "as larger fuel reprocessing plants are built, it may become necessary to remove krypton from gaseous effluents in order to maintain local exposure limits within applicable radiation guides."****

Human beings may be exposed to released radioactive materials either internally (following ingestion as via plants or other food , or inhalation, followed in many instances by incor-

features of major nuclear facilities. Environmental Reporter (Federal Laws), pp. 21: 0262, 51: 1602.
*This means that one half of a given amount of tritium will decay in 12.25 years, half of the remaining half in another 12.25 years, and so on.
**Hearings, pt. 1, supra at 157.
***Environmental Quality,1st Annual Report of the Council on Environmental Quality (August 1970), p. 144.
****Hearings, pt. 1, supra at 255.

poration of the material into some body tissues), or externally as by radioactive krypton in the atmosphere.

Low-level liquid wastes are usually released directly to condenser cooling water and discharged following some holdup time for radioactive decay. Tritium is extremely difficult to remove from liquid discharges. According. to AEC Commissioner Clarence E. Larson,"much more research needs to be done on control of tritium releases in effluents."*

After liquid contaminants are released, principal human exposures may be from drinking water and consumption of food, e.g., radioactivity may concentrate in fish, or contaminated water may be used for agricultural irrigation.

> "Some waterplants and animals tend selectively to remove and concentrate certain radioactive wastes . For example, radioactive species of cobalt, cesium, and manganese are concentrated in the edible tissues of shellfish, while in dairy country radioactive iodine vapors that condense on grass may appear in the milk of the cows that eat the grass."**

Human exposure is also possible through recreational use of contaminated water.

The AEC has set standards for permissible doses, exposures and concentrations of radiation, as well as issued regulations relating to the discharge of radioactive effluents from major nuclear facilities,*** e.g., nuclear power reactors, fuel reprocessing plants, fuel fabrication plants, and the transport of radioactive materials. The AEC standards are based in large measure on recommendations of the NCRP, ICRP, and FRC.

---

*Environment Reporter (Current Developments), p. 756 (Nov. 20, 1970).
**Energy Report, supra at 110.
***10 C.F.R. pt. 20.

The current standards for maximum, annual allowable doses
of radiation from   man-made sources, over and above the natural background exposure, are 170 millirems (mr) (average) for
the entire population and 500 mr for individuals within the
general population.

The average annual dose to the general population from natural background radiation, i.e., cosmic rays, radiation in soil
and materials, is about 100 to 150 mr.*

To date, controlled discharges of radioactivity during normal operation of nuclear power plants have generally been substantially within the maximum allowable limits, i.e., within a
few per cent of the limits; and, the AEC projects that radioactive
releases from future power plants will generally be at equally
low levels.**

It has been estimated that exposure of people living near
the boundary of commercial power plant sites has ranged between
one and ten mr per year, or in other words, has averaged about one

---

*The difference between living in a wood house and a stone
house is about 20 to 30 mr per year; and between living in
Denver and Washington, D.C. is about 70 mr per year. Hearings,
Pt. 1, supra at 107.

** Hearings (Pt. 2, Vol II), supra at 2438-39.

per cent of the 500 mr standard for individuals.*

Based on a linear hypothesis, i.e., absence of a threshold,

> "doses even as low as an average of 10 mrem/yr. to the
> entire U.S. population would be expected to introduce
> into the population between 1,000 and 5,000 deaths per
> year, as a consequence of genetic mutation, leukemia,
> thyroid cancer, other tumors and life shortening."**

Assuming that annual exposure of the entire population to radiation from the entire nuclear industry, i.e., power facilities, fuel reprocessing and fabrication facilites, ranges from 2 to 10 mr, deaths from such exposure have been estimated to range from a minimum of 200 to a maximum of 5000 per year.*** Deaths from natural background exposure (100 to 150 mr) would, on a similar basis, range from 10,000 to 75,000 per year.

Others, postulating that average population radiation dose from current nuclear power facilities and related activities does not exceed 1/2 of one per cent of the 170 mr limit deemed acceptable by the AEC, estimate an actual cumulative total of 18 deaths per year as a result of such activities.****

---

*Environmental Quality, supra at 143; Hearings, Pt. 1, supra at 107; Abrahamson Report, supra at 13.
**Testimony of Dr. Karl Z. Morgan, Director, Health Physics Division, Oak Ridge National Laboratory, Hearings (Pt.2), supra at 1269.
***Abrahamson Report, supra at 13.
****Dr. Karl Z. Morgan, quoted in Nucleonics Week, August 27, 1970, p. 2.

The operating results of nuclear fuel reprocessing facilities
have been somewhat worse than those for existing power plants.
For example, despite the fact that the facility in West Valley,
New York has not operated in excess of 50 per cent of its annual
capacity (300 tons of spent fuel), its liquid effluents have ranged
from 6 to 18 per cent of maximum allowable concentrations of an
annual basis.*

8.   Indirect Radiation Hazards

Radiation hazards are also associated with the fabrication
of nuclear fuels, (i.e., plutonium or uranium) and the mining
and milling of uranium. For example, radioactive isotopes may
escape to contaminate areas surrounding the manufacturing plant,
as recently occurred at the AEC's plutonium factory at Rocky
Flats, Colorado, where a fire resulted in leakage of substantial
amounts of toxic plutonium oxide beyond the plant boundaries.
The New York Atomic and Space Decelopment Authority recently
revealed plans to establish a plutonium fuel fabrication complex
in West Valley, New York.

Also, uranium miners are exposed to dangerous concentrations
of radioactive gas, as well as particles of radioactive radon.
Studies by the United States Public Health Service show that underground uranium miners are subject to lung cancer "to a degree
substantially greater than the general population, or that of
miners in other kinds of underground mines."**

About 2,600 miners are now producing uranium from underground mines. Because of the increasing uranium requirements, the
number could increase to 10,000 by 1980.

---

*Hearings pt. 2 (Vol. 1), supra at 1701.
**Energy Report, supra at 67.

Substantial amounts of uranium tailings, i.e., solid residues,
are sometimes left in the area of mines or uranium ore-concentrating
mills. They contain substantial amounts of radium from the ore and
can be scattered by the wind or find their way into nearby streams
and rivers. "How best to dispose of tailings actually remains an
unanswered question for the present."*

Also, low-level liquid wastes are discharged at the over 20
such mills in the country into ponds or lagoons "at a rate of 300
to 500 gallons per minute (for an average mill processing 1000 tons
of ore per day.)"**

---

*Fox, Radioactive Wastes, supra at 22.
**Fox, Radioactive Wastes, supra at 4.

C. Thermal Pollution and Fish Kills are Major Problems posed
    by Disposal of Vast Amounts of Waste Heat Produced by
    Steam-Electric Plants

Fossil fueled and nuclear plants are the major source of thermal

pollution, i.e., the discharge of heated water, of the nation's and

state's waterways. Significantly, nuclear plants discharge about

50 per cent more heated water than fossil-fueled plants. of the same size?

All steam-electric plants produce large amounts

of waste heat as a result of the very low level of efficiency now

achieved in the generation of electricity. About two-thirds of the

heat energy cannot be turned into electricity; rather, it must be dis-

charged into the air or water as waste heat. Most often the bulk of

the waste heat is absorbed by cooling water withdrawn from a waterway,

passed through the plant's condenser, and returned to the waterway.

The rise in temperature of the cooling water is usually in the range

of 10 degrees to 20 degrees Fahrenheit, with the average rise about

15 degrees. Temperature rises of 30 degrees Fahrenheit, however, are

not uncommon.

Massive amounts of water are needed to cool the condensers: on

a national basis, electric power generation accounts for over 80 per

cent of total cooling water use, and nearly 1/3 of the total water

used for all purposes. The total amount of water used for cooling

power plants now is about 120 billion gallons per day, or about 10 per

cent of the average daily runoff of water in the continental United

States.

The projections of enormous growth in generating capacity,

particularly nuclear, and the fact that at least 85 per cent of the

electric energy planned to be produced over the next two decades

-52-

will be produced by steam-electric plants, make clear that the problem of thermal pollution is going to become of increasingly greater significance and reach awesome dimensions. "In absolute terms, it has been estimated that the annual waste heat discharge would increase from the present 6 x 10^{15} Btu to more than 20 x 10^{15} Btu in 1990."[8] Cooling water requirements are expected to increase to 200 billion gallons per day by 1980 and 600 billion gallons per day by 2000, the equivalent of 50 per cent of the average daily natural runoff of water in the continental United States (excluding Alaska).**

1. Environmental Damage

Thermal discharges can drastically affect aquatic life and water quality, e.g., density, viscosity, gas solubility. For example, a rise in water temperature increases respiration of marine organisms but at the same time decreases the capacity of the water to hold oxygen. This imbalance between increased respiration and decreased available oxygen may have harmful effects on marine life.

Sizeable increases in water temperature kill aquatic life;*** increase the occurrence of disease in fish populations; decrease spawning success and endanger the survival of young fish; interfere with normal biological rhythms and migration patterns and stimulate

*Problems in Disposal of Waste Heat from Steam Electric Plants, prepared by the staff of the FPC's Bureau of Power (1969) ("Waste Heat Study"), p. 2.
**Daniel Merriman, The Calefaction of a River, Science (May, 1970).
***Voluntary reports to the Federal Water Pollution Control Administration of fish kills by heated waste water discharges from power plants indicate that about 735,000 fish were killed by such discharges between August, 1962 and June, 1969. Hearings Pt. 1, supra at 377.

the development of less desirable species. Often, what is not recognized

> "...is that in many of our waterways the waste heat may
> be imposed upon an environment which is already near a
> critical point for certain segments of the aquatic life
> we seek to protect, for the process we hope to limit and
> for certain uses we propose to make of the water resources."*

Increases in water temperatures also increase algae growth, particularly in a nutrient rich area near a source of sewage or industrial waste; speed the eutrophication process in waterways; and trigger excessive plant growth, decreasing water flow and increasing siltation. Higher temperatures can also create conditions enabling bacteria in domestic sewage "to multiply in astronomic numbers."**

Increasing the temperature of water substantially reduces the waste assimilation capacity of the receiving body.

> "One situation which has been documented is in Alabama's
> Coosa River where raising the temperature 9°F. above the
> existing summer temperature of 77°F. resulted in a reduction
> of the waste assimilative capacity of the stream by 11,000
> pounds per day of oxygen demanding wastes if the same dis-
> solved oxygen levels were to be maintained....
>
> One of the major pollution problems today is from municipal
> and other oxygen demanding wastes. If thermal pollution is
> not controlled, this problem will become more difficult and
> costly."***

Thermal pollution also reduces the recreational value of water by heating or increasing growth of algae; results in local fogging on water and land; and reduces the value of water for industrial cooling.

---

*EPE Report, supra at 3.
**Albert C. Jensen, Assistant Director, Division of Marine and Coastal
Resources, DEC, Thermal Pollution in the Marine Environment, in The
Conservationist, p. 13 (Oct.-Nov. 1970)
***Dean E. Abrahamson, Environmental Cost of Electric Power, pp. 9-10
(Scientists Institute for Public Information - 1970) ("Abrahamson
Report").

Also, power plants act "as very efficient predators"*   of
small marine organisms, e.g., fish eggs, larvae, plankton, that
pass through the condenser cooling system and have resulted in substantial mechanical fish kills at the cooling water intakes.
Chemicals, such as chlorine, placed in the coolant water to keep
the condensers free from clinging organisms may also adversely
affect fish and fish food organisms.

---

* Jensen, supra at 13.

2. Thermal Pollution in New York State

Fossil fueled and nuclear power plants are the largest man-made source of thermal discharges into the waters of New York State.*

On the Hudson River, one nuclear and two fossil plants now discharge about 500,000 gallons per minute (gpm) of heated water. At least one fossil plant and four nuclear plants are scheduled for installation over the next decade. According to Albert C. Jensen, Assistant Director, Division of Marine and Coastal Resources, DEC, these future plants (with current technology) can be expected to add about 2,000,000 gpm of hot water to the Hudson, with temperature additions of about 25°F. above the normal river temperature.** The thermal pollution would occur in areas of the river that serve as important spawning and nursing grounds for many valuable types of fish, e.g., striped bass.

On Long Island Sound, there are now five fossil fuel plants which, together with a new unit scheduled for 1972, will require about 1,800,000 gpm of cooling water.

Moreover, the six nuclear plants planned to be located on the Sound by the early 1980's will use astronomical volumes of coolant water.*** The 4,000 MW proposed for David's Island

---

*A Thermal Profile of the Waters of New York State, a Report of the New York State Atomic and Space Development Authority (1970).
**Jensen, supra at 10.
***Jensen, supra at 11.

by Con Ed would require 3,000,000 gpm; and LILCO's two new 820 MW plants on Long Island Sound will require about 600,000 gpm each.* Three existing fossil plants and three planned nuclear plants on the Connecticut shore of Long Island Sound would require 2,100,000 gpm. The total volume of coolant water that would be required by all existing and planned fossil and nuclear plants on the Sound is at least 7,200,000 gpm-more than the 6,000,000 gpm flow of the American side of Niagara Falls.**

The Sound, like the Hudson River, is still very productive in terms of marine life. These waters produce a wide variety of shellfish and finfish, which support major commercial and recreational fishing activities.*** Marine ecologists and the commercial fishing industry are very concerned that the vast amount of heated water discharged into the Sound may adversely affect the marine environment. Of particular concern are the "serious permanent ecological changes that may be induced by the total discharge of a number of plants into a given body of water."**** Authorities at the Marine Sciences Research Center at the State University at Stony Brook, Long Island estimate that such an ecological change - a "regional warming"- of the Sound will occur within the next 20 years as a result of thermal discharges from power plants in the western portion of the Sound.

_____

*Significantly the Federal Water Quality Administration, which oversees water quality in interstate and coastal waters, has recently urged the United States Atomic Energy Commission to reject LILCO's application to build an 820 mw plant at Shoreham, L:I. because the thermal discharge facilities proposed by LILCO are, in its view, inadequate to protect marine life. Newsday (12/8/70).
**Jensen, supra at 11.
***About 1,000,000 persons fish in the state's marine waters and contribute more than $10,000,000 to the local economy. Jensen, supra at 9.
****Jensen, supra at 13.

The thermal pollution problem in the Sound is exacerbated by the 4,000,000 gpm of hot water discharged into the waters surrounding New York City by Con Ed's 11 steam-electric stations. Some of this water passes into the Western end of the Sound through the East River.

Moreover, the waters around New York City and western area of Long Island Sound are heavily loaded with nutrients owing to the outfall of sewage from disposal plants, leaching from cesspools on Long Island and surrounding areas of Westchester and Connecticut, and industrial wastes. These materials deplete the dissolved oxygen in the water. The heat discharged from power plants furthers the depletion of oxygen, particularly during periods of peak electricity use in the summer. As noted above, oxygen depletion can lead to fish kills, excessive algal growth and production of putrid, hydrogen sulphide gas.

The precarious biological condition of waters surrounding New York City justifies concern regarding the addition of the waste heat from only a few hundred megawatts of electric capacity. Such concern has recently been expressed by scientists at the Marine Sciences Research Center at the State University at Stony Brook. They have advised against any increase in electric generating capacity in New York City because of thermal pollution problems.*

The seriousness of the thermal pollution problem posed by electric power generation has been recognized by the New York State Legislature. It recently passed legislation requiring a utility,

*See, e.g., Letter from D. Squires, Director of Marine Sciences Research Center, State University at Stony Brook, to Mayor John V. Lindsay (August 10, 1970).

prior to construction or increasing the capacity of a steam-
electric generating plant, to submit an environmental feasibility
study to the DEC and to obtain from the DEC a certificate
allowing thermal discharges from the plant.* The State has
adopted thermal discharge standards which provide the basis for
issuance of such certificates. The basic standard is extremely
broad: no heated liquids can be discharged into the State's
waters "at such temperatures as to be injurious to fish life...
or impair the waters for any other best usage (e.g., drinking,
swimming, fishing)...".** Specific criteria were adopted
(effective August, 1969) which establish maximum permissible
temperatures and changes in temperature for specific types of
water bodies, e.g., coastal waters, estuaries. The criteria
do not, however, apply to the discharges from existing power
plants; rather, they are "intended only to be a frame of
reference in determining whether existing discharges comply
with the broad, general standard for thermal discharges".***

Also, the criteria only apply to individual plants. The
problem of regional warming from cumulative discharges of
several plants into a single body of water, deemed critical by
marine ecologists, must also be confronted.**** For example,
Con Ed plans to add two nuclear units totaling about 1850 MW,

_____
*Public Health Law, §1230.3(b).
**6 NYCRR §701.3 et seq.
***6 NYCRR § 704.4.
****Jensen, supra at 13.

at Indian Point on the Hudson River by 1973. These new plants,
together with Indian Point No. 1, will discharge about 2,100,000
gallons of hot water per minute into the Hudson, and produce
an effuent channel temperature rise of about 15° Fahrenheit.*
The DEC has issued a permit to Con Ed to construct a single discharge
canal and outfall structure, providing for a submerged discharge
of all cooling water released by the three units. The DEC is, however,
still evaluating the environmental effects of the thermal discharges
from Con Ed's existing and planned plants at Indian Point on the
Hudson River on the basis of the combined discharge of these
plants. The study "is on-going and will be carried on for at
least another year."**

*Environmental Impact of Indian Point Station, Nuclear Unit No. 2,
prepared by Con Ed (Dec. 17, 1970), p. 52.
**Letter from Henry L. Diamond, Commissioner of DEC to Neil Fabricant,
EPA, dated Oct. 13, 1970

3. Fish Kills in New York State

Operation of once-through cooling systems - the only kind currently employed by utilities in this state - has resulted in massive mechanical fish kills in the Hudson and Long Island Sound.

Con Ed's Nuclear Unit No. 1, placed in service at Indian Point on the Hudson, January, 1963, has been involved in at least two large fish kills. The first occurred shortly after it began operation. Many thousands of white perch and striped bass, attracted by the heated water discharged from the plant, were sucked into the condenser cooling intake located near the point of discharge and killed.

Some alterations were made in the system to cure the problem but, in January, 1970, Con Ed disclosed that about 150,000 fish had been killed as a result of getting stuck in a screen on the water intake conduit.

In March, 1970, Con Ed announced that 120,000 more fish - mostly white perch - were killed at the plant site for "unknown reasons." As a result of these fish kills and thermal discharges into the river, the New York State Attorney General instituted legal action in May, 1970 charging Con Ed with thermal and toxic pollution of the Hudson and negligent operation of its plant. The State is seeking $5 million in damages for alleged fish kills attributed to plant operations. The Attorney General argues that Con Ed should not be allowed to operate the plant "until suitable methods and procedures are instituted which will enable the defendant to withdraw water from and discharge water into

-61-

the Hudson River in such a manner as to avoid the killing of fish and other forms of marine life and to further avoid endangering the ecology of the Hudson River."*

Con Ed's plants are not the only ones that have destroyed massive amounts of marine life. In 1966, "at least two truck-loads" of small menhaden and white perch were hauled away from LILCO's fossil fueled plant in Port Jefferson, New York.

In January of last year, more than a thousand bluefish were killed at LILCO's Northport power plant when they were driven from the warm water discharge area (52°F.) into the cold "normal" water of the Sound (31°F.). The actual force that propelled the fish into the cold water is still unknown.**

*New York Times, May 13, 1970.
**Jensen, supra at 12.

D. Utilities are Seeking Millions of Acres of Valuable Land for Sites and Transmission Lines to Meet Projected Growth

1. Increasing Demands on Decreasing Land Resources

The magnitude of the land use problem is well illustrated by a recent study of the availability of land resources to satisfy demands from electric utilities and all other possible sources by the year 2000. The study concludes that to meet all projected demands for land in the nation by 2000 would "require the use of every acre in the 48 contiguous states, including deserts, mountain peaks and marshes and still leave a net shortage of 50 million acres."* (emphasis added).

In order to quadruple generating capacity within the next two decades, the utility industry estimates it will require about 300 new sites for units of 500 MW or larger, over and above substantial additions at existing plants and replacement of older units.

They will seek 170 sites between 1970 and 1980, and 130 sites between 1981 and 1990.**

Currently there are about 300,000 miles of electric power transmission lines in service throughout the country, which occupy about 4,000,000 acres of land. Only 2,400 miles - (0.008 per cent) of these lines are underground.***

---

*Hans H. Landsberg, Natural Resources for U.S. Growth - A Look Ahead to the Year 2000 (Baltimore, The Johns Hopkins Press - 1964), cited in EPE Report, supra at 21.
**Letter from John Nassikas, Chairman of the FPC, to Spiro T. Agnew, President of the United States Senate, dated 9/30/70. Of the new sites, about 105 are expected to be for fossil-fuel plants and 195 for nuclear power.
***EPE Report, supra at 21-22.

It is estimated that to transmit the electricity that the industry projects will be required by 1990, 200,000 additional miles of transmission lines will be required, bringing the total to about 7,000,000 acres of land for rights-of-way, or more than 11,000 square miles (the area of the State of Connecticut is 5,000 square miles). Rights-of-way will average from 145 feet for single circuit lines to 200 feet or more for high voltage lines.*

Land would also be required for fuel storage and handling facilities, docks and railroad trackage, pipelines for oil and gas, offshore facilities for oil tankers and, in the case of coal fired plants, ash removal facilities. As regards nuclear power, land would be required for storage of wastes, as well as fuel reprocessing and waste handling facilities.

New York State utilities reportedly estimate that 35 to 40 additional sites within the state will be required to meet projected demands during the next two decades.

Millions of acres of valuable land, including a substantial amount of waterfront property are at stake. The Federal Office of Science and Technology estimates that the space requirements for a 3,000 MW generating station, including land required for fuel storage and sulfur dioxide removal facilities (2-4 acres), would be as follows: coal - 900 to 1200 acres; nuclear - 200 to 400 acres; oil - 150 to 350 acres.**

Con Ed's site at Indian Point, which is expected to house 2200 MW of nuclear capacity by 1973, is about 240 acres. LILCO recently acquired 425 acres of property on Long Island Sound to

---

*Energy Report, supra at 116. A width of 175 feet is equivalent to about 21 acres per mile of line.
**Considerations Affecting Steam Power Plant Site Selection, The Energy Policy Staff, Office of Science & Technology, pp. 10-15 (1968).

be used for additional electrical generating units. About 1300
acres of a 2300 plot recently acquired by the New York State Power
Authority will house a 820 MW pumped storage facility.*

Together with the tendency to locate several units at one
site, the increased size of new units will certainly require pro-
portionately more cooling water. Steam-electric plants will have
to be built on large lakes and rivers, many of which are already
seriously polluted.

Based on current projections, 80% of power generated in the
Northeast in 1990 will be nuclear, as opposed to 1% in 1966. "And
every major body of water in the area will be rimmed with nuclear
power plants."** The proliferation of power plants around major
waterways is well illustrated by the fact that sixteen nuclear
plants, with a capacity of 11,632 MW, are operating or planned for
operation within the next five years along the shores of the Great
Lakes.*** 24 generating plants already operate along the 1,661-mile
shore of Lake Michigan. The Department of Interior has now expressed serious concern over additional discharges of waste heat
into that body of water.****

Of the seven major utilities in New York, four have plants
on the Hudson River. By the early 1980's Con Ed itself intends to
add four nuclear plants at its Indian Point complex on the Hudson
with a total rated capacity in excess of 4,000 MW.

*PASNY 1969 Annual Report, p. 9-10.
**Why Utilities Can't Meet the Demand, Business Week (Nov. 29, 1969).
***A New River (Staff Report), Environment (Jan. - Feb. 1970) pp.
36-41.
****Environment Reporter (Current Developments), p. 491 (Sept. 4, 1970).

Eight of Con Ed's eleven plants in New York City are located along the East River.

If current plans for nuclear plants are carried out, Long Island Sound will be rimmed with generating facilities pouring at least 7.2 million gallons per minute of heated water into the Sound - more than the 6 million gallon per minute flow of the American side of Niagara Falls.* Con Ed proposes to locate 4000 MW of capacity on David's Island; two nuclear plants are planned for Lloyds Neck and Shoreham, Long Island; and three nuclear plants are planned for the Connecticut shore - all by the mid 1980's.

2. <u>Virtually All Transmission Lines are Overhead Lines Which Impair Scenic Beauty, Create Safety Hazards and Depress Property Values</u>

The vast majority of electric transmission lines throughout the nation and New York State are overhead lines. The utilities claim that underground lines cost too much and that, in any event, no one has developed the technology necessary to utilize underground lines on a large scale.

At present in New York State, the major investor-owned utilities and the New York State Power Authority have in service about 16,400 miles of overhead transmission lines and only 1500 miles of underground lines.** Three utilities (New York State Gas & Electric, Orange & Rockland, Central Hudson) have a combined total of 5070

---

*Jensen, <u>supra</u> at 11.
**<u>Statistical Year Book of the Electric Utility Industry for 1969</u>, p. 56 (Edison Electric Institute, September 1970).

miles of overhead lines and just 30 miles of underground lines.*
The New York State utilities intend to install at least 2000 additional miles of lines during the next decade, most of which will
be overhead.**

The huge 75-110 feet high towers strung across the land mar
the natural beauty of the landscape, withdraw land from other uses,
and decrease property values. In addition, they pose safety problems, and cause considerable interference with reception of television and radio signals. According to Charles Luce,

> "Radio interference is going to get more and
> more serious as we build lines with voltage of 500
> KV and higher. As the designers of transmission
> lines reach toward one million volts we may find
> radio interference a constraint that will limit the
> voltages we can use in certain areas."***

While the trend toward extra higher voltage lines   could
reduce the number of actual miles of lines required, they will use
larger rights-of-way and larger, higher towers than the lower voltage lines.****

---

*Attachment No. 1 to Letter from Howard J. Read, Staff Counsel, PSC,
to Robert Hallman, EPA (1/26/71).
**Northeast Power Coordinating Council, Data on Coordinated Bulk Power
Supply Programs, FPC Order 383-2, Docket R-362, Appendix A (Sept. 1,
1970).
***Address Before the FPC 50th Anniversary Ceremony, June 3, 1970.
****Energy Report, supra at 116.

III. Major Methods for Dealing Directly With Environmental
      Damage Associated With Electric Power and Assessment
      of Industry, as Well as Governmental, Efforts

A. Introduction

This section contains a discussion of the primary methods
for dealing with environmental harm caused by electric power
production and supply, as well as an assessment of the efforts
of industry and government to reduce such environmental harm.
Generally, it is fair to say that neither the electrical industry
nor government has committed anywhere near enough time or money
to research and development to solve environmental problems posed
by electric power; to develop more efficient methods of power
generation; or to study the short and long term effects on
ecological systems, human health, plant, animal and aquatic
life of effluents from nuclear and fossil-fuel plants.

Moreover, the federal research and development effort for
civilian energy production, conversion and transmission is
dominated by research and development for nuclear fission energy. A
pitifully small amount is spent to develop more efficient and
less polluting methods for recovering and using fossil fuels,
or other potential fuels such as municipal solid wastes. For
example, in fiscal year 1970, over 84 per cent of the $368
million devoted to energy research and development by the
federal government was spent on atomic energy and, the major
portion of atomic energy research and development went toward
development of liquid metal fast breeder reactors.* Significantly,
the AEC's fission power program, which cost about $276 million

*Hearings, Pt. 1, supra at 25, 495-98 .

-68-

in fiscal 1970, was almost 10 times larger than any of the other
federal, energy research and development programs and almost three
times as large as the sum of all the others.*

Further, only a very small portion of atomic energy research
and development funds are allocated to development of a controlled thermonuclear fusion** reactor (about $34 million in fis-
cal 1970), although "its potential for increasing the world's
energy supply with a minimum of environmental problems dwarfs
even the breeder program."*** Significantly, the White House has
recently announced that further cuts will be made in spending for
fusion research in order to provide additional support for development of liquid metal fast breeder reactors which, according to
President Nixon's science adviser, Dr. Edward E. David, Jr.,
has become one of the country's "chief technological goals."****
The primary reason advanced by federal authorities for pressing
ahead with breeders is that technology for such reactors is much
further developed than fusion technology and, thus, is likely to
be available to serve increasing power demands in the next decades.
While fusion in the United States is still in the basic research
stage and commercially useful technology is probably more than
twenty years away (assuming expenditures rising to $200 million
annually,)***** it appears to offer substantial advantages in

---

*Hearings, Pt. 1, supra at 496.
**In fission reactors, energy is released by splitting heavy nuclei,
which gives rise to neutrons, energy in the form of heat and fission
products. In fusion, energy is released by the combination of two
light nuclei such as nuclei of deuterium. This is the basic reac-
tion taking place in a hydrogen bomb and the sun.
***Hearings, Pt. 1, supra at 497.
****Walter Sullivan, Clean Reactors Delayed in a Drive for Atomic
Power, N.Y. Times, 3/8/71, p. 18.
*****EPE Report, supra at 45.

terms of resource conservation.* The environmental impact of
fusion reactors has not been thoroughly studied, although most
authorities estimate that fusion reactors would not create vast
amounts of radioactive wastes, could not give rise to a runaway
reaction, and that fusion reactors may prove particularly adapt-
able to direct conversion technologies which would produce relatively little thermal pollution.**

As regards research and development efforts by the electric
utilities, in 1969 they spent only $41 million dollars on re-
search and development - the equivalent of 1/4 of one per cent of
gross revenues - as against $323.8 million on sales promotion
and advertising.*** Except for a few token grants, most research
and development money was directed toward improvement of existing
systems.**** Notwithstanding the utilities' increasing public
claims that they are striving to decrease environmental harm,
utility spending for research actually declined from 0.269 per cent
of operating revenue in 1966 to 0.226 per cent in 1969.*****

The industry's failure to conduct research and development,
absent governmental compulsion, is a clear example of social ir-
responsibility. In this connection, former Chairman of the
Federal Power Commission, Lee C. White, has recently

*It has been estimated that "the energy obtainable from the
deuterium contained in 30 cubic kilometers of seawater would be
about equal to that of the earth's initial supply of fossil
fuels." Abrahamson Report, supra at 21.
**See Sullivan, N.Y. Times 3/8/70, supra at 18; W. C. Gough, E. J.
Eastlund, The Prospects of Fusion Power, Scientific American (Feb.'71).
***Statement of United States Senator Lee Metcalf of Montana, quoted
in Safety, the New Republic (Jan. 23, 1971) p. 18.
****L. Lessing, New Ways to More Power With Less Pollution, Fortune
(November, 1970), p. 78, 136.
*****J.N. Nassikas, FPC Chairman, Regulation of the Electric Utili-
ties in the 1970's, address before 38th Annual Convention of the
Edison Electric Institute, Boston, Mass. (June 1, 1970).

stated: "It has always mystified me that, as important and
as financially strong as the electric utility industry is, it
has left so much of the research and development to the
manufacturers of electrical equipment."* Moreover, PSC Chairman
Swidler has recently indicated dissatisfaction with the
electrical industry's research and development efforts, stating
that the utilities "devote a pitifully small amount to research"
and that "electric equipment manufacturers carry on individual
research programs, but mostly on problems having immediate
commercial potential."**

Frederick H. Warren, advisor to the Chairman of the FPC
for Environmental Affairs, as well as Charles Luce, Chairman
of Con Ed, has suggested that the electric power industry
should invest about one and one-half per cent of its $20 billion
gross revenues, or about $300 million per year, for research
and development.*** A similar level of expenditure, i.e., one
to two per cent of electric utilities' revenues, was suggested
by the Federal Interagency Committee in its report entitled
"Electric Power and the Environment."****

Whether the above-cited amount is sufficient or not,
there is widespread agreement that to accomplish the requisite
research and development necessary to eliminate environmental
damage caused by electric power "will require funding levels

*Remarks by Lee C. White before the Annual Meeting of the
Missouri Basin Systems Group (February 4, 1970.)
**Statement of Joseph C. Swidler, Before the Subcommittee on
Intergovernmental Relations of the Senate Committee on
Government Operations on S.2752 (August 3, 1970.)
***Environment Reporter (Current Developments,) p. 756
(Nov. 20, 1970); Remarks of Charles F. Luce, entitled "Our
Polluted Environment: Business Searches for Solutions," at
Indiana University of Pennsylvania (Oct. 19, 1970.)
****EPE Report, supra at 42.

significantly above those now being provided by the government and industry."* In fairness to the utilities it should be noted that the regulatory process may discourage expenditures for research and development. Generally, research and development costs unrelated to specific facilities are not included in a utility's rate base upon which it is entitled to earn a fair return. Rather, such costs are only recoverable as operating expenses, although some regulatory bodies, e.g., the FPC, PSC, allow a utility under certain circumstances to amortize the costs over a period of years (as opposed to charging them against revenues in the year they are actually incurred.) The usual practice has been to expect manufacturers to make product improvements, with the utility paying a portion of the development expenses through the cost of the product (which would go into the rate base.)

It may be desirable in order to encourage utility management to accelerate and expand research and development efforts to permit all or a portion of research and development expenditures (approved by appropriate environmental authorities) to be included in a utility's rate base.** At least one group of authorities has recently urged

> "the regulatory commissions at the federal and state level to take positive action to assure that the utility industry can recover research and development expenses in its rates and that the utilities devote a reasonable portion of their large revenues to such expenditures."***

*EPE Report, supra at 41.
**E.g., AEC Authorizing Legislation, Fiscal Year 1971 (Pt. 3) p. 1257 (March 11, 1970); Nuclear Safety (May-June, 1970), p. 192.
***EPE Report, supra at 44.

B. Steam-Electric Plants Waste Fuel, Produce Vast Amounts
    of Excess Heat and Air Pollutants Largely Because the
    Process Now Used to Generate Electricity is Very Inefficient

Steam electric generating plants* - which now supply about
80 per cent of all electricity in the nation and 75 per cent of all
electricity in New York State - waste large quantities of fuel,
produce vast quantities of waste heat and air pollutants as a
result of the very low level of efficiency now achieved by these
plants in the generation of electricity.

Steam electric plants generate electricity by the thermodynamic
process known as the Rankine Cycle. Heat produced by burning
fossil fuel or nuclear materials turns water into steam. The
steam passes through a turbine at high pressure and temperature,
turning the turbine which in turn drives a generator to produce
electricity. After leaving the turbine, the steam goes into a
condenser, where the steam gives off its excess heat to the cooling
water circulating in the condenser, is condensed to water and
returned to the boiler or reactor to repeat the cycle.

For technical reasons, the best overall efficiency attainable
by fossil-fueled plants is about 38 to 40 per cent; at least 60 per
cent of the heat energy produced by burning fossil fuel is not converted to electricity, but is discharged into the air or water as
waste heat.**

Because of limitations on temperatures and pressures in the
reactor, current nuclear fueled, light-water reactor plants are

_____
*Steam-electric generating plants include fossil-fueled and nuclear
powered plants.
**The heat equivalent of 1 kilowatt hour of electricity is 3413 Btu's.
Thus, a plant that is 40 per cent efficient would need 8,533 Btu's
of heat energy to produce a single kilowatt of electricity. Waste
Heat Study, supra at 1-2.

-73-

even less efficient than fossil-fueled plants, i.e., they require
more heat to produce a unit of electricity. Present nuclear plants
operate at any where from 25 to 33 per cent efficiency.

The inefficiency of steam electric plants means that, for
every three units of heat formed by combustion or fission, only
one unit goes to produce electricity and about two units must
be discharged to the environment as waste heat. In other words,
each kilowatt hour of electricity produced by steam-electric
plants requires more than the equivalent of a kilowatt hour to
be thrown away.

> "The air and water, in essence, are used as a sink for
> the waste heat....[F]from 60 to 67 per cent of all fuel
> consumed in a central powerplant ultimately serves only
> to heat up the air and water in the vicinity of a power
> plant."*

Electricity is also lost during transmission and distribution.
While such losses vary, a fair estimate is that up to 10 per
cent of electricity generated can be "wasted" during transmission
and distribution. Thus the total process - for a fossil fuel
plant under the best conditions - would only be 34-36 per cent
efficient.

The inefficiency of steam-electric plants is deplorable from
an environmental - as well as an economic and resource preservation
- point of view, particularly when one considers that 85 per cent
of electricity expected to be produced over the next two decades
will be produced in steam-electric plants. Air pollution and
thermal pollution could be significantly reduced by increasing

---

*Energy Report, supra at 93.

the efficiency of the present means of producing electric energy.
At the same time, substantial amounts of valuable fuel could be
saved and the costs of producing electric energy reduced. As one
observer has recently stated:

> "Efficiency is the key. The higher the efficiency
> of an energy system, the more usable power is produced
> per unit of fuel, and the less pollution and waste....
> [H]owever, the steam-generating process, which currently
> accounts for over three-fourths of the nation's power,
> is essentially a ponderous, three-stage mechanical
> system.... Energy is lost at each stage, and more is lost
> in transmission lines. The whole system still reflects
> nineteenth-century attitudes that the earth's resources
> are so limitless that we can afford as the shortest route
> to the greatest profit, to waste most of them."*

1. Growing Use of Inefficient Electricity is Wasting
    Valuable Resources

A rather alarming indication of the wastefulness of inefficient electric power is that its growing use is directly related
to the increasing consumption of energy resources necessary to
yield a dollar of gross national product. For the 50 years
preceeding 1966, the relationship between total energy consumption
and real gross national product, i.e., total output of goods
and services (GNP), was that a decreasing amount of energy was
required per dollar of GNP.

Since 1966, however, the consumption of energy has begun
to rise faster than GNP. In other words, the amount of energy
consumed per each dollar of GNP is increasing as shown by the
following chart.

*Lessing, New Ways to More Power with Less Pollution, Fortune
(Nov. 1970), p.78.

GROWTH OF ENERGY CONSUMPTION IN THE U.S.

Year	Total Energy Consumption in (Trillion BTU)	Per Capita Consumption in (Thousand BTU)	Consumption per $ of GNP in (Thousand BTU)
1947	32,870	228,132	106.1
1950	34,153	224,886	96.1
1955	39,956	242,056	91.2
1960	44,816	248,989	91.9
1961	45,573	248,955	91.6
1962	47,620	256,173	89.8
1963	49,649	263,169	90.1
1964	51,515	269,188	88.8
1965	53,791	277,507	87.2
1966	56,948	290,655	86.7
1967	58,873	297,543	87.3
1968	62,432	312,363	88.2
1969*	65,645	325,102	90.2

Source: These figures were derived from U.S. Government sources
          and compiled in Competition in the Energy Markets, a re-
          port by the National Economic Research Associates, Inc.**

Significantly, several authorities have concluded that a

major reason for the increased consumption of energy per unit of

GNP is:

> "That the technical efficiency of new electric power
> plants and many other energy conversion devices is no
> longer increasing and may even decrease over the next
> several decades. This factor, coupled with the in-
> creasing share of end uses being supplied by electricity
> is at least an important item working in the direction
> of changing the historical relationship."***

---

*Preliminary GNP in constant 1958 dollars.
**Swatek, The User's Guide to the Protection of the Environment
(1970) p. 86.
***Energy Policy Staff of the United States Office of Science and
Technology, comments on Review and Comparison of Selected United
States Energy Forecasts prepared by Battelle Memorial Institute
(1969), quoted in Man's Impact on the Environment: Assessment and
Recommendations for Action (M.I.T. Press, 1970). Paul W. McCracken,
Chairman of the President's Council of Economic Advisors and
Committee on the National Energy Situation recently expressed a
similar view. New York Times, 11/3/70.

It would be wrong to assume, however, that an increase in the efficiency of electric power production will necessarily result in a reversal of the present trend towards increased energy consumption per dollar of GNP. The number of end uses requiring electricity may continue to expand and could become more accessible to the consumer by reason of lower costs.

Moreover, an increase in efficiency is likely to give rise to lower unit costs and an increase in the use of electricity in industrial processes. Increased use is further encouraged by the current promotional rate structure wherein the unit cost of electricity decreases as the amount used increases. Thus, the present trend is likely to continue unless government is willing to intercede in order to implement rational energy utilization and environmental policies.

2. Electric Heat as Prime Example of Inefficiency

The wastefulness and increased environmental damage caused by the inefficiency of the present mode of generating and supplying electric power is well illustrated by comparing electric home heating to direct heating by gas, oil or coal, and to steam heat. As noted above, conversion of fuel to electricity at a power plant under the best conditions occurs at 38-40 per cent. Moreover as much as 10 per cent of the electricity produced may be lost during transmission and distribution. Accordingly, while electricity is converted to heat in a home at about 100 per cent. efficiency, the total process is only about 34-36 per cent efficient.

By contrast, the conversion of fuel to useful heat when burned
in a home furnace has been estimated as follows:

Type of Furnace*	Efficiency*
Stoker-Fired Coal	60%-70%
Gas & Oil-Fired	
(a) Boiler	70%-80%
(b) Atomizing Burner with Forced Air	80%
Oil-Fired with Pot-Type Burner	70%

It therefore appears that the electric heating process is
165 to 700 per cent more wasteful in converting fuel to useful
heat than burning fuel in a home furnace. For example, to produce 100 u
of useful heat by home furnace, one must burn fuel with an energy
content of 125 to 167. To obtain the same result with electric
heating, 278 to 295 units (in fuel terms) must be burned which
means correspondingly more air pollution - up to 135 per cent
more. In terms of waste heat, this means that electric heating
wastes 178 to 195 energy units, as against only 25 to 67 for the
home furnace; or, in other words, from 2.5 to 8 times as much
waste heat is discharged into the environment as a result of using
electrical heating.

Commercially-purchased steam heat is also much less wasteful than electric heat. A comparison of the environmental impact of
using electric or steam heat in three New York City Housing Developments (Waterside, Twin Parks and Harlem River Park) is set forth below. This analysis assumes that(a) steam heat is twice as efficient
as electric heat in terms of fuel economy; (b) each apartment unit on
the average requires 800 gallons of fuel oil per year; (c) the
sulfur content of the oil is 0.3 per cent.

*Swatek, The User's Guide to Protection of the Environment (A Friends
of the Earth/Ballantine Book, October, 1970) p. 37.

		FUEL OIL USAGE PER YEAR (GALLONS)		SULFUR OXIDE EMISSIONS PER YEAR (TONS)*	
DEVELOPMENT	APTS.	STEAM HEAT	ELECTRIC HEAT	STEAM HEAT	ELECTRIC HEAT
Waterside	1,471	1,176,800	2,353,600	28	56
Twin Parks	2,099	1,679,200	3,358,400	40	80
Harlem River Park	1,655	1,324,000	2,648,000	31	62

*The use of electricity for light and air conditioning would add approximately 2 tons of sulfur oxides per year to each of the above emission figures (assuming 2 air conditioners per apartment).

3. <u>Re-examination of Combination Electric and Gas Companies</u>

In New York State, electric utilities are authorized to engage in the business of producing, acquiring and supplying gas,
e.g., natural gas, for light, heat and power.* The seven major
investor-owned utilities in the state sell both electricity and
gas. Thus, a large number of consumers are dependent on a single
company for both gas and electricity.

Natural gas and electricity are, of course, competitive
forms of energy. The gas industry has become a strong competitor
of electric power for large installations (e.g., office buildings
and shopping centers), and for central air conditioning households and businesses; also, electric household appliances such
as ranges and water heaters are competing strongly with gas appliances.**

"Certainly, such combination companies are at odds with a
policy of encouraging health inter-[energy]...competition at
the retail level."*** Electric utilities are highly unlikely
to market natural gas in a way which will undermine the growth
in the demand for electricity - particularly in the area of space
heating.

The utilites' argument in support of the dual electric-gas
monopoly is that they achieve certain operating economies in
meter reading and overheads. A question that demands careful

*Transportation Corp. Law, Article 2.
**In 1960, about 320,000 more gas ranges were sold than electric
ranges. In 1969, the difference was only 129,000. As regards
water heaters, in 1960, gas models outsold electric models by
1,950,000. In 1969, the difference was reduced to 1,200,000.
Merchandising Week (A Billboard Publication) Feb. 23, 1970, pp.
20-21.
***Testimony of S. David Freeman, Director, The Energy Policy Staff,
Federal Office of Science and Technology, before the Subcommittee on

reexamination is whether it is in the public interest to permit
two monopolies to be run by a single company, particularly where
the end products are directly and actually competitive and the
use of one may have significantly less impact on the environment and
result in less waste of resources than the other. Incidentally, any
cost benefits to the consumer achieved by combination companies could re-
appear as the result of meaningful price competition between the two
sources of energy.

4. Prospects for Improving Efficiency

The amount of heat required by a steam electric plant to
generate a kwh of electricity depends largely on the temperature,
pressure and moisture content of steam, which in turn depends
on the ability of boilers and fireboxes to withstand high temperatures, pressures and hot corrosive combustion gases. "The
higher the temperature and pressure of the steam and the less
its moisture, the more heat energy is carried to the turbine by
each pound of steam and the greater is the plant efficiency."*

The prospects for significant improvements in overall efficiency of steam electric power plants are not good, at least
for the next decade or two. A significant increase in the efficiency of steam-electric plants could only be attained by
much higher steam temperatures and pressures, which would
require structural materials capable of withstanding them. Such
materials are not now available.** Otherwise, increased efficiency
is dependent upon the development of more efficient energy systems,

Judiciary, May 5, 1970.
*Energy Report, supra at 93.
**See Waste Heat Study, supra; Abrahamson, Environmental Cost of
Electric Power, p. 10 (Scientists' Institute for Public Information
-1970) ("Abrahamson Report"); Bloom, Heat - A Growing Water Pollution
Problem, Environmental Reporter, Monograph No. 4, May 1, 1970.

-81-

such as the combined-cycle units, and fuel cells, and more efficient conversion processes, such as thermionics, or magnetohydrodynamics (MHD). MHD is a method for converting heat directly into electrical energy without the need for a conventional turbine and generators, which has been in existence at least since the early 1920's. It could make possible efficiencies as high as 60 per cent, thereby reducing fuel use by about one-third with a consequent reduction in the generating facility's impact on the environment.* However, the electrical industry and government have essentailly ignored MHD. In 1970 the total amount of federal and non-federal funding for MHD research was $500,000, whereas it is estimated that an initial annual effort of $2 to $4 million and a total of $500,000,000 are needed to develop the process for use in 15 to 25 years.** The Nixon Administration has requested only $1,000,000 for MHD research in the 1972 budget.***

Other more efficient forms of generation have also been virtually ignored ****in favor of nuclear "breeder" reactors, projected for commercial use in the 1980's. Such reactors will, however, only be about as efficient as present day fossil-fuel plants, i.e., 38 to 40 per cent.

---

*Energy Report, supra at 88 and n.1. A recent study done for The National Electric Research Council Task Force on MHD found that current knowledge could produce a combined-cycle MHD plant (coal-fueled; total capacity about 2000 MW) with an efficiency of 49-50 percent "if certain engineering problems are resolved." Environ-mental Report (Current Developments) pp.1050-51 (1/29/71).
**EPE Report, supra at 45.
***Environmental Reporter (Current Developments), p. 1071 (2/5/71).
****In 1970, no federal or non-federal funds were spent on research for fuel cells or combined cycle units. The total amount of funding needed to develop these forms of generation has been estimated at $100,000,000. EPE Report, supra at 45.

C. Methods for Controlling Air Pollution Hazards
Associated with Fossil-Fuel   Plants Have Not
Been Adequately Developed.

There are essentailly two methods of controlling pollutants
caused by the production of electric power at fossil-fueled
plants: (a) the application of control technology; (b) regulation of the type and sulfur and ash content of fuel.   Low
polluting fuels, i.e., natural gas and low sulfur coal and oil,
are in short supply, a situation which will not be abated in
the immediate, and perhaps the foreseeable, future. Nor has
technology for the control of emissions of sulfur oxides or
nitrogen oxides from combustion processes been adequately
developed to reduce such emissions to a level compatible
with reasonable air quality goals.

1. Unavailability of Control Technologies

   (a) Sulfur Oxides

"Contrary to widely held belief, commercially proven
technology for control of sulfur oxides from combustion processes
does not exist.

"...Positive action will be required to prevent the emission of sulfur oxides into the ambient air from more than
quadrupling by the year 2000.

"The demand for electric power is increasing so rapidly
that sulfur oxides emissions may increase even allowing for:

   (1) projected construction of nuclear power plants;

   (2) substitution of gas or low sulfur fuel oil at locations
       where they are available

   (3) use of coal of reduced sulfur content to the extent
       that can be expected;

- 83 -

(4) introduction of improved combustion methods; and

(5) application of improved stack-gas treatment and sulfur recovery processes."*

These conclusions reflect the considered judgement of a panel of experts chosen in large measure from industry itself.**

The Academy's report outlines the control processes currently under development. Suffice it to say that at the current level of industrial and governmental expenditure, we are years away from achieving acceptable levels of emissions from electric power generating facilities through the employment of post-refinery, sulfur removal processes.

(b) Nitrogen Oxides

Techniques for altering the combustion process within the boiler appear to be available which can substantially reduce nitrogen oxide emissions. These techniques, however, are now only being employed by two utilities in California.

On the other hand, there are no commercially proven methods for removing nitrogen oxides from stack gases emitted by power plants. Aside from California, no meaningful effort is being made by industry or government to develop adequate technology for controlling nitrogen oxide emissions.

As previously indicated, the levels of nitrogen oxides in New York City have risen alarmingly in the recent past. More power generation - regardless of the fuel employed - means more

*Abatement of Sulfur Oxide Emissions from Stationary Combustion Sources, National Academy of Engineering, National Research Council (1970). See also Environmental Reporter(Current Developments),p.835 (12/11/70).
**The panel included among its members top executives from firms such as General Electric, DuPont, Commonwealth Edison and Con Ed.

nitrogen oxides. Adequate emissions controls must be made

available.

Basic Reason for Lack of Adequate Controls

A basic reason for the lack of adequate control technology is that

 neither   the federal nor the state governments, the utilities

nor their suppliers have committed a significant amount of time

or money to the development of such technologies. For example,

in 1970, the total amount of federal and non-federal funds spent

to develop processes for the removal of sulfur oxides and

nitrogen oxides from stack gases was $15 million - 10 per cent

of the estimated $150 000,000 needed to develop a workable

process in a minimum of five years.* Research and development on

precombustion processes is similarly inadequate. For example,

total federal and non-federal spending on the development of a

sulfur removing process from coal was about $2 million in 1970.

It has been estimated that $20 million will be needed to develop

a process in 4 to 7 years.**

Until entering into the August 22 Memorandum of Under-

standing with the City last summer, Con Ed had made virtually

no effort to develop stack gas removal processes, although

they are vital to the protection of the public health and suc-

cess of the City's proposed air pollution control program.

Parenthetically, we note that the failure to recover sul-

fur results in a shameful waste of resources: about 12 million

*EPE Report, supra at 44.
**Idem.

tons of sulfur are emitted into the air each year, while the
country consumes about 16 million tons - all of which is mined.*

2. Shortages of Low-Polluting Fuels

The FPC has estimated the amounts of fuel which will be
required to meet the projected demand for electric energy over
the next two decades as follows (expressed in tons of coal
having a heat equivalent of 25 million Btu):

PROJECTED FUEL USE BY ELECTRIC UTILITIES
(AMOUNTS IN MILLIONS OF TONS)

	1970		1980		1990	
	Amount	Percent	Amount	Percent	Amount	Percent
Coal	304.6	56.7	472.0	42.5	613.6	38.8
Natural Gas	145.9	27.2	195.9	17.2	245.9	11.6
Oil	59.5	11.5	86.8	7.8	91.8	4.3
Nuclear	27.2	5.0	365.5	32.1	1,176.1	55.3
Total	537.2	100.0	1,111.2	100.0	2,127.4	100.0**

(a) Coal

Approximately 90% of the total reserves of low sulfur coal
(less than 1% sulfur content) are located west of the Mississippi
and are not readily obtainable for electric power generation
in New York State. Low-sulfur coal reserves in the East, for
the most part, are already committed to the domestic and foreign
steel industry. Meaningful supplies of such coal are presently
unavailable for use by power generating facilities in New York
State.***

*Your Right to Clean Air, A Manual for Citizen Action, p. 14
(The Conservation Foundation, Washington, D.C., August 1970)
**"All forecasts of the relative energy mix for power generation are
based on the assumption that those fuel resources will be available at
the requisite quality level of prescribed environmental standards, at an
economically feasible price." J.N. Nassikas, FPC Chairman, An Outline
of National Energy Policy: Some Personal Reflections, Remarks at FPC
50th Anniversary Program, June 3, 1970, p.4.
***Considerations Affecting Steam Power Plant Selection, Office of
Science and Technology, (December, 1968).

Some studies and experimental projects for reducing the
sulfur content in coal have been undertaken by industry and
governmental agencies. They reveal that feasible methods of
reducing sulfur content to acceptable air quality levels are
still in the developmental stage and will not be available for
use in electric power generation for many years.* In sum, it
is unrealistic to anticipate the use of low sulfur coal as a
fuel for electric power generation in New York State within the
foreseeable future.**

The development of effective and economically feasible
methods for controlling sulfur oxide emisssions from coal should
be given the highest priority, however, since this would increase
the usefulness of the immense coal resources in this country
and abroad for electric power production.Compared to estimates
of oil and gas resources, domestic coal reserves are vast,
estimated by the United Stated Bureau of Mines to equal 1000
to 1500 times estimated annual coal production of 856,000,000
tons in the year 2000. According to Joseph C. Swidler, PSC
Chairman, coal "constitutes the national guarantee of adequacy
of fuel supply for a good many generations, although at constantly
increasing costs."***

(b) Residual Fuel Oil

Here again, the country is faced with the two-pronged problem
of unproven technology and critical shortages.

---

*See also A.M. Squires, Clean Power From Coal, Science (August 28, 1970)
pp 821-27 which discusses a technology based on high pressure combustion
of coal to achieve sulfur oxide removal.
**Control Techniques for Sulfur Oxide Air Pollutants, United States De-
partment of Health, Education and Welfare (January, 1969)
***Problems of Energy Supply In a Crowded World (Oct. 15, 1970), supra .

A primary reason for the shortage of domestic supplies
of residual oil has been the desire of United States refiners
to maximize profits. Residual oil has traditionally sold for a
much lower price than other oil products, such as gasoline and
jet fuel. From 1959 to 1969, the output of residual oil has
dropped from 14.4% of refinery production to 6.8% on a national
basis, and from 17.6% to 7% on the East Coast.

Notwithstanding several relatively advanced, desulfurization processes for obtaining low-sulfur residual fuel oil, increased cost and unstable supply problems have not been resolved.
The estimated capital investment to construct a desulfurizing
plant is $260 per barrel of daily capacity. Without regard to
the scarcity of fuel oil itself, whether of a high or low sulfur content, the added refining step of reducing sulfur content
to less than 1% has been estimated at 50 to 80 cents per bar-
rel. The desulfurization process would raise fuel oil prices
to the utilities anywhere from 20% to 35% with a concomitant increase in consumer prices for electricity.

Fuel prices have already risen astronomically throughout
the East Coast. Industry spokesmen claim that increased transportation costs, political problems in North Africa and unfavor-
able import quotas have compelled a rising price structure.*
While these factors account for some portion of the increased

*See, e.g., Mayer, Why the U.S. Is In An 'Energy Crisis,'
Fortune (Nov. 1970), pp. 75,77.

costs, there is some evidence that extraordinary profiteering and the playing off of one low sulfur region against another are at least equally important in explaining the unprecedented price increases.

Additionally, there is a general shortage of residual oil necessary for desulfurization. According to a study by the Petroleum Industry Research Foundation, domestic and Caribbean refiners (the major source of residual oil) are expected to achieve only a slight increase in production during the next

year, despite an anticipated increase in East Coast require-

ments of 13-14% over the period.* Low sulfur distillate oil,

which is mixed with high sulfur residual to meet the legal requirements

ments, is also in short supply.

John N. Nassikas, Chairman of the FPC, recently confirmed

the severe fuel shortage and suggested that it may assume crisis

proportions in the near future when he stated:

> "...the supply prospects for residual fuel oil over the
> next few years are not encouraging. Most of the world supply
> of residual is high in sulfur content. Thus far, the east
> coast utilities have not experienced serious difficulties,
> other than higher costs, in switching from coal to low
> sulfur residual fuel oil to meet air pollution control
> regulations. Their experience has encouraged some mid-
> west utilities to apply for permits to import low sulfur
> oil.... The hard fact is that we cannot assume that
> adequate supplies of low sulfur fuels will become available
> simply because they are needed. Not only does it take
> time and money to open new coal mines, build new refineries,
> expand the capacity of our transportation network, and take
> the many other necessary steps to bring the desired fuels
> to the ultimate consumers, it also requires coordinated
> long-range planning by utilities, the fuel suppliers, and
> the air pollution control officials, but we have not yet
> made the institutional arrangements to facilitate this
> type of planning."**

Mr. Nassikas' remarks make it abundantly clear that we

are in deep trouble with respect to meeting projected fuel and

energy demands over the next several decades, while at the same

time achieving adequate environmental protection.

(c) Natural Gas

The availability of natural gas, the least polluting of

the fossil-fuels, seems even less certain than the availability

of low sulfur coal or residual fuel oil.

---

*See W. Smith, "East Faces Fuel Shortages" (N.Y. Times, Sept. 27,1970).
See also Oser "Owners In City Start to Feel Credit Squeeze."(N.Y. Times
October 18, 1970, Section 8, p.1).
**An Outline of National Energy Policy:Some Personal Reflections,
(June 3, 1970) supra.

Ten years ago, 32 million customers used 12 trillion
cubic feet of natural gas. Last year over 40 million consumers
used 20 trillion cubic feet. Industry studies have projected
that total consumption of 761 trillion cubic feet will be required
over the next two decades.

Currently, one sixth of domestic natural gas is used for
power generation. The FPC has projected a decline in the use
of this fuel by the utility industry from its present level
of 27.2% of fuel requirements to 11.6% in 1990.

About 12 years ago, the rate of drilling oil and gas wells
began to level off. Production and consumption continued to
increase. Proven reserves declined for the first time in 1968
and again in 1969, as production outstripped new discoveries.*
The utility companies have faced difficulty in retaining even
their present allotments. The PSC's staff has prepared a report indicating that the shortage of natural gas may be approach-
ing a crisis level and that some restrictions on the addition of
new industrial customers, as well as on the promotional activities
of gas suppliers, are likely to be imposed.

According to Joseph C. Swidler, Chairman of the PSC, "The
crux of the gas problem is that producers have not been looking
for gas, and without an assured supply, the pipeline companies
have not been building pipelines to carry additional gas to
market."** We anticipate that the FPC will accede to industry

*Not Enough Gas in the Pipelines, Fortune Magazine (November, 1969).
**Statement before Subcommittee on Special Small Business Problems
of Select Committee on Small Business, House of Representatives,
Oct. 8, 1970.

requests for significant increases in wellhead prices, in
the near future. While the price increases may lead to increased
exploration for and production of natural gas, there is a time
lag of several years between exploration and production. Thus,
even with added incentives, production is likely to continue to
fall short of demand for at least the next several years.

There has been increasing interest in the importation of
liquified natural gas (LNG) to supplement our domestic supply.
Here again, economic and technological problems plus the critical
shortage of tankers equipped to transport sizeable quantities of
LNG raise serious doubts as to the availability of this alternative,
either in the long run or immediate future.

El Paso Natural Gas Company and the Philadelphia Gas Works
plan to import approximately 1,500,000 Mcf per day from Algeria
and Venezuela by 1974. Even if these large-scale projects
are completed by 1974, they will represent less than 2% of projected demand. According to FPC estimates, LNG imports are unlikely to account for more than 5% of natural gas consumption in
the United States by 1980.*

More than a year ago, FPC Commissioner John Carver warned that:

"(a)t a time when we are seeking incentives for increased
exploration and production, when increased imports from
Canada and transport in liquid form are being planned and
when research on conversion of coal to gas is being accelerated
it would seem very foolhardy in the extreme to count it heavily
in our inventory of potential electric power sources."**(Emphasis
added)

*FPC, Staff Report on Natural Gas Supply and Demand,pp.60-64(Sept. 1969).
**Remarks at the Annual Conference of the Atomic Industrial Forum
(12/1/69), quoted in Energy Report, supra at 62.

FPC Chairman John N. Nassikas, at a recent conference on energy in

the 70's also cautioned that:

> "we cannot realistically expect to meet all incremental
> demands for gas in the course of the next five years, be-
> cause the development of new gas by exploration, overland
> or LNG imports, or supplementary technologies for more
> efficient recovery for production of gas from coal, will
> require several years before making substantial contribu-
> tions to the gas stream."*

Moreover, should significant amounts of natural gas become

available, it is unlikely that utilities will receive the major

portion thereof unless the FPC reverses its present policies. For

example, during the Con Ed-Astoria debate last summer, the FPC told

the City that it was "unrealistic" to expect that Con Ed could ob-

tain natural gas to burn in its proposed 1600 MW units.

In any event, there is serious doubt whether from an air pol-

lution standpoint, the limited supply of natural gas available to

New York City should be allocated for use in electric power genera-

tion, rather than space heating. While the combustion of natural

gas does not result in sulfur oxide emissions, when burned at power

plants in large steam boilers, at high temperatures, it does result

in high emissions of nitrogen oxide.

Space heaters, using natural gas and operating at lower tem-

peratures, emit less nitrogen oxides. Thus, some experts, among

them Dr. Robert Rickles, Commissioner of the City's Department

of Air Resources, feel that available supplies of natural gas

should be used in space heaters rather than power plants.

---

*Public Utilities Fortnightly (Feb. 4, 1971), p. 50.

* * * * *

In sum, the prospects for securing an adequate supply of low polluting fuels for use by electric generating facilities in New York State within the foreseeable future are exceedingly poor.

The shortage of low-polluting fuels is largely the result of ill-advised, piece-meal policies of the federal government, such as the oil import quota system, and proration laws which restrict domestic production of oil.* These policies are designed to favor special interests (oil interests) rather than the public welfare.

The availability of low-polluting fuels is critical to improving the quality of the City's air and maintaining power supplies during air pollution alerts - when natural gas is required to be burned.

In an **effort** to reduce the amount of sulfur oxides in the City to a level commensurate with federal and state standards, EPA has included in its proposed air pollution control law a requirement that all fossil-fueled units in the City utilize low-sulfur fuel, effective October 1, 1971, on the following basis: distillate oils used for space heating, - 0.2% sulfur; residual oils - 0.3% sulfur; coal - 0.3% sulfur.**

---

*See, e.g., <u>Cold Facts About the Fuel Shortage</u>, Consumer Reports (Feb. 1971). State proration laws are authorized and assisted by the federal government under the Connally Hot Oil Act, 15 U.S.C. § 715-715M, which prohibits as contraband any shipment in interstate commerce of oil produced, stored or made available in excess of state-imposed limits.
**At present there is a 1% sulfur content limit on fuels used in the City. State law now in effect will require any power plant built after April 1, 1971 within the New York City Metropolitan Area to burn 0.37% sulfur fuel.

- 94 -

APCO has warned, however, that even with full enforcement of these requirements, annual average sulfur dioxide concentrations will be about 0.04 ppm, still above the acceptable level of 0.03 ppm. According to APCO, the only apparent way to achieve a level of 0.03 ppm would be through a large-scale conversion to natural gas, at least in Manhattan.

Unfortunately, as noted above, prospects for securing an adequate supply of natural gas for use by electric generating facilities within the foreseeable future are exceedingly poor. It is essential for federal and state governments to encourage the development of methods for removing pollutants from high polluting fuels before burning, as well as to encourage the discovery, production and distribution of low-polluting fuels at fair prices.

In discussing fuel shortages, we should not lose sight of the fact that the production, as well as transport, of fossil-fuels may have serious adverse health and other environmental effects. For example, underground coal mining exposes miners to coal dust, which has been related to chronic respiratory diseases. Strip mining of coal, which is likely to increase substantially to meet projected demands, results in deforestation, erosion and general uglification of land, as well as drainage of acid wastes, e.g., sulfuric acid, into streams and burning of abandoned mines and waste. Oil spills from the development of off-shore wells, e.g., the recent Santa Barbara Channel case in California and blow-outs at Chevron Oil Company's facilities in the Gulf of Mexico, and discharges from tankers result in substantial damage to beaches, wildlife refuges, and seafood resources.

An additional disturbing factor in connection with the above-
described fuel shortages is that the petroleum industry, with
the aid of the federal government, is rapidly acquiring ownership
of all the nation's energy resources, including nuclear fuel.
Increasing concentration in the energy production market may
eliminate meaningful inter-fuel competition and result in the
vesting of substantial political and economic power in the hands
of a select few.

Many public officials are alarmed over the rapid concentration
of firms in the energy market.   United States Senator George
D. Aiken, a member of the Joint Congressional Committeee on Atomic
Energy, warns that:

> "There is some group determined to get control of electrical
> energy in this nation.... When you control energy - and
> oil interests now control coal and are on their way to control-
> ling nuclear fuel - then you control the nation. I see this
> as a very serious threat to political democracy."*

Since the mid-1960's, oil companies have been actively
acquiring interests in other energy resources. Six of the ten
largest oil companies now have interests in every other fuel. The
petroleum industry is now reported to provide at least 25 per
cent of the country's coal production.

On a national basis, only two of the ten largest coal
companies are independently owned - the remaining eight are
owned by oil companies, other mineral companies or other large
industrial concerns with stakes in the energy field.   The
two largest owners of coal reserves are both oil companies:

---

*Mintz & Warner, Electricity for the Future - I, The Washington
Post (August 23, 1970).

Standard Oil of New Jersey and Continental Oil Co. According to PSC Chairman Swidler, this concentration of coal reserves in the hands of oil companies "has been abetted by the federal government by the sale of public land coal reserves to oil companies."*

Oil and gas are major competitive fuels; but most natural gas is produced by integrated oil companies. The twenty-five largest oil companies all have natural gas interests.

The petroleum companies are also rapidly entering the nuclear fuel business. At least eighteen oil companies have invested in producing and processing uranium. In 1969, oil companies accounted for about 14 per cent of domestic uranium production and did about 37 per cent of the drilling for uranium exploration and development. As of January 1, 1970, they controlled about 45 per cent of known uranium reserves.**

Kerr-McGee, an oil company, owns 27 per cent of total uranium milling capacity, which exceeds that of any other firm. It also is one of the two companies in the business of converting uranium into the form in which it is used to enrich nuclear fuel. The other company is Atlantic Richfield, one of the nation's largest oil companies.

Oil companies, portraying their investments as efforts to diversify, are in fact obtaining control of their actual and potential competitors. Walter B. Comegys, Deputy Assistant

---

*Statement before Subcommitteee on Special Small Business Problems of Select Committee on Small Business, House of Representatives, Oct.8,1970.
**Testimony of S. David Freeman, Director, Energy Policy Staff, federal Office of Science and Technology, before the Subcommittee on Antitrust and Monopoly Legislation of the Senate Committee on the Judiciary (May 5, 1970).

Attorney General in the United States Department of Justice,
recently testified before the Antitrust Subcommittee of the
Senate Committee on the Judiciary that: "we cannot lightly
forego interfuel competition as the most effective long-term
force for consumer protection in the energy field."* Neither
Congress nor the Justice Department, however, has made any
apparent attempt to prevent further concentration of energy
resources or to compel energy producers to divest themselves of
interests in competing firms.

PSC Chairman Swidler has also criticized the trend toward
concentration in energy markets, as follows:

> "It seems to me to be vital to the best interests of the
> nation that we not only maintain competition between
> companies, but also between energy sources. Effective
> competition can assure economic efficiency in production
> and consumption and avoid misallocation of our scarce
> productive resources. At the moment competition in the
> energy market is fast waning, and soon will be extinct if
> the present trend continues."**

*Mintz & Warner, The Washington Post (August 23, 1970), supra.
**Statement before Subcommittee on Special Small Business Problems
of Select Committee on Small Business, House of Representatives
(October 8, 1970).

D. Thermal Pollution: Current Condenser Cooling Methods Pose Serious Environmental Problems.

The method most often employed by utilities for dissipating waste heat is the "once-through" cooling process in which water is withdrawn from a lake, stream, river, passed through the condenser and returned heated to the source. Although this cooling method is the most damaging in terms of thermal impact, it is used by utilities primarily because it is cheaper and more convenient than other possible cooling methods. Some utilities even refuse to recognize the thermal pollution problem. For example, J. Harris Ward, Chairman of the Board of Directors of Commonwealth Edison Co., recently remarked that "raising the temperature of the water a few degrees is no reason for civilization to commit suicide."*

Cooling ponds and cooling towers, which transfer waste heat to the air rather than the cooling water source, are often mentioned as possible alternatives to wasteful, damaging once-through cooling. However, they pose significant environmental problems.

Cooling ponds and associated drainage areas require large amounts of land. Approximately one acre of pond plus ten acres of drainage area to supply water for the pond is needed for each megawatt of generating capacity.**

*Why Utilities Can't Meet Demand, Special Report published in Business Week, (November 29, 1970).
**Energy Report, supra at 98.

There are two types of cooling towers: "wet" or evaporative towers, where heat is dissipated by evaporation with the flow of air provided by mechanical means or natural draft; and "dry" towers, which discharge only dry heat to the air by conduction and convection. Wet cooling towers can involve the diversion of substantial amounts of water from the cooling source. For example, Southern California Edison Company has estimated that, by the year 2000, the amount of water that would be evaporated if it had to utilize wet cooling towers for its plants would equal over one million acre feet of water a year - or about 25 per cent of California's allocation of Colorado River water.* This, of course, is only one utility in one portion of the country.

A recent report by engineers at Batelle Memorial Institute, Pacific Northwest Laboratory, found that:

> "Studies of evaporation show that roughly twice the water loss can be expected from cooling tower operation as from systems using ponds or lakes. To put this in proper perspective, if...the total national energy requirement from 1970-2000 had to be served by direct evaporation devices such as cooling towers, the incremental electrical capacity of 1,040 gigawatts requires a consumptive flow of 31,200 cu. ft./sec. of water for evaporation alone. This sums to a total of approximately 24,000,000 acre feet per year, about twice the flow of the entire Colorado River."**

Natural draft cooling towers require the erection of large structures that are generally unsightly, e.g. 30 stories high, 400 feet in diameter at the base. Also, evaporative cooling towers release damaging chemicals and large quantities of moisture

---

*Remarks of C.F. Luce, Chairman of the Board of Con Ed, before the FPC 50th Anniversay Ceremony (June 3, 1970).
**Jaske, R. T., Fletcher, J.F., & Wise, K.R., Heat Rejection Requirements of the U.S., Chem. Engineering Progress (Vol.66, No.11) p.20 (Nov.1970)

to the atmosphere which can cause fog and icing on roads.
Icing can also form on powerlines, thereby contributing to the
unreliability of power supply. At fossil-fueled plants,
smoke plumes can intereact with water vapor from a cooling tower,
thereby precipitating sulfuric acid solutions.

Significantly, in March of last year, James G. Cline,
Chairman of The New York State Atomic and Space Development
Authority (NYASD), expressed serious doubt as to the feasibility
of employing evaporative-type cooling towers throughout New
York State. He said:

> "under the high humidity and low temperature conditions
> which prevail over much of New York, wet cooling towers
> could potentially produce unacceptable atmospheric effects."*

Dry cooling towers are either much larger in size or greater
in number than evaporative towers. They are also considerably
more expensive than evaporative towers.

Dry towers are likely to release large amounts of warm
dry air into the atmosphere, the environmental effects of which
are unknown. Also, dry towers do not cool water as much as
wet towers, which reduces plant efficiency and requires more
fuel per kilowatt hour of electricity generated.** None have
been installed in the United States.

In sum, at the present time, there are no environmentally
acceptable or proven alternatives to once-through coooling for disposing of the vast quantities of waste heat produced by steam-

---

*NYASD, Eighth Annual Report (4/1/69-3/31/70), p.22.
**Energy Report, supra at 100.

electric plants. One promising alternative may be to develop
beneficial uses for waste heat, such as fish farming, space heating,
desalination of water, power generation in "combined cycle" units,
and industrial production.* To date, however, little research
or money has been devoted by government or the utilities to developing such productive uses.

Some reduction in thermal pollution might also be possible
if and when more efficient methods of electric power generation
are developed. According to PSC Chariman Joseph Swidler:

> "We know that the discharge of thermal effluents may have
> severe impact...[and] that if we are not soon to be in trouble,
> we must find ways to reduce the proportion of the heat released
> by combustion or nuclear fission into fresh water bodies
> and many salt water areas....
>
> If we are to eliminate the problem of waste heat as a pressing
> universal concern, we must conduct a major research effort to
> discover a means of achieving substantial higher efficiency levels.**

NYASD which has recently completed the first thermal survey
of waters throughout New York State, has concluded that additional
electric power generation, with its attendant cooling water releases, can only be undertaken "if careful ecological research and
engineering analysis serve as the basis for the siting of future
power stations and the design of their cooling water release structures."*** There is little evidence to date, however, of the willingness of industry or government to undertake the research essential to
develop acceptable methods for disposing of waste heat. For example,

---

*See Remarks of Joseph C. Swidler, Chairman, PSC, entitled "Problems
and Opportunities in Waste Heat Disposal, " before Conference on the
Beneficial Uses of Thermal Discharges, Albany, N.Y. (Sept. 18, 1970).
**Idem.
***A Thermal Profite of the Waters of New York State, A Report of
NYASD, p.3 (1970).

despite suggestions that dry cooling technology is a "must"
for utilities "and a very hard and slow thing to develop,"*
virtually no public or private money was spent in 1970 on heat
transfer studies for dry towers or dry tower demonstration,
which is estimated to take 3 to 7 years and cost $5 million
to $10 million.**

---

*Remarks of C.F. Luce, Chairman of the Board of Con Ed, before the
FPC 50th Anniversay Ceremony, June 3, 1970.
EPE Report, supra at 44.

E. The Problem of Adequately Controlling Radiation Ha-
    zards Associated with Nuclear Power Development and
    Fully Informing the Public Concerning Them

    1. Projected Growth in Nuclear Power Facilities
        Increases Potential Hazards from Radiation and
        Requires Reexamination of Regulatory and In-
        dustry Policies, Particularly Those Raising
        Questions of Public Credibility.

The number and size of nuclear power plants throughout the
country and this state are expected to increase dramatically over
the next 30 years. There are now a total of 20 nuclear plants
operating throughout the country, the largest of which is 800 MW.
During the next 8-10 years, about 90 nuclear plants are scheduled
to come on stream throughout the country; more than a third of
them will be larger than 1000 MW. The commitment of industry to
nuclear power is illustrated by the fact that, at current prices,
nuclear plants now ordered represent an investment for plants and
nuclear fuel of about $80 billion, over a 30-year operating per-
iod.*

The AEC projects that, by the end of 1980, 150,000 MW of nuclear capacity will be in operation, supplying about 25 per cent
of electricity demands, and that within the next 30 years, about
900 nuclear plants will be built, the majority of which will be
1000 MW or larger.

A substantial portion of the projected nuclear expansion is
planned for New York State.** As of December 31, 1970, three of
the seven major utilities in New York State were operating nuclear
plants, with a total capacity of 1,191 MW. Only one other state -

*Environmental Reporter (Current Developments), p. 1119 (2/12/71).
**See also Section V. B. infra.

Connecticut - has more nuclear generating capacity (1227 MW).

Eight nuclear units - all larger than 800 MW - are planned for New York State within the next 10 years. Almost one-half of Con Ed's additions will be nuclear. Long Island Lighting Company intends to build an 820 MW nuclear plant at Shoreham, Long Island - about 50 miles from New York City - by 1975, and another plant in the same area in the early 1980's. The Power Authority of the State of New York (PASNY) is building an 800 MW nuclear unit near Oswego, New York.

By the early 1980's, Con Ed plans to install about 4,400 MW of nuclear capacity at its Indian Point complex - about 25 miles from New York - and four 1000 MW nuclear units on David's Island, about one-half mile off the shore of New Rochelle and about 14 miles from the Empire State Building. The Company has also announced that it is considering placing large nuclear plants on off-shore islands in waters surrounding New York - at points about 10-15 miles from City Hall, which means about 2-3 miles off the shore of Brooklyn or Staten Island.

As regards nuclear fuel reprocessing facilities, the only commercial facility in operation in the nation is located about 30 miles south of Buffalo in West Valley, New York. The facility is owned by Nuclear Fuel Services, Inc., (NFS) a subsidiary of Getty Oil Company, with Skelly Oil Company, a Getty subsidiary, holding a minority interest. NFS recently announced plans to triple the annual capacity (300 tons per day of spent fuel) of its existing plant, which will make it larger than two other plants now planned south of Chicago, Illinois and in South Carolina in the near future.

Also, NYASD
has recently opened a plutonium storage facility in West Valley,
New York, as a first step toward the establishment of a plutonium
fuel fabrication complex with private industry.* Plutonium is the
major fuel to be used in new breeder reactors, projected for commercial use in the 1980's.

At present, no one has even remotely adequate experience with
reactors of the types and sizes projected for future use - especially
the electrical industry. Milton Shaw, Director of the AEC's Division
of Reactor Development and Technology, in commenting on the difficulties being encountered by the industry in meeting nuclear plant
construction schedules, testified before the Joint Committee on Atomic
Energy last year that:

> "Probably the biggest problems still being encountered are
> due to the fact that there are 71 utilities, mostly inex-
> perienced in advanced technologies, actively involved with
> nuclear power plants. Most of these utilities are going
> through their first experience with a large nuclear plant,
> along with the architect-engineers, and the construction
> forces in many various locations....** (emphasis added)
>
> [T]he translation of any reactor system from the laboratory
> to a maturity sufficient for safe, reliable, and economic
> widespread applications to utility power generation is an
> extremely difficult and costly undertaking, requiring the
> highest level of technical management, professional compe-
> tence and organizational skill. Nowhere are these needs
> more apparent than in the breeder program, which is perhaps
> the most difficult reactor development effort in the his-
> tory of the AEC."***

---

*NYASD Eighth Annual Report (3/31/69 - 4/1/70).
**AEC Authorizing Legislation Fiscal Year 1971, (Pt. 3), p.1428
(March 11, 1970).
***Id., at 1419.

Just recently he told the same Congressional committee that it is

> "important to note that there are still too many first-of-a-kind components not being proof-tested until after installation in the plant and there are many new features which remain to be proven out until the plants operate at full power. Moreover, only limited experience has been gained with one commercial type 800 MWe light water plant - the Dresden-2 unit supplied by General Electric. Experience is yet to become available with many first-of-a-kind components for 800 MWe and larger size plants designed by the other manufacturers."*

*Testimony on FY1972 Authorization, Hearings before the Joint Committee on Atomic Energy (March 4, 1971).

-107-

Moreover, the projected proliferation of large nuclear facilities will result in expansion of nuclear fuel reprocessing activities, more radioactive wastes to transport and dispose of, and increased risk of nuclear reactor accidents. As the number of plants increases, radioactive wastes will build up and emissions may increase. Also, as nuclear plants are clustered together, the total amount of radioactivity to which a region may be exposed will be greater than that released by any single plant.

The potential increase in radiation hazards associated with the projected expansion in nuclear facilities compels a careful examination of the propriety of current regulatory mechanisms and policies for protecting against such hazards, as well as the adequacy of basic information disclosed to the public and governmental officials with responsibility for environmental protection, for enabling them to evaluate intelligently the benefits and risks involved in making a substantial commitment to expansion of nuclear power. Whether or not nuclear experts in industry or government possess adequate information, it is essential that the public be fully and completely informed.

Now, under the Atomic Energy Act of 1954, as amended (42 U.S.C. §2011 et. seq.),the AEC has the basic responsibility for regulating the location, as well as safety of and radioactive emissions from, major nuclear facilities in a manner which protects "the health and safety of the public." At the same time, the AEC has the responsibility for _promoting_ the development of atomic energy for peaceful, military and industrial purposes. Until recently, it also was re-

-108-

sponsible for establishing radiation exposure and emission standards governing virtually all man-made sources of radioactivity
and had established such standards. The standards do not, however,
apportion the maximum allowable exposure among the various sources
of radiation, i.e., power plants, reprocessing facilities, medical,
industrial and military sources. Moreover, the adequacy of current
standards is presently the subject of widespread debate and proposals
have been made to revise the existing standards downward to
approximate more closely actual practice and the apparent design
capabilities of power facilities.

The AEC has consistently taken the position that no state or
local government should have the right to establish stricter
standards for radiation exposure and emissions from major nuclear
facilities than are set by the federal government, or to regulate
reactor safety. Recently, this position has been challenged by
several states which have imposed limits on radioactive emissions
from nuclear power plants which are stricter than the AEC requirements. The projected proliferation of nuclear power facilities,
as well as an increasing awareness of the environmental problems
posed by nuclear power development, is generating increased
interest and activity on the part of state and local officials
in exercising their inherent police powers to protect against
possible harm to the public health and welfare from radiation
hazards associated with nuclear power (as they do now regarding
thermal pollution and air pollution from fossil-fueled plants).
Unfortunately, however, the State of New York is in an untenable position in this regard. Several years ago, Governor

-109-

Rockefeller ceded to the AEC exclusive regulatory authority with
respect to the radiation hazards associated with major nuclear
facilities (such as power plants and reprocessing facilities).*

A credibility gap exists with respect to assurances by
the AEC and the nuclear power industry, including utilities,
regarding the safety of and potential hazards associated with
expanded nuclear power development. Significant factors contributing
to the lack of public confidence in the "nuclear power experts" are:
(1) the dual responsibility of the AEC for promotion of nuclear
power and for protection of the public health and safety from
radiation hazards; (2) the ambiguous attitude of the AEC toward
siting nuclear plants near densely populated urban areas, as well
as the economic incentive for utilities to locate such plants
as near as possible to major load centers; (3) the federal Price-
Anderson Act, strongly backed by the nuclear power industry and
the AEC, which limits the liability of reactor manufacturers,
utilities and nuclear fuel reprocessors to a very small percentage
of possible damages from a nuclear accident; (4) the refusal of
the AEC to inform the public fully as to the risks and all possible
consequences of an accident involving the large reactors now
being placed in service; (5) the AEC's opposition to permitting
state and local authorities to impose restrictions on major nuclear
facilities regarding radioactive emissions which are stricter than
those the AEC imposes; (6) the AEC's failure to set radiation
exposure and emission levels specifically for nuclear power plants

*The situation in New York State, as well as the reasons militating
against exclusive federal regulation of radiation hazards, is
discussed in Section V. D. infra.

-110-

and reprocessing facilities ; (7) the AEC's recent decision essentially to terminate safety research and development on light water reactors (expected to be increasingly placed in service for at least the next 15 years) and to shift responsibility in this area to industry which, historically, has not made any substantial effort to carry out such research and development; (8) the rush of industry and the AEC to place light water reactors in service (reinforced by the economic incentive for utilities to increase reliance on nuclear facilities) although they (a) offer no resource conservation benefits, (b) contribute 50 per cent more thermal pollution than fossil-fuel plants, (c) a critical need exists for more safety research and development on these reactors (but the AEC is cutting back in this area), and (d) create substantial amounts of high-level radioactive wastes which must be isolated from man for many centuries. As regards management of such wastes, the AEC is attempting to develop a safer method than the current one of storing the wastes in boiling, liquid form in metal containers which must be changed at least every 20 years to protect against corrosion and leakage; but, the AEC's current estimates are that the new method (solidification and storage in salt mines) will not be available for large-scale commercial use for at least another five to seven years. Moreover, the safety, as well as environmental implications, of this approach remain to be studied, as well as independently evaluated, in detail.

The issues of credibility raised by the foregoing must be resolved promptly. Whether or not nuclear experts in industry and government possess adequate information and are willing to rely on "conservative"

-111-

designs, they have a clear obligation, and our objective must be, to provide full and complete information to the public regarding all possible risks and benefits of nuclear power development. Dependence on nuclear experts with a stake in, or substantial ties to, development of nuclear power must be drastically decreased and replaced with independent, objective evaluations of proposals to expand nuclear facilities. Moreover, the public, as well as state and local authorities with responsibility for environmental protection, must expand their participation in and control over development of nuclear power.

2. Controversy Surrounding Adequacy of AEC Standards

John W. Gofman, formerly Associate Director of the Biomedical Division of AEC's Lawrence Radiation Laboratory, and Arthur R. Tamplin, Research Associate at Lawrence Radiation Laboratory, have recently called for "the earliest possible revision downward, by at least a factor of tenfold, of the allowable radiation dosage (i.e., 170 mr per year)...."* They predict a 10 per cent increase in all forms of cancer plus leukemia if the population receives the AEC's maximum allowable radiation exposure. Assuming the population increases 50% during the next 30 years, Gofman and Tamplin maintain there will be about 32,000 additional cases of leukemia and cancer caused by radiation each year.**

They also assert that present AEC radiation limits could

---

*Energy Report, supra at 112.
**Gofman and Tamplin, Radiation: The Invisible Casualties, Environment (April, 1970) p. 12.

lead to 150,000 to 1.5 million cases of genetic damage per year.*

The Gofman and Tamplin projections regarding increased deaths are based in part on the conservative assumptions that there is a linear relationship between radiation exposure and adverse health effects, i.e., a linear extrapolation from high dosages down to very low dosages,** and that risk of harm is directly proportional to exposure.

Other authorities have questioned the AEC's maximum permissible dosage levels and supported the call for a ten-fold reduction in AEC's allowable radiation dosage. Dr. Linus C. Pauling estimated in an article in the September 1970 issue of the Bulletin of the Atomic Scientists that 96,000 additional deaths from cancer would occur each year if the general public were exposed to such levels. Also, Dr. Joshua Lederberg, Professor of Genetics, Stanford School of Medicine, has predicted that exposure to the permissible levels would result "in genetically determined diseases that would mean $10 billion a year in additional health costs."***

*Long Island Press (9/9/70), p.27.
**Hearings, Pt. 1, supra at 642.
***CPR National Journal, p.2488 (Nov. 14, 1970).

Other scientists and the AEC have sharply criticized the above-mentioned predictions as unrealistic and misleading, primarily on the ground that power plants do not in fact emit more than a small fraction of the permissible amounts of radiation, and are projected to emit less radiation in the future. The late T. J. Thompson, a former member of the AEC, estimated that the average annual radiation dose to population within 50 miles of large nuclear power plants is 1000 times smaller than the additional dose from natural sources to which a passenger is exposed on a single coast to coast jet flight.* Moreover, estimates of the actual biological effects of current and projected controlled emissions from power plants (not fuel reprocessing facilities) are often cited as evidence that the problem is miniscule. For example, Dr. Ralph Lapp, projecting a total of 300 nuclear power sites (the AEC, as noted above, projects 900 power reactors by the year 2000), estimates "a maximum of 5 cancer deaths per year, and more probably less than one" attributable to nuclear-power effluents. **

The AEC's critics admit that, at the present time, no appreciable portion of the U.S. population is receiving radiation dosage from major nuclear facilities which is very near the maximum permissible dosage. They maintain, however, that it is unsound for the AEC to assume that current standards are adequate to cope with the projected rapid increase in number and size of nuclear power reactors and resultant increase in fuel reprocessing activities and

---

*Nucleonics Week, August 20, 1970, p. 5.
**Lapp, Radiation Risks, The New Republic (Feb. 27, 1971), p. 19; see Lauriston S. Taylor, "What We Do Know About Low-Level Radiation," supra .

waste products.

Apart from this, the AEC's estimates of present emissions, doses and their effects may also be misleading:

(1) The predicted effects of current waste discharges are based on computed estimates of the radiation doses that result from the measured, discharged radioactivity. These computations can be correct only if based on full knowledge of the main pathways by which this radioactivity enters human tissues and of the tissues that are most affected. For example, commonly, in absence of contrary information, the allowed concentration of waste radioactivity in environmental waters is based on the assumption that its worst effects will be those owing to people's drinking the water. But this basis would prove too optimistic if it should later turn out that radioactivity in the water is taken up and greatly concentrated by aquatic organisms important in the human food chain. In that case, the radiation dose from the given level of radioactivity in the water could be far greater than if the sole human intake were via drinking the water.*

(2) Even if the true radiation doses from power plant discharges are very much smaller than doses from natural sources, and cause only one new genetic mutation per 10,000 or per 100,000 births, such effects need not be accepted if they are avoidable. While the great majority of such mutations will be harmful, they will also be mainly recessive, i.e., most will have no effect on the individual by whom they are inherited, but will be propagated

*E.P. Radford, et. al. _Environment_ (Vol. 11, No. 7) pp . 20-27. (September, 1969).

in the human gene pool "unexpressed" until an individual inherits
the same mutation from both parents. No estimates can be given of
the severity of the disability that most such individuals will carry,
of the proportion that will be directly eliminated as nonviable
fetuses, nor of the total number of progeny who will inherit the
defect and suffer with it before it is finally eliminated from the
human gene pool because its bearers have died childless.*

(3) Certain subgroups of the population may turn out to be
far more vulnerable to radiation than is suggested by the average
risk as estimated, for example, by Gofman and Tamplin. Such subgroups may be more sensitive to radiation than the population at
large either because radiation compounds damage done by some other
toxic agent or for other reasons. This is illustrated by the
recent evidence that the risk of lung cancer among uranium miners
who are smokers is three times as high as the sum of the separate
risks they would incur by mining uranium and by smoking.**

Regardless of the precise accuracy of the estimates of either
the promoters or critics of nuclear power and the AEC, concededly
there is a risk, as the FRC reasoned in 1961, that there is no
level of exposure to radiation that will not harm living tissue.
Why then should nuclear power plants be permitted to make any
avoidable discharges of radioactive wastes into the environment?

The primary reasons the AEC is reluctant to lower the permissible levels appear to be: (a) it is uncertain what the operating

---

*Report of The United Nations Scientific Committee on Effects of
Atomic Radiation, General Assembly, 21st Sess. (1966), pp. 7-8.
**F.E. Lundin, Jr., V.E. Archer, et.al., Health Physics (Vol. 16),
pp. 571-78 (1969).

results will be for the very large power plants planned to be constructed at a rapid pace over the next thirty years;* (b) lower toler-
ances might jeopardize and increase criticism of the AEC's other
programs involving civilian and military uses of nuclear explosives
(e.g., Plowshare Program to develop nuclear explosives for civilian
use); (c) an "operating cushion" is deemed essential to anticipate
possible increases in emissions above the one per cent levels;**
(d) the AEC is under continuing pressure from the utilities and reactor manufacturers to limit plant construction and operating costs;
(e) the AEC appears to believe that it can limit biological effects
to a "negligible" level, by keeping exposures significantly below
natural background exposures.

One response of the AEC to the current controversy has been to
promulgate several amendments to its regulations which appear designed
to show an increased concern for environmental problems but which,
in fact, lack much substance. For example, the AEC recently amended
its radiation emission regulations to require licensees of power reactors (but not nuclear fuel reprocessing or fabrication facilities)
to make

> "...every reasonable effort to maintain radiation expo-
> sures and releases of radioactive materials in effluents
> to unrestricted areas as far below the limits specified
> ... as practicable."***

---

*Hearings, Pt. 1, supra at 207-09. With respect to the lack of ex-
perience with the larger reactors projected for future use, AEC Commissioner James Ramey has stated that: "it is not possible at this
stage, particularly on these newer, bigger plants, to take a certain
percentage and say this design is going to end up or should end up
with a level of two per cent of standards...." Ibid.
**Hearings, Pt. 1, supra at 206.
***Energy Report, supra at 111; 10 C.F.R. Pt. 20.

In effect, this directs utilities to do whatever is economically
practicable - which is exactly what they are doing now. No specific criteria as to what constitutes "as low as practicable" were
provided by the AEC.

Moreover, it has proposed to require applicants for power
plant licenses to estimate the range of maximum potential annual
radiation doses to individuals and population groups that would
result from estimated releases of radioactive wastes.* Merely
gathering such clearly relevant information, of course, cannot
serve as a substitute for measures necessary to reduce (or eliminate) emissions to acceptable levels.

Largely as the result of the current controversy surrounding
the AEC's standards and the substantial increases in number and
size of reactors under construction and planned,** former Secretary of Health, Education and Welfare, Robert Finch, who served
as Chairman of the Federal Radiation Council, in January, 1970,
called for a careful re-evaluation of present standards. In so
doing, he expressed agreement "with the concept that the radiation standards should be developed on the assumption that any increase in radiation exposure will be accompanied by a commensurate
increase in the risk of cancer.***

The newly formed EPA has recently commissioned the National
Academy of Sciences to do a two-year study of current radiation

*Environmental Reporter (Current Developments), p. 1185 (2/26/71).
**Hearings, Pt. 2 (Vol. 1), supra at 1129.
***Letter from former Secretary of HEW Robert Finch to Senator
Edmund Muskie, dated January 28, 1970, reprinted in Hearings, Part
2 (Vol. 11), supra at 2363-64.

standards to obtain an independent check on the work of the NRCP, which recently issued a report concluding there is no need for "any drastic reductions in the recommended exposure levels despite the current urgings of a few critics."*

> 3. Prudent Public Health Policy Requires That Every Effort Be Made to Eliminate Routine Discharges of Radiation from Major Nuclear Facilities or Reduce Them to as Near Zero-Release as Possible.

From a public health point of view, every effort should be made to prevent radiation from escaping into the environment. The fact that everyone is exposed to some natural background radiation, as well as the prudent assumption that exposure to any radiation involves a risk of biological damage, is additional reason for keeping all man-made sources as low as possible, not a justification for more radiation.

There is growing concern about the disposal techniques for lower level radioactive wastes, as well as solid wastes, and the potential hazard they pose - particularly in view of their rising volume and radiation levels. The National Academy of Sciences warned over four years ago that:

> "The current practices of disposing of intermediate
> and low-level liquid wastes and all manner of solid
> wastes directly into the ground above or in the fresh-
> water zones, although momentarily safe, will lead in
> the long run to a serious fouling of man's environ-
> ment."**

---

*New York Times, Jan. 25, 1971.
**National Academy of Sciences - National Research Council report of the Committee on Geologic Aspects of Radioactive Waste Disposal (May, 1966), reprinted in Underground Uses of Nuclear Energy, Hearings Before the Subcommittee on Air and Water Pollution, Committee on Public Works, U.S. Senate, 91st Cong., 1st Sess. (Nov. 1969), p. 462, 501.

Another authority has sharply criticized the practice of discharging krypton -85 into the air, urging that "a prudent public-health policy requires (krypton)... to be trapped and sealed up in steel bottles never to be opened again by man."*

While it is often said that a perfectly "clean" plant is not technologically feasible, as regards power plants, there is substantial evidence that the technology is now available or easily attainable for virtually eliminating radiation releases. It appears that the use of zirconium cladding, as opposed to stainless steel, on fuel elements will significantly reduce re-leases of tritium into the reactor coolant. Westinghouse Elec-tric Company has recently announced the availability of an "es-sentially zero radioactivity release" plant, although it stresses that this applies primarily to krypton and to tritium released to the coolant system. Westinghouse estimates that the system would add about $1 per kw to the capital cost of a new plant.**

The only discharge of radioactive gases from this type plant would occur when the containment structure is ventilated during refueling (amount estimated at about 80 curies, compared to 7,000 curies now).

General Electric maintains that its plants are designed at about 1 to 5 per cent of AEC limits.***

Other radioactive waste treatment systems are available that can keep radioactive liquid effluents at one-quarter of 1 per cent

---

*Dr. Ralph E. Lapp, The Four Big Fears About Nuclear Power, New York Times Magazine (Feb. 7, 1971).
**Nucleonics Week (May 7, 1970), p. 1.
***Hearings, Pt. 2 (Vol. I), supra at 1686. LILCO claims that its proposed 820 MW plant at Shoreham, Long Island will emit less than 1% of the allowable limits for radioactive discharges.

of permissible limits and reduce radioactive gas releases by a
factor of twenty below the level achieved with traditional 30-
minute hold-up systems.*

Babcock & Wilcox and Combustion Engineering have stated that
reduction to virtually any level of radioactive release is feasible, depending on the amount of money the utility is willing to
spend.**

The problem then appears to be essentially higher costs for
utilities. According to Dr. Morton Goldman, Vice President and
General Manager, Environmental Safeguards Division, NUS Corporation,

> "If one restricts consideration of the "zero release"
> concept only to liquids, the process becomes somewhat
> more feasible to achieve, but with many problems. For
> example, although most radionuclides can be very ef-
> fectively separated from most process waste liquids,
> tritiated water cannot be separated from normal water.
> Thus in a "zero liquid release" plant, the operator
> must be resigned to the accumulation of tritium, at
> least, in his plant systems."***

As far as industry is concerned, the primary constraint on
reducing, and perhaps eliminating, radioactive discharges is economic. Technology is available to collect radioactive gases and
bottle them up so that they can be stored below ground like many
other radioactive wastes.****

Milton Shaw, Director of the AEC's Division of Reactor Development and Technology, has recently conceded that "we know there is a

---

*Hearings, Pt. 2., (Vol. I), supra at 1695-96.
**Nucleonics Week (May 7, 1970) pp. 1-2.
***Hearings, Pt. 2, supra at 1552.
****Ralph E. Lapp, The Four Big Fears About Nuclear Power, in the
New York Times Magazine, p. 28 (February 7, 1971). See also Hear-
ings (Pt. 1), supra at 1971.

practical method for removing krypton and xenon from effluents."*

While it is apparently more difficult to eliminate radioactivity from liquid effluents, utilities and nuclear fuel reprocessors must make every effort and commit the resources necessary to achieve near-zero releases. Radioactive waste treatment systems are now available that can keep radioactive liquid effluents at one-quarter of one per cent of AEC limits.**

The fact that economics, not technology, is the primary reason for the failure to limit radioactive releases to zero or near-zero at fuel reprocessing facilities was conceded by T. C. Runion, President of Nuclear Fuel Services, Inc., which owns the only commercial reprocessing facility in the country, located 30 miles south of Buffalo. Mr. Runion recently testified before the Joint Congressional Committee on Atomic Energy that:

> "We have, as a primary objective, the aim to retain and contain and to keep the products of our nuclear combustion stored and controlled. The degree to which we may accomplish this is generally offset simply by economics; that is to what extent it is economically attractive versus the effect on the environment to do otherwise."*** (emphasis added).

The National Academy of Sciences' committee on radioactive waste disposal has expressed a strong (and persuasive) dissent from the philosophy

---

*Fiscal Year 1971 (Pt. 3), supra p. 1201.
**Hearings, Pt. 2 (Vol. 1), supra at 1695-96.
***Hearings, Pt. 2 (Vol. 1), supra at 1705-06.

"that safety and economy are factors of equal weight in radioactive-waste disposal, and that the relative desirabilities of disposal practices can be assessed on the basis of hazard times cost. Certainly the present problems of stream pollution by industrial and municipal wastes have arisen from the use of this philosophy in the past. The Committee remains convinced that economics is a criterion secondary to that of safety."*

*NAS Waste Study, supra at 505.

4. A Comprehensive, Independent Examination of
   Reactor Safety is Required, Together with
   Full Public Disclosure of the Risks and All
   Possible Consequences of Reactor Accidents.

   (a) The AEC has refused to inform the public
       of the risks and consequences of Major Re-
       actor accidents.

Despite the projected growth in size and number of nuclear

power plants, the AEC has refused to publish a new accident re-

port updating its 14-year-old analysis of the consequences of an

accident involving a 100-200 MW reactor. The AEC has, however,

conceded that the conceivable harm and damages from an accident

involving larger reactors "under some circumstances would be sub-

stantially more than the consequences reported in the ...(1957)

study."* It should be noted that a 1000 MW power reactor, at the

end of one year of operation, contains in its fuel elements as

much long-lived, radioactive material as is produced by a 50 mega-

ton fission bomb. If the reactor were disrupted or an accident

occurred, the radioactive material released in the worst case

would approximate that released if such a bomb exploded.

   (b) The utility industry is virtually immune from
       full financial responsibility for nuclear ac-
       cidents and radiation damage.

The liability of the utilities and reactor manufacturers

in the case of a reactor accident is now limited by the federal

*"Questions and Answers About Nuclear Power," document prepared
by Con Ed (March 31, 1970), Par. 27.3.

-124-

Price-Anderson Act passed in 1957 (currently in effect until 1977), to a maximum of $560 million - $478 million of which will be paid by the Federal Government.* This is only 8 per cent of the maximum $7 billion property damage estimated in the AEC's <u>outdated</u> 1957 Accident Report.

Significantly, the Price-Anderson measure was pushed through Congress in 1957 shortly after the AEC's Accident Report was released and was sponsored by Senator Clinton Anderson of New Mexico and Congressman Melvin Price of Illinois, both members of the Joint Congressional Committee on Atomic Energy (the leading spokesmen for nuclear power in Congress). The law's prime purpose was to get the atomic power development program "off the ground." According to Representative Price, private insurers would not provide insurance against atomic reactor accidents; and, neither the utilities nor the manufacturers "would risk going into this uncharted area without indemnification protection."**

When this measure was being reconsidered by Congress in 1965, several reactor manufacturers and utilities testified that they would probably abandon the nuclear power business if the limitation on liability were dropped. For example, Mr. Mel Frankel, on behalf of the Department of Water and Power, City of Los Angeles, testified that:

> "without the protection which presently is provided
> by the Price-Anderson Act it is doubtful that any
> utility would consider it prudent to build nuclear
> plants."***

---

*The limitation of liability also applies to nuclear fuel reprocessing and transport of nuclear fuel.
**Curtis and Hogan, <u>The Perils of the Peaceful Atom</u>, p. 254 (1969).
***<u>Id</u>. at 254.

Thus, the power industry is certainly not convinced that nuclear plants are entirely safe and it has secured ample protection for itself in the event of an atomic accident. The existence of the Price-Anderson law raises a serious question regarding the credibility of the power industry's public assurances of the "total safety" of nuclear reactors. Further, greater and more responsible efforts to deal with reactor safety would undoubtedly result if the nuclear industry were forced to assume full financial responsibility for radioactive hazards.

(c) Safety Research and Development on Light Water Reactors Has Been Drastically Reduced by the AEC.

Although the AEC has spent about $250 million on nuclear power safety to date, overall reactor safety funding in recent years has fallen below the agency's estimates of need and safety research on large-scale water reactors now in use, and planned for increased use during the next 15 - 20 years, is being significantly reduced.*

A special analytic study on Reactor Safety completed in October, 1969 by the AEC Division of Reactor Development and Technology, in cooperation with the AEC Regulatory Staff (primarily responsible for licensing major nuclear facilities), concluded that:

> "major efforts are still required to resolve safety issues currently facing both reactor suppliers and those charged with safety assessment for the surge of light

*AEC Authorizing Legislation, Fiscal Year, 1971 (Pt. 3), Hearings Before the Joint Committee on Atomic Energy, 91st Cong., 2d Sess., p. 1619 (March 11, 1970) (hereinafter cited as Fiscal Year 1971 Pt. 3).

-126-

water power reactors announced in the 1965-68 period. Concurrently, there is a need to accelerate work on the advanced reactors. An increased funding level will be required for the AEC to properly carry out its responsibilities."*

Nevertheless, the AEC's total funding request for its nuclear

safety program for fiscal year 1971 was $35.0 million, a decrease

of $1.4 million from 1970. 75 to 80 per cent of this program is

related to the breeder reactor, projected for service in the mid-

1980's.**

Owing to budgetary restrictions and the need "to meet pro-

grammatic needs related to advanced reactors,"*** i.e., breeder

reactors, funding for testing of engineering safety features for

water reactors, i.e., features designed to prevent and control

major accidents, was cut by almost 35 per cent in fiscal 1971

(from $8.7 million in 1970 to $5.8 million). This has resulted in

termination of a program for testing the reliability of reactor

containment systems during loss-of-coolant accidents in water

cooled reactors, and a program for testing the behavior of re-

actor fuel under loss-of-coolant conditions. Moreover, certain

emergency core cooling analytical studies, important for under-

standing the reliability of such accident control devices, have

been deferred "pending the availability of resources."**** Ac-

cording to Milton Shaw, Director of the AEC's Division of Reactor

*Fiscal Year 1971 (Pt. 3), supra at 1374.
**The same amount has been requested for the AEC's nuclear safety program in the 1972 budget. Environmental Reporter (Current Developments), p. 1068 (2/5/71).
***Fiscal Year 1971 (Pt. 3), supra at 1241.
****Id. at 13

Development and Technology, the terminated programs "are in the category of those producing rather important safety information even today. They are not facilities that we would prefer to have closed down.... However, they must be phased out in order to give higher priority attention to the newer safety facilities...."*

Additional decreases in "important safety activities" have been made in the AEC's funding requests for fiscal year 1972, e.g., the program related to failure modes of zirconium clad fuel rods used in light water reactors "will be closed out...."**

Termination of the above-described programs is particularly significant in view of the AEC's 1967 report on "Emergency Core Cooling" which concluded that it was not possible to "assure the integrity" of reactor containment systems because reliable methods for containing the large molten masses of fuel which would result from a meltdown "do not exist today...."

Moreover, the AEC continues to acknowledge that reactor responses following loss-of-coolant accidents and the effectiveness of emergency core cooling systems is the "most critical safety problem facing all water reactor plants... [and that] the need for information in this area has been strongly emphasized by regulatory groups."***   Yet, the AEC has never actually assessed the reliability of emergency core cooling systems under actual accident conditions in a power reactor and does not plan to carry out such an experiment until 1975 at the earliest (the LOFT program).

*Id. at 1338.
**Testimony of Milton Shaw, Director, AEC's Division of Reactor Development and Technology, FY1972 Authorization Hearings Before the Joint Committee on Atomic Energy (March 4, 1971).

*** Fiscal Year 1971 (Pt. 3), supra at 1539.

Strangely enough, the test reactor scheduled for use (50 MW reactor) differs significantly from the large water reactors scheduled for future use in terms of size and components.* Moreover, some authorities maintain that the area of greatest uncertainty, viz, flow distribution of core cooling water, cannot adequately be studied in the planned experiment.** On the other hand, reactor manufacturers and members of the AEC regulatory staff, which evaluates reactor license applications, reportedly oppose the planned LOFT experiment in large part because of their belief that problems posed by loss-of-coolant accidents can be "handled by conservative design."***

In any event, if the LOFT program is implemented, it would seem essential, as the AEC's Advisory Committee on Reactor Safeguards (ACRS)**** has recommended, that "every reasonable effort must be made to accomplish it on an improved time scale (to start high temperature tests before 1975)...."*****

The ACRS has recently criticized the AEC's research efforts regarding reactor safeguards. In a letter dated November 12, 1969, addressed to AEC Chairman Seaborg (which was not publicly revealed until mid-1970), the ACRS complained to the AEC that (a) only small or modest efforts have been initiated for additional research on fuel failure and partial or large scale core melting; (b) high-

*Fiscal Year 1971 (Pt. 3), supra at 1621.
**Ibid.
***Fiscal Year 1971 (Pt. 3), supra at 1621.
****ACRS is a committee composed of scientists and engineers established by law to advise the AEC on safety aspects of reactors, including reviewing and commenting upon nuclear facility license applications. 42 U.S.C. §2039.
*****Fiscal Year 1971 (Pt. 3), supra at 1621.

priority safety research and development on liquid metal breeder reactors is currently being neglected; and (c) little is being done about ACRS's recommendations for more safety research on light water reactors to be constructed during the next decade, "including work on reactor design concepts that might provide more confidence on how to deal with primary-system rupture followed by failure of emergency core-cooling."*

As regards water cooled reactors, the AEC has determined that major financial responsibility for safety programs should be assumed by the nuclear industry to permit the AEC to concentrate on its higher priority, breeder reactor program. The AEC recently declared that it will

> "reduce its support of the Light Water Reactor Safety research and development...to be consistent with anticipated greater industrial participation, although a critical need still exists for water reactor safety research and development...for the many such reactors under construction or on order."** (emphasis added)

Whether industry will prove to be an adequate source of safety research is subject to serious question. As noted above, the utilities have traditionally not provided any substantial support for research and development. Moreover, although reactor manufacturers spend substantial sums in designing and producing equipment, their efforts are generally channeled into areas that offer the greatest commercial potential. It is unclear how much of their efforts can accurately be described as experimental research on safety features.

*Nucleonics Week, June 30, 1970, (p. 3-4). The ACRS letter is reprinted in Fiscal Year 1971 (Pt. 3), supra at 1619-21.
**Fiscal Year 1971 (Pt. 3), supra at 1534.

One authority has recently reported that General Electric and Westinghouse, which together account for about 80 per cent of nuclear orders, "do little safety research with their own funds and the utilities do practically nothing...."*

As regards advanced (high-temperature) reactors, the AEC, as well as the nuclear industry, acknowledges the need to develop proven design methods and criteria for structural analysis of pressure vessels, reactor cores and other components, but,

> "to date, no effective means have been found to fund such a program on a cooperative basis at a meaningful level.... [A]dditional data are required to establish proven design methods and design criteria for the temperature systems for many aspects of the problem."**

While considerable information may be able to be developed within a two to three-year period, implementation of this, as well as certain other, safety studies relating to breeders has been lagging with the probable result, according to the ACRS, that "many safety-related design decisions will have to be made by applicants and the regulatory groups without the benefit of needed safety research...."***

Regardless of the adequacy of industry or AEC reactor safety research, the adoption of conservative reactor designs (promised by industry) or a conservative attitude in licensing reactors (promised by the AEC), the credibility of the AEC, as well as the nuclear industry, on the issue of reactor safety is open to serious question. As noted above, the AEC has persistently refused to inform the pub-

---

*Dr. Ralph E. Lapp, Safety in the New Republic, (Jan. 23, 1971), p. 18.
**Fiscal Year 1971 (Pt. 3), supra at 1362.
***Fiscal Year 1971 (Pt. 3), supra at 1620.

lic conerning the risks and consequences of reactor accidents;
and, the nuclear industry has failed to assume full financial
responsibility for reactor accidents. The AEC's lack of
credibility has led some authorities, including Stewart L.
Udall, former Secretary of the Interior, to call for the transfer
of the AEC's regulatory authority over reactor safety to the
newly formed EPA.*

5. The Problem of Urban Siting: Pressure is Increasing
    From Utilities to Site Nuclear Plants in Urban Areas
    for Primarily Economic Reasons.

Under the Atomic Energy Act of 1954, the AEC has the responsibility for licensing major nuclear facilities, including power
plants. A two-stage licensing process has been established
pursuant to which a construction permit, which can be granted
only after a public hearing held by a three-man Atomic Safety
and Licensing Board, is required to build the facility and an
operating permit is required to run the facility. Issuance
of the latter permit does not require a public hearing unless
an acceptable issue is raised by some affected party who is
prepared to intervene legally.** An applicant for a construction
                 is required to file
permit /a formal application describing the design and location

*Environmental Reporter (Current Developments), p.786 (Nov. 1970).
A similar proposal has been made by Dr. Ralph E. Lapp.
**According to AEC Commissioner Ramey, the AEC is considering two
basic changes in this procedure: (a) an early site review, before
any substantial commitment has been made by the utility or changes
have been made to the landscape; and, (2) elimination of the opportunity for a hearing at the operating license stage. The prime
purpose of such changes is to eliminate what the AEC deems to be
unnecessary delays in licensing nuclear power plants. Statement
of James T. Ramey, at Hearings before the Subcommittee on Fisheries
and Wildlife Conservation of the House Committee on Merchant Marine
and Fisheries, regarding Implementation of the National Environmental
Policy Act (Dec. 8, 1970).

of the proposed plant, as well as the safeguards to be provided, and, since January, 1970, an environmental impact statement in conformity with the National Environmental Policy Act of 1969. Such materials are reviewed by the AEC's regulatory staff, the ACRS, and other relevant federal agencies.

In a study entitled Civilian Nuclear Power, A Report to the President - 1962, the AEC declared that: "Until experience is gained and adequate safeguards are proved out, prudence dictates that large reactor installations be fairly far removed from population centers."* About the same time, the AEC adopted "interim" reactor site criteria, which it describes as "deliberately flexible," to assist the Commission in evaluating the suitability of proposed sites for nuclear power plants.** The criteria are extremely vague but, in essence, they require a judgment to be made balancing engineered reactor safeguards, proposed operation, e.g., maximum power level and inventory of radioactive materials, the number and density of residents in the environs of the site, together with the means available to protect these people in case of a serious reactor accident and the physical characteristics of the site. The criteria do not specify a permissible population density or total population to be located in the area immediately surrounding the site.

In evaluating a proposed site, the applicant is required to postulate a maximum credible accident which would result in release of "appreciable quantities of fission products" and then

*Civilian Nuclear Power, A Report to the President (Dec. 1962), p.54.
**10 C.F.R. Pt. 100.

to determine: (a) an "exclusion area" (the area immediately surrounding the reactor under control of the licensee) where exposure to individuals located at any point on its boundary for two
hours after an accident is not to exceed a specified amount*;(b)
a "low population zone" (defined as the area immediately surrounding the exclusion area which contains a number and density of residents such that "there is a reasonable probability that appropriate protective measures could be taken in their behalf in the
event of a serious accident") where exposure to any individual
at any point on its outer boundary during the entire time of passage of the radioactive cloud generated by the accident is not to
exceed a specified amount**; and, (c) a "population center distance"
of at least one and one-third times the distance from the reactor
to the outer boundary of the low population zone.*** "Population
center distance" is defined as "the distance from the reactor to
the nearest boundary of a densely populated center containing more
than about 25,000 residents."**** The criteria also provide that
a greater distance may be required if "very large cities are involved...because of total integrated population dose consideration."*****

There is, however, no AEC requirement for utilities to "back-
fit" facilities after permits have been granted,i.e.,modify facilities

---

*Total radiation dose to the whole body of 25 rem or a total radi-
ation dose of 300 rem to the thyroid from iodine exposure. 10 C.F.R.
Pt. 100, §100.11(a)(1). According to the AEC, these doses are merely
"site criteria guides" and do not "constitute acceptable limits for
emergency doses to the public under accident conditions." Ibid. See
also USAEC Document TID-14844 (March 23, 1962),Calculation of Distance
Factors for Power and Test Reactor Sites.
**Ibid.
***10 C.F.R. Pt. 100, §100.11(a)
****10 C.F.R. Pt. 100, §100.3(c)
*****10 C.F.R. Pt. 100, §100.11(a)(3)

or add new technology designed to provide additional environmental protection, despite the probability that many circumstances deemed relevant to initial site approval in the AEC's reactor site criteria, e.g., total number and density of nearby population, ability to evacuate such persons, may change over the years. In fact,the AEC recently rejected a suggestion by various environmental groups to adopt a "backfitting requirement."*

The AEC further states in its siting criteria that it expects reactors, by reason of design, construction and operation to reflect "an extremely low probability for accidents that could result in release of significant quantities of radioactive fission products" and that the site location, as well as engineered reactor safeguards,"should insure a low risk of public exposure" to such radioactivity in the event of an accident.**

As noted above, the projected expansion in the number of power plants from about 20 today to 900 in the year 2000 (the majority of which will be 1000 MW or larger) vastly increases the likelihood of a serious accident within the next thirty years. The Assistant Director of the Oak Ridge National Laboratory (one of the AEC's several research arms), Dr. Walter Jordon, however, is willing to accept the possibility of a nuclear accident and has recently announced that the public should accept the risk as well:

"We and the public should be prepared to face the possibility of a nuclear accident, just as we live with the possibility

*35 Fed. Reg. No. 235 (Dec. 4, 1970), p.18471.
**10 C.F.R. Pt. 100, §100.10.

- 135 -

of major earthquakes which will exact a large toll in property and lives."*

Nothwithstanding the AEC's public posture of minimizing the likelihood of nuclear accidents, AEC officials appear to be concerned over the possibility of a nuclear accident, as pointed out in a recently published article on Nuclear Safety:

"That high AEC officials harbor their own doubts about reactor safety engineering comes out piecemeal in their speeches or may be read between the lines. (It comes out directly if you talk to AEC personnel at the operating or bench level. Reactor engineers tend to be somewhat habituated to their machines and most utility men are not very well informed about reactors.) None other than the AEC's Director of Regulation, Harold L. Price, put his finger on the real problem in mid-1967 when he said:

'The basic safety issue presented by metropolitan sites for large power reactors is whether, in lieu of partial dependence on distance from population centers, full reliance can or should be place on the inherent safety of the reactors and their engineered safety features.'"**

The first attempt by a utility company anywhere in the nation to locate a nuclear power plant in a major city was made by Con Ed in 1962 when it proposed placing a 1000 MW plant in Ravenswood, Queens. Upon hearing of the proposal, David E. Lilienthal, former Chairman of the AEC, remarked that he "would not dream of living in Queens if a huge nuclear plant were located there."*** The then Chairman of the company said in response, that Con Ed could build a nuclear plant in the middle of Times Square without hazard to the community."*** Con Ed withdrew the proposal in 1964.

Con Ed acknowledges that urban siting is contrary to the

---

*"Benefit vs. Risks in Nuclear Power - A logical facts-and-figures comment on the current anti-atom literature,"in Oak Ridge National Laboratory Review, quoted in Safety, The New REpublic, Jan. 23, 1971 p. 21.
**Dr. Ralph E. Lapp, Safety, in The New Republic, (Jan.23,1971), p.19
***Quoted in Curtis & Hogan, supra at 126.

AEC's purported policy of locating nuclear power plants in
remote, unpopulated areas - a policy based on the view that a
key criterion for siting nuclear plants should be the number of
people potentially exposed to radioactive byproducts from a
plant,* but maintains that nuclear plants "can be built and
operated in total safety...in the cities of the world."**
This assertion of "total safety" is nonsense. As noted above,
there are many dangers associated with nuclear plants, a fact
well known by the utility and its suppliers who have refused
to assume full financial responsibility for reactor accidents -
their liability is limited to $84 million by federal law.
Moreover, apart from the known dangers, no one has any significant
experience with the large reactors Con Ed wants to place in New
York City.

The fact is that Con Ed wants to site nuclear plants in
the metropolitan area near its load center for economic reasons.
According to Louis Roddis, Jr., President of Con Ed, a "key
advantage" that fossil-fuel plants now have over nuclear plants
is:

> "being able to site such plants in an urban setting,
> thereby saving the need for costly...transmission facilities....
> The in-city siting of nuclear plants would erase the economic
> advantage fossil plants enjoy, one that has required instal-
> lation of long distance transmission facilities at great
> cost to bring nuclear generated power to load centers."***
> (emphasis added.)

*Statement of Dr. K.Z. Morgan, Director, Health Physics Division,
Oak Ridge National Laboratory, quoted in New York Times, Aug. 12, 1970
**Louis H. Roddis, Jr., President, Con Ed, "Metropolitan Siting of
Nuclear Power Plants" presented at IAEA Symposium on Environmental
Aspects of Nuclear Power Stations, August 10-14, United Nations,N.Y.,N.Y
***Roddis, Metropolitan Siting, supra Mr. Roddis noted that the
transmission cost required to bring power from Indian Point to the
City is about $180 per KW more than for an in-city site.

In sum, there is a powerful economic incentive for Con
Ed to locate nuclear plants as near as possible to its major
load center - regardless of the relative safety of locating a
nuclear plant in a very densely populated urban area, (as opposed
to a remote, open area) - an economic incentive which is made
even more attractive by the limited liability Congress has
provided for utilities and their suppliers regarding the potential
catastrophic consequences of nuclear accidents.

Con Ed's plan to engage in urban siting has the support
of NYASD, whose Nuclear Power Siting Committee is now investigating
off-shore sites on existing or artificial islands near New York
City. In a recent address, James Cline, Chairman of the Authority,
clearly tipped his hand in favor of urban siting of nuclear
power plants, while alluding to the need for additional experience
and development of improved safety systems, when he stated:

> "looking to the future and to the desirability of locating
> nuclear power generating facilities in urban areas to replace
> the fossil fueled plants now located there, there is a vital
> need to develop, test and demonstrate the improved safety
> systems and features of plant design in reliance upon which
> such urban siting will be undertaken." (emphasis added).*

The AEC's present attitude toward urban siting is at best
ambiguous, as indicated by its vague reactor siting criteria out-
lined above. Moreover, the AEC's alleged policy of siting plants
in remote areas seems to bear slight resemblance to the agency's
actual practice, particularly as regards Con Ed. For example,
while Con Ed's Indian Point Units No. 1, 2, and 3 are about 24
miles from New York City, they are actually located about one

*NYASD Eighth Annual Report, p. 22. (1970).

mile from a "population center," i.e., an area with 25,000 people.
Based on the 1960 census, about 53,000 people lived within a five-
mile radius; the number is expected to increase to 108,000 by 1980.
In 1960 there were 327,000 people within a 15-mile radius of Con
Ed's nuclear plant complex at Indian Point. The estimated 1980
population is 670,000.* Although some improvements in reactor
safeguards may have been made since Indian Point No. 1 came on
line in 1962, it is disturbing at the least to recall that the
outdated, 1957 AEC Reactor Accident Report showed several thousand
people being killed at distances up to 15 miles and injured at
distances up to 45 miles from the reactor, which was assumed to
be 100-200 MW in size - 5 to 10 times smaller than the combined
capacity of units 1 and 2 at Indian Point, and 20 to 40 times
smaller than the 4,000 MW of nuclear capacity Con Ed plans to
place on David's Island, 14 miles from the Empire State Building.

6. Management of High-Level Radioactive Wastes Poses a Major Hazard.

Presently, about 80,000,000 gallons of high-level radioactive
wastes are stored in liquid form in about 200 concrete encased,
steel tanks buried at AEC sites in Washington, South Carolina
and Idaho.** At the Western New York Nuclear Service Center (WNSC),
30 miles south of Buffalo, in West Valley, New York, about 520,000

---

*Con Ed, Environmental Impact of Indian Point Station, Nuclear
Unit No. 2 (December 17, 1970), p. 4. For other instances in
which power reactors have been sited within ten miles of population centers, see Curtis & Hogan, supra at 127-28.
**(footnote next page)

gallons of high level, radioactive wastes are stored in liquid
form in two 750,000-gallon, carbon steel tanks and two 15,000-
gallon, stainless steel tanks owned by NYASD.

Some tanks are cooled, others are allowed to boil with
steam siphoned off to prevent rupture. Aside from the possibility
of an accident, there is a clear risk that the tanks will corrode
and leak. At best, the tanks are expected to last about 20 years
(though the wastes within them remain deadly for 600 - 1,000
years) before requiring replacement to protect against deterioration of protective materials. Catch basins, designed to collect
material which does escape are generally placed beneath tanks.
To date, there have been fifteen reported leaks; and tanks at
the AEC's Savannah River Plant in South Carolina have sprung
leaks at least four times - in one case, about 700 gallons of
wastes soaked into the ground.*

In 1970, commercial reactors produced about 700,000 gallons of high-level wastes. The AEC estimates that 3,500,000
gallons of such wastes will accumulate from commercial reactors
between 1970 and 1980. By the year 2000, the amount will rise

(footnote from previous page)
Prior to 1967, the AEC dumped limited quantities of radioactive
wastes in the ocean. The majority of radioactive disposal sites
were in the Atlantic. Other countries still engage in ocean
dumping of radioactive wastes.
*Dennis Farney, Finding Places to Put Nuclear Waste Proves a
Frightful Problem, Wall Street Journal, p. 1 (Jan. 25, 1971);
Curtis & Hogan, supra at 176.

to about 60,000,000 gallons. These wastes are expected to be 10 to 30 times as radioactive as most of the weapons - related wastes now stored at AEC sites.*

The AEC concedes that tank storage constitutes at best an interim approach to management of long-lived, radioactive wastes.** According to a recent AEC publication entitled "Radioactive Wastes," the needs for continuous surveillance of stored liquid wastes to ensure against escape and for transfer of wastes from tank to tank every decade or two owing to corrosion failure compel the development of a safer, long-term solution.***

The AEC has determined that a safer method for dealing with the high-level wastes is to convert the liquid wastes to solids, such as glasses, ceramics or calcines, and to store the solidified matter in dry geologic formations, such as salt mines.**** Storage of wastes as solids is considered to provide significantly more safety than storage as liquids because the solid wastes are expected to be: (i) immobile; (ii) less soluble in water; (iii) considerably smaller in volume; and (iv) more rugged physically than wastes in liquid form.***** Moreover, the wastes are easier to transport in solid form. "Safety considerations militate

---

*Dennis Farney, Finding Places to Put Nuclear Waste Proves a Frightful Problem, Wall Street Journal, p. 1 (Jan. 25, 1971).
**Fiscal Year 1971 (Pt. 3), supra at 1424-25.
***Fox, Radioactive Wastes, supra at 26.
****E.g., McLain & Bradshaw, Status of Investigations of Salt Formations for Disposal of Highly Radioactive Power-Reactor Wastes, Nuclear Safety (March - April, 1970).
*****Schneider, Bradshaw, et. al., "Status of Solidification and Disposal of Highly Radioactive Liquid Wastes from Nuclear Power in the U.S.A.," presented at IAEA Symposium on Environmental Aspects of Nuclear Power Stations, U.N. Headquarters, New York (Aug. 10-14, 1970).

against the bulk shipment of high-level waste liquids or slur-ries."*

Solidification, however, will <u>concentrate</u> the highly radio-active wastes sixfold or more, and the solids will continue to give off intense amounts of heat while the wastes decay.** After solidification, the wastes must be stored "virtually forever, under stable, controlled conditions."*** In other words, solidi-fication will not reduce the level of radioactivity of the wastes, it merely will change their form to make them easier to handle and store in isolated environments for the centuries that the material must be contained.

Salt mines are considered good locations for wastes because they are generally very dry (free of circulating ground waters and isolated from underground acquifiers) and located in areas of low seismic activity. Also, according to the AEC, "salt has good structural properties and its compressive strength and nuclear shielding characteristics are similar to concrete...;"**** salt has good thermal conductivity and heat capacity; and, is relatively plastic so that fissures should seal or close rapidly. Desir-able salt formations for storage of wastes are considered to be ones that are at least 200 feet thick and within 2000 feet of the surface.*****

*<u>Id</u>. at 9.
**Farney, <u>supra</u> at 1.
***Schneider, Bradshaw, et. al., <u>supra</u> at 1.
****Testimony of Milton Shaw, Director, AEC's Division of Reactor Development and Technology, FY72 Authorization Hearings, Before Joint Committee on Atomic Energy (March 16, 1971).
*****<u>Id</u>. at 10.

The National Academy of Sciences Committee on Radioactive
Waste Management concluded in November of last year that "the
use of bedded salt for the disposal of radioactive wastes is
satisfactory.... [I]t is the safest choice now available, provided the wastes are in an appropriate form and the salt beds
meet the necessary design and geological criteria."*

Since beginning a waste solidification engineering program in 1966, the AEC has tested four processes for solidification of high-level wastes on a pilot plant scale. Only one is
now considered ready for commercial use.**

The AEC expects to complete and report on the results to
date of its solidification development program within the next
two years. Additional developmental work is required to scale-
up existing processes for work on high-level wastes of the kind
to be produced by the large reactors scheduled for future use,
at a rate beyond one ton a day.*** Moreover, detailed studies
must still be carried out regarding the short and long-term
physical, chemical and radiological properties of solidified
wastes and their effects on storage materials. When recently
asked about the progress being made in the AEC's solidification
program, AEC Commissioner Ramey gave the following guarded and
rather unenthusiastic response: "we are sufficiently confident
that we can achieve some solidified waste disposal of high-level
wastes."****

---

*Conclusions attached to testimony of Milton Shaw before Joint
Committee on Atomic Energy (March 16, 1971), supra.
**Schneider, Bradshaw et. al., supra at 4-5.
***Ibid. The AEC's Annual budget for development of methods for
managing high-level wastes has averaged about $2.6 million over
(footnotes continued next page)

Citing the availability of solidification technology, the
AEC has recently adopted a waste disposal policy based on solidification of high-level wastes and storage of such wastes at
federally-owned repositories. The policy in essence is: (1)
fuel reprocessing plants need not be located on federally-owned
or controlled land; (2) high-level liquid waste inventory must
be limited in volume to the quantity produced in the prior five
years; (3) all high-level wastes must be transferred in solidified
form to a federal repository no later than ten years following
separation of wastes from used fuel; (4) federal government has
physical responsibility and industry has financial responsibility
for disposal of high-level wastes.* The commercial fuel reprocessor is thus required at his expense to solidify liquid radioactive
wastes no later than five years, and to ship the solidified wastes
to federal disposal sites within ten years, after separation of
the wastes from reusable fuel. Hence, as many as eleven years
(includes about one year for cooling and transport of fuel rods
containing wastes from power reactor to reprocessing facility)
may elapse from the time used fuel rods are removed from a reactor
until high-level wastes are finally delivered to a federal repository.

The AEC's decision to permit storage of high-level wastes at
the fuel reprocessing site for up to ten years after separation
from used fuel appears in large part to be based on economics, not

(footnotes continued from previous page).
the last two years. Fiscal Year 1971 (Pt. 3), supra at 1538.
****Hearings (Pt. 1), supra at 123.

*10 C.F.R., Pt. 50 (Appendix F).

- 144 -

safety. Preliminary cost estimates of high-level waste management
involving solidification indicate a total cost varying from about
equal to about 20 per cent higher than total costs for perpetual
liquid storage. These cost estimates, however, assume interim
liquid storage of one to five years, interim solid storage from
one to ten years, and burial in salt after an additional aging
of one to ten years at the federal disposal site.* It appears
that

> "there is a distinct economic advantage in permit-
> ing the short-lived isotopes in the waste to decay
> and thereby drastically reduce its heat-generation
> rate before carrying out final disposal. The econ-
> omics of this interim storage period are such that
> very little is gained by storing the wastes for per-
> iods longer than five to ten years."**

Since industry has financial responsibility for waste disposal and interim storage for ten years reduces the cost of ultimate disposal, there is little chance that fuel reprocessors will
choose to store the wastes for less than ten years. The fuel reprocessors have a clear economic incentive to retain the wastes
during the time they are in a form that is most dangerous to the
public. According to several scientists at Oak Ridge National
Laboratory who have done considerable work on solidification,

> "the most important concern is during the first ten
> years after solidification when the heat removal pro-
> blems, temperature, radioactivity, and rate of tem-
> perature change are the greatest, and during trans-
> portation to the long-term disposal site."***

*Schneider, Bradshaw et. al., supra 13-14.
**McLain & Bradshaw, Nuclear Safety, supra at 131.
***Schneider, Bradshaw, et. al., supra at 6.

It also bears mention that no one as yet has any experience in the design, operation, safety and environmental problems posed by waste solidification plants which will be added to fuel reprocessing sites.

As regards disposal sites, the AEC announced last summer that it has tentatively selected a 1,000 acre site near Lyons, Kansas as an initial salt-mine depository to demonstrate long-term storage of high-level solidified wastes.* According to the AEC, the major purpose of the project "will be to provide technical data and experience on operational methods and costs of long-term storage of solidified high-level wastes."**

The wastes will be packed in sealed, 10-foot long steel containers and set in holes in the floors of rooms mined in the salt formations about 1000 feet below the surface. Each cylinder to be buried will contain a million or more curies of radioactivity. Also, the heat given off while the wastes decay is expected to raise the temperature in the underground caverns to 200 degrees Fahrenheit or more.***The AEC maintains that the fission product decay heat should not create a significant problem, however, at least as long as it does not exceed 200 degrees Fahrenheit, because of the plastic nature of the salt, i.e., the salt is expected to consolidate and recrystallize into its undisturbed state "within a few decades."**** According to Milton Shaw of the AEC,

---

*The site will also be used for long-lived, low-level radioactive wastes.
**Environmental Reporter (Current Developments), p. 179 (June 19, 1970).
***Farney, supra at 8.
****Schneider, Bradshaw, et. al., supra at 11.

however, "in situ experiments are necessary to confirm what we believe to be good heat transfer and subsidence calculations."[*]

The AEC intends to carry out geologic and detailed safety studies regarding the Kansas project during 1971. The safety study will cover the safety "of both the operational aspects as well as the long-term environmental considerations."[**] One area that must be investigated in detail is the long-term behavior of the wastes. Water contained in salt could lead to stress - corrosion - cracking of waste containers within a few years.[***] The National Academy of Sciences has identified a number of problems to be resolved before beginning operations at the Lyons, Kansas site, including designing spacing of high-level containers "to prevent the release of water included in the salt" and "developing mining and backfill methods to maintain subsidence within acceptable limits."[****]

The total estimated cost of the demonstration project is $25 million. The AEC has requested an initial funding of $3.5 million to acquire the site in fiscal year 1972. The AEC currently estimates that a minimum of three years will be required to design and prepare the site once authorization is granted.[*****]

A conceptual design study is now being made by Oak Ridge National Laboratory for the facility in Kansas which the AEC ex-

[*]Testimony of Milton Shaw before Joint Committee on Atomic Energy (March 16, 1971), supra.
[**]Fiscal Year 1971 (Pt. 3), supra at 1427.
[***]Schneider, Bradshaw, et. al., supra at 12.
[****]Attachment to Testimony of Milton Shaw before the Joint Committee on Atomic Energy (March 16, 1971), supra.
[*****]Environmental Reporter (Current Developments), p. 180 (June 19, 1970); Schneider, Bradshaw, et. al., supra at 12.

pects to be capable of handling all high-level wastes produced by commercial power reactors in the United States until about the end of the century. Other major salt deposits in the country (Southeastern Michigan and West Central New York) are considered of adequate size by the AEC to accommodate additional high-level wastes produced by power reactors through at least the next century.*

As regards transport of high-level wastes, the AEC concedes that the total amount of high-level liquid wastes from commercial power reactors will almost triple over the next thirty years and that the level of radioactivity of such wastes will increase. Thus, notwithstanding the development of a workable disposal process, the transportation of liquid and solid wastes along public thoroughfares will increase as the volume of waste continues to grow. When operating at full-scale, the AEC estimates that up to 400 railroad cars per year (about one train every three months) will arrive at Lyons, Kansas, carrying about 1200 or more separate cylinders of wastes.**

---

*Schneider, Bradshaw, et. al., supra at 10.
**Farney, supra at 1.

F. Possible Methods for Rationalizing Land Use

1. Sound Environmental Planning May Require that Utilities Be Precluded from Purchasing Land for Sites.

The industry traditionally has sought to acquire land without public disclosure so as to avoid possible public opposition and an increased price, e.g., Con Ed's acquisition of the Storm King site and rights-of-way; LILCO's recent purchase of 425 acres next to its Shoreham site from the Brooklyn Catholic Diocese.*

Moreover, the utilities, encouraged by regulatory policies, are now anxious to acquire a broad inventory of sites well in advance of actual need.** The push is on to acquire quickly as many sites as possible, before, in the words of the Chairman of NYASD, the land is put "to less vital land uses."*** In our view, the notion that electric power generation is inherently more vital than, for example, public health or educational facilities - or conservation of resources - is clearly contrary to the public interest.

The policies of the PSC encourage land acquisition well in advance of actual use for power supply by permitting a utility to include land purchased "for future use" in its rate base, even though it will not utilize the particular site for some time.**** This practice was recently reaffirmed by the PSC in approving a $100 million rate increase (the largest in history) for Con Ed.

*Long Island Press (12/11/70).
**See also EPE Report, supra at 29.
***James G. Cline, Chairman of NYASD, Letter to the Editor, New York Times, August 13, 1970.
****The FPC has adopted a similar policy designed to encourage advance acquisition of sites. It recently amended its regulations to permit electric utilities and natural gas pipeline companies to include the cost of land held for future use in the rate base. Environmental Reporter (Current Developments), p. 994 (11/15/70).

The Commission, overruling objections by its staff, held that
Con Ed could include in its base rate $18 million of land which
it intends to use at a vague future time for electric power service, reasoning that:

> "We believe that electric utilities such as Con Ed
> should be encouraged, particularly at the present
> juncture in which sites for utility plants are be-
> coming increasingly difficult to find, to acquire
> properties on which electric plants may be located
> in the future. We can hardly urge on utilities a
> broad vision of future land requirements while insisting
> on use of an accounting technique that indefinitely
> postpones compensation for land acquisitions or on
> strict proof of specific need for every parcel."*
> (emphasis added)

In our judgment, any policy that encourages utilities to buy
up land for future use is inconsistent with sound environmental
planning and totally unnecessary. Acquisition of sites in advance
of approval by appropriate governmental authorities is not crucial
to a rational planning process; in fact, it seriously undermines
any effort to devise or implement rational land use policies.

There is no apparent need for utilities to buy or own land,
much less to acquire interests in land prior to obtaining requisite
governmental approval. In fact, purchasing land for future use
which is eventually disapproved may tie up capital and impose an
unfair, extra cost on the consumer.

Utilities should be precluded from purchasing land: instead,
they should be required to identify desirable sites and inform the
public and appropriate regulatory authorities of the sites well in

*Re Consolidated Edison Co. of New York, Inc., 85 PUR 3d 276, 290
(August 12, 1970). Of 24 locations, 15 were labelled, "after 1973."

advance of alleged, actual need, and, thereafter, to proceed to obtain requisite approvals. Once approvals have been granted, the locality wherein the facility is to be located could, if it desires,
purchase the property and lease it to the utility. If the locality
were unable to make the purchase, then the state could provide necessary financial assistance. Public ownership would eliminate the
cost of the land from the rate base which would (a) benefit the
consumer of electricity* and (b) could reduce a utility's debt financing requirements and, thereby, make it easier to finance research
and development in environmental areas.**

   2. **Neither** the Utilities, nor the Federal and State Governments
   Have Made Meaningful Efforts to Develop Adequate Methods
   for Undergrounding Transmission Lines.

The utilities may be able substantially to reduce environmental and safety problems posed by transmission lines by placing
them underground. Undergrounding may also, however, involve some
imposition on the landscape, e.g., trees are cut down, roads are
needed and must be maintained, at intervals there must be large
manholes and pumping stations to circulate oil used for cable
cooling, and some safety problems where,for example, liquid hydrogen is used for cooling superconductive cables.***

---

*Rental payments under a lease, however, would be recoverable by
a utility as operating costs; but, a net benefit would accrue to
the consumer.
**Real estate taxes, which might be lost as a result of public
ownership, could be recouped through lease payments or by requiring the lessee to pay a portion of the tax.
***P.H. Rose, Underground Power Transmission, Science, p. 272
(October 16, 1970).

The primary constraints on undergrounding, according to the
utilities, are cost - it is claimed that undergrounding high voltage cable costs 10 to 20 times as much as comparable overhead lines -
and lack of technology to move power underground on a reliable
basis for long distances.*

According to Mr. Luce, research is needed to develop new
types of cable insulators, improved AC-DC converters, and new forms
of transmission such as cyrogenic (i.e., superconducting and super-
cooled) cables.** Also, it appears that "automation or other improvements in the techniques of trenching and cable laying must
be considered along with improved cable designs. In congested
areas...deep service tunnels may provide an answer."***

Despite the mounting public concern with overhead lines,
neither the utilities nor government have directed much effort to
developing improved materials and processes for placing transmission
lines underground. In 1970, for example, no federal or state money
was spent on gas insulated cable development; and, only $100,000
of private funds was spent, although total funding required is
about $3 to $5,000,000 to develop such cable in 4 to 7 years.****
Further, no industry funds, and only $25,000 of government money,
were spent on superconducting cyrogenic cable, which is expected to

---

*Short lengths of cables insulated with compressed gas, which
are basically able to match overhead lines in capacity and voltage
handling capability, have been placed in service. Rose, supra
at 269.
**Remarks before FPC, 50th Anniversary Ceremony, June 3, 1970.
***Rose, supra at 272.
****EPE Report, supra at 44.

require at least $8,000,000 to develop within 5 to 7 years.*

Utilities not only have failed to spend money to develop suitable undergrounding technology, but continue to treat the public's land as their private preserve. A recent example of utility insensitivity to environmental values and community interests occurred in Wallkill Township in Orange County, New York.

---

*Idem.

There surveyors hired by Con Ed reportedly trespassed on lands
and cut trees in an effort to hurry along completion of an overhead transmission line which the local zoning board held could not
be erected because it would greatly decrease local land values.
The locality has no objection to the line, so long as it is placed
underground.

Con Ed's proposed route cuts right through an unscarred, 645-
acre wetlands called Basherkill, which people in the area, as well
as conservationists, are eager to retain in its natural state. Con
Ed's route - needless to say - is shorter and, thus, less expensive
than a route prepared by conservationists which avoids the nature
area.*

The traditional utility approach of seeking lower cost at the
expense of the environment - well illustrated in the Wallkill in-
cident - cannot be tolerated, particularly in view of the vast increase in electric power facilities which the utilities assert will
be required over the next two decades. An immediate program is
needed - funded by public and private sources - to seek economically feasible, environmentally sound and safe means of undergrounding existing and future transmission lines.

3. Multiple Use of Rights-of-Way Should be Encouraged

In addition, it will be necessary for regulatory authorities,
as well as utilities, to discard the present practice of establishing exclusive, single purpose, rights-of-way for individual utilities, e.g., railroads, telephone, gas, and electric companies.

*New York Times (11/13/70)

This practice "can no longer be accommodated with the land avail-able for the rapidly expanding population."*

The regulatory authorities, i.e., PSC, DEC, Department of Transportation, should make every possible effort to have utili-ties make joint use of rights-of-way, consistent with safety, re-liability and sound environmental considerations. Joint use has recently been vigorously endorsed in a report on Electric Power and the Environment prepared by a federal interagency committee, sponsored by the Office of Science and Technology of the Execu-tive Office of the President. The Committee concluded that the principle of joint use

> "needs major emphasis in future planning and right-of-way acquisition programs. To move in this direc-tion will require major innovations in land-use plan-ning...as well as utility practices."**

Moreover, this principle was recently approved by the New York State Legislature in creating the new state Department of Transportation. The legislature authorized the Commissioner of Transportation in connection with planning, designing and con-structing any state transportation facility "to provide, to the extent he deems feasible and in the best interest of the state, for multiple use outside the City of New York of the right of way appurtenant thereto."***

---

*EPE Report, supra at 24.
**EPE Report, supra at 25.
***Transportation Law, §14-b.

IV.   Utility and Regulatory Practices Which Hinder Environmental Planning

A.   Introduction

The consumption of energy in general and electricity in
particular have been growing rapidly - faster than population since
the late 1940's, and their rates of growth have increased markedly
in the last few years. Overall energy consumption has been growing at about 5 per cent a year since 1965, as compared with a rate
of growth of 2.8 per cent in the period 1947 to 1965. Per capita
consumption of energy in 1969 was 42.5 per cent higher than in
1947. Overall energy demands are predicted to double in the
next 15 years.*

The rate of growth in electricity use has even exceeded that
of energy consumption. Electricity use has grown at an annual
compound rate of 8.4 per cent since 1947, growing at about 9
per cent for the past two years.** Per capita consumption of
electricity increased about 3.5 times from 1950 to 1970.

The utility industry projects that per capita demand for electricity will continue to grow much faster than population for the next
several decades. Important assumptions underlying the industry's bul-
lish projections are: (a) that the total environmental costs of producing and supplying electric power will continue to be omitted from
the sale price of electricity and a continuation of the present

_____

*See, e.g., Testimony of S. David Freeman, Director, Energy Policy
Staff, Federal Office of Science & Technology, before Subcommittee
on Anti-Trust & Monopoly Legislation Senate Committee on the Judi-
ciary (May 5, 1970); L.A. Mayes, Why the U.S. Is In An "Energy
Crisis," Fortune (Nov., 1970); A. Gerber, Energy, Electric Energy
& The Environment, Pub. Utilities Fortnightly (2/4/71).
**EPE Report, supra at 2; Gerber, supra at 16.

promotional pricing structure, pursuant to which the unit cost
of electricity decreases as the amount of electricity consumed
increases; and, (b) that the electrical industry, including the
utilities, will be permitted to continue to engage in large
scale advertising and promotional activities designed to promote
consumption of electricity.

The principal areas in which the utilities are seeking to
foster increased demand are: (1) electric heating and air conditioning in residences, as well as industrial and commercial establishments; (2) the use of electrical processes in conversion industries,
e.g., steel, petroleum, aluminum; and (3) the use of additional and
upgraded electric appliances.*

The growing use of electric power and its impact on the environment is causing an increasing number of concerned people to
question seriously whether all proposed electric power facilities
are actually needed, or constitute the best alternative in terms of
avoiding environmental damage for meeting actual needs; and,to
seek a reevaluation of current policies which encourage demand for
electric power, as well as a reexamination of the traditional
operating policies and procedures of the electrical industry, including electric utilities and the power-oriented regulatory bodies.

The public's changing attitude was recently demonstrated by a
television quiz on the environment.

> One question that was put to a nationwide sampling
> of viewers was whether they were for "progress" in the
> form of new power plants, highways, and airports to
> meet the growing needs of society, or whether they were
> for "conservation" to preserve the environment against

---

*See, e.g., 21st Annual Electrical Industry Forecast, Electrical
World (9/15/70).

the damage caused by such developments. A sizable
majority voted for "conservation" over "progress."*

Also, some governmental officials are beginning to question
the desirability of continuing to increase use of electric power.
For example, the authors of a report published in September, 1970,
entitled "Electric Power and the Environment", sponsored by the
Energy Policy Staff of the Office of Science and Technology of the
Executive Office of the President reached this conclusion:

> The relative costs and benefits of present policies as
> contrasted with a policy of discouraging growth in energy
> use should be carefully evaluated. It may well be time-
> ly to reexamine all of the basic factors that shape the
> present rapid rate of energy growth in light of our re-
> source base and the impact of growth on the environment.**

In Los Angeles, as a result of the serious air pollution problems in the Los Angeles Basin, the Air Pollution Control District
recently promulgated a regulation which in effect bans the construction of new, fossil-fuel electric power plants in Los Angeles
County. Last year, the Los Angeles Department of Water and Power
sought a variance from the regulation to construct a 460 MW fossil-
fuel plant. The Department argued that the additional capacity was
necessary to meet an expected 7.6 per cent annual increase in demand for electricity and to maintain a reserve capability adequate
to avoid the hazards of total or partial blackouts in the City during the years 1972 to 1976.

In a decision issued on July 9, 1970 the Superior Court of
Los Angeles County upheld the denial of a variance by the Air Pol-

---

*S. David Freeman, Policy Alternatives for Resolving the Power Plant
Siting Problem, presented at IAEA Symposium on Environmental Aspects
of Nuclear Power Stations, August 10-14, United Nations Headquarters,
New York, New York.

**EPE Report, supra at xi.

lution Control District. The Court noted that only about 1.75 per
cent of the historical (and projected) 7.6 per cent annual increase
in demand for electric power was attributable to population growth;
the remaining 5.85 per cent was the result of increased per capita
consumption, "due primarily to the aggressive advertising of the
Department, urging a greater use of electricity by every resident."
Finding that projected peak demands could be significantly reduced
if the Department curtailed its advertising and that alternative
sources of power were likely to be available to meet a modest increase in demand, the Court held that:

> "the public interest in preventing any increase in the
> levels of air pollution and in seeking a diminution in the
> current levels of air pollution in the Los Angeles Basin,
> is an overriding public interest which must stand para-
> mount and supreme when contrasted with the public interest
> of the residents of Los Angeles in obtaining all of the
> electrical power they may desire. No substantial evidence
> has been presented to prove that the residents of Los An-
> geles are in any real danger in the foreseeable future of
> having an insufficient amount of electrical power to sat-
> isfy their basic needs. They may not have sufficient elec-
> trical power to supply all of their peripheral needs or
> demands created by good and effective advertising copy...
> but if the residents of the Los Angeles Basin are ever to
> live in an atmosphere having air of a satisfactory quality,
> it may be essential that they be willing to make some sac-
> rifice in the amount of electricity they use and enjoy over
> the next few years."*

Some of the   questions being raised are: Do we need all the
additional electric power projected by the utility industry? What
role should electric power play in meeting total energy needs? Should
the present and projected rate of growth in demand be decreased and,
if so, by what means? What demands represent essential needs? What

---

*Department of Water and Power of the City of Los Angeles v. Hearing
Board of the Air Pollution Control District of the County of Los Angeles et al, 1 Environmental Rep. 1580, 1606(9/18/70).

factors are responsible for increased demand and what are the uses
to which electric power is being and is planned to be put? What
would be the effect on the rate of growth in demand of making the
user pay for all environmental costs of electric power? What are
the social costs and benefits, including economic, public health,
and environmental costs and benefits of electric power? What
reforms are necessary in the present regulatory structure to make
it more responsive to the public interest? What changes are required in the management, organization and policies of the electric utility industry to assure that essential power needs are
met in the most efficient way with the least possible environmental harm? What actions can and should be taken to eliminate the
adverse environmental consequences of producing and supplying
electric power?

The substantial and dangerous impact on the environment
associated with electric power; the lack of adequate pollution
control technology and supply of low polluting fuels; and, the
extreme inefficiency of current methods of producing and supplying
electric power convince us that demand for electricity cannot be
permitted to grow at the rate and in the manner desired by the electric industry. Government must take immediate steps: (1) to discourage growth in demand for electrical energy by assessing the total societal costs of harm to health and the environment   caused by the pro -
duction and distribution of energy in general and electricity in particular
and factor such costs into the rate and pricing structure of energy
suppliers;   (2) to ensure that essential energy needs are
met with the least possible harm to the environment; (3) to maximize efficiency in the production, distribution and consumption

of electrical energy; and (4) if less stringent measures fail to increase efficiency and scale down electricity use, to impose direct
legal restraints on production and use of electrical energy. This
program may entail, for example, a total rejection of electric
heating - which results in considerably more pollution and waste of
resources than direct home heating; total replacement of incandescent
lighting by flourescent lighting, which is three times more efficient;
limits on the use of lighted billboards and neon signs for advertising;
new design concepts for large office buildings, e.g., natural
draft and/or regenerative heating and cooling systems; adequate
insulation in all buildings; an immediate prohibition on utility
promotional practices; and replacement of promotional rates with
rates designed to reflect the social costs of electric power
generation and distribution.

The industry's efforts to broaden and expand the use of electricity as an energy source, if permitted to continue uncontrolled,
will inevitably result in irreparable damage to the environment and in
crisis-rationing of power. The recent blackouts and load-shedding
in New York City, together with the dangerously high air pollution
levels, are examples of an unplanned and irrational reduction in
electric consumption without substantial benefit to the environment.

The current commitment of industry and several governmental
officials (including Governor Nelson Rockefeller* to maximum growth for
electric power and the philosophy of maximum consumption of resources,
goods and services must be replaced with a rational energy policy and
environmental action plan. Criteria must be developed for separating
essential from non-essential uses of electricity. We are opposed to the massive consumption of resources in the
*See Sections V. A. and C., infra.

name of economic development without adequate consideration of
environmental and resource utilization consequences, i.e.,
without environmental planning and rational resource management.
We would hope that any rational energy policy and environmental
action plan which is developed will serve to channel economic
development into environmentally sound areas.

1.   Industry's Projections of Continued Growth in Demand

The electric utility industry and the Federal Power Commission
estimate that demand for electricity will continue to grow at an
average rate of 7 per cent a year, with a doubling time of every 10
years, at least for the next two decades. Electric energy is projected to rise from 23 per cent of total energy requirements in 1970
to 33 per cent in 1980 and about 50 per cent in the year 2000.*

Consumption of electricity is expected to increase from 1.52
trillion kilowatt-hours (Kwh) in 1970 to 5.83 trillion Kwh in
1990, an increase of 284 per cent. For the 25 year period 1965-
1990, the increase would be 450 per cent. At least $350 billion
of capital investment is estimated to be required to install
plant and equipment to meet projected demands by 1990. By the
year 2000, the FPC estimates electrical energy requirements will
reach 10 trillion Kwh.**

The Federal Power Commission (FPC) and utilities estimate
that in order to meet the demand forecast for the two decades

_____

*Testimony of Milton Shaw, Director, AEC's Division of Reactor
Development and Technology, FY 1972 Authorization. Hearings
Before the Joint Committee on Atomic Energy (March 4, 1971);
Energy Report, supra 81.

**Energy Report, supra at 81-82; FPC Environmental Statement on
the Proposed Electric Power Environmental Policy Act of 1970,
p. 3 (9/30/70).

ahead, net electric power generating capacity must be <u>quadrupled</u> -
going from about 344,000 MW in 1970 to an estimated 1,260,000 MW in
1990. By far the greatest growth is expected in nuclear capacity,
which would increase dramatically from 3.4 per cent to about 40 per
pent of the total generating capacity by 1990. Fossil-fueled capacity would decrease from 76 per cent to 44 per cent.*

(a) <u>New York State</u>

New York State accounts for about 5 per cent of national demand for electricity.**According to the utilities, demand for electricity will continue to double in New York State every twelve years,
at least for the next 25 years.   The largest growth is forecast for Southeastern New York.

The Governor's Electric Power Committee reported in 1967 that
electric generating capacity will have to increase by at least 270
per cent by 1990, based on 1965 requirements.***The Governor recently stated that rising demands will require:

---

*FPC projections of kind and amount of electric generating capacity
required in 1970 and the next two decades to meet projected demands
are as follows (set forth in letter from J.N. Nassikas, FPC Chairman,
to Honorable Spiro T. Agnew, President of the Senate, dated Sept. 30,
1970).

	1970		1980		1990	
	Megawatts	Percent	Megawatts	Percent	Megawatts	Percent
Conventional Hydro	51,400	14.9	68,000	10.2	81,945	6.5
Pumped Storage Hydro	3,600	1.1	27,000	4.0	70,000	5.5
Fossil Steam	261,200	75.9	396,000	59.3	559,000	44.3
Internal Combustion & Gas Turbine	16,000	4.7	30,000	4.5	50,000	4.0
Nuclear	11,600	3.4	147,000	22.0	500,000	39.7
Total:	344,000	100.0	668.000	100.0	1,260,945	100.0

**Remarks of Joseph C. Swidler entitled "Problems and Opportunities
in Waste Heat Disposal," at the Conference on the Beneficial Uses of
Thermal Discharges, Albany, N.Y. (9/18/70).
***Report of the Governor's Electric Power Committee (12/15/67).

"Additional power equal to that now required to light
up every city, power every industry, and run every household appliance in New York State."*

Utilities in this state are planning to install about 21,000
MW of new capacity between 1970 and 1980. This would increase their
total installed capacity to about 40,000 MW: approximately 8,000 MW
will be nuclear (including eight plants of 500 MW or larger) and
4,000 MW will be conventional fossil-fueled plants (including six
plants of 500 MW or larger); about 3,000 MW will be pumped storage;
and, the rest will be primarily gas turbine.**

(b) New York City

During 1970, Con Ed supplied 32.4 billion Kwh of electrical
energy to customers in its service area, which includes the five
boroughs of New York City plus 70 per cent of Westchester County.
Con Ed supplies about one-half the state's entire load to the state's
smallest service area in size.*** Its service area is uniquely re-
stricted to a very densely developed and populated peninsular area,
which seriously aggravates the environmental hazards associated
with electric power production and supply.

From 1948 to 1968 demand in Con Ed's service area grew at a com-
pounded annual rate of 5.8 per cent (doubling every 12 years)****.
In 1970, total sales increased by about 6.9 per cent over 1969.
In January 1970, Charles Luce, Chairman of the Board of Di-

*Nelson A. Rockefeller, Our Environment Can Be Saved, p. 78
(Doubleday & Co., 1970).
**Northeast Power Coordinating Council, Data on Coordinated Regional
Bulk Power Supply Program (September 1, 1970).
***The service area is about 660 square miles in size and has about
8,900,000 residents. Other utilities, with small portions of the
states' load, serve areas of many thousands of square miles.
****New York City's Power Supply, prepared by Development and Resources
Corporation (October 1969) p. 8.

rectors of Con Ed, forecast growth of about 350-375 MW per year for
the next 10 years. He stated that to meet this rate of growth "and
provide adequate reserves, now requires a new 1,000,000 KW plant
approximately every two years."* In other words, every two years
the Company will need an additional plant, larger than the contro-
versial new unit planned for Astoria, Queens in 1974.

The Company's forecast, however, appears to be too low. Recently Con Ed informed the City that it is reviewing its load forecasts and that "preliminary indications are that upward revision
will be necessary." The predicted peak load for the coming summer
exceeds last summer's predicted peak load by 400 MW. The company's
1970 Annual Report projects an annual growth rate for electric loads
of about 4-1/2 to 5 per cent.

To meet even the most conservative load forecasts, Con Ed intends to install about 6,660 MW of new capacity between now and
1980: about 3,100 MW will be nuclear (including three plants of
850 MW or larger); about 1600 MW will be fossil-fueled (two 800
MW units); and, the rest will be gas turbines. The Company's total
installed capacity is expected to increase by about 46 per cent,
from 9,360 MW to 13,700 MW in 1980. Con Ed has also projected a requirement for 22.5 million KW of additional generating capacity
by the year 2000 - an increase of <u>240 per cent</u> based on current installed capacity.

2. <u>Promotional Activities and Pricing Policies are
   Directed at Increasing Average Per Capita Consumption.</u>

The primary factor in the utilities' projected growth in de-

---

*<u>Power for Tomorrow: The Siting Dilemma</u>, address by C. Luce, printed
in <u>The Record of the Association of the</u> Bar of the City of New York
(January, 1970).

mand is a continual increase in average consumption per customer.
On a national basis, population is only expected to account for 20
per cent of growth in demand over the next 30 years, with the remainder based on projections of economic development and increased
per capita use. * According to Charles Luce, "even if we achieved
zero population growth, the demand for energy would continue approximately to double every decade.... Average residential use of
electricity has increased five times since World War II. People are
buying more appliances and demanding more comfort: television,
frost-free refrigerators, air conditioning, and so on...."**

Three basic factors underlie the projected increase in per
capita consumption: First, environmental costs of producing and
supplying electric power have not been included in the price charged
the consumer. The reason such costs exist, as pointed out above in
the discussion of environmental damage caused by electric power, is
that the utility industry, as well as state and federal regulatory
agencies, have refused to take the action necessary to prevent environmental harm: low unit costs rather than environmental protection have been their major objective.

A major reason for the rising per capita consumption is
that the price of electricity has steadily decreased - even in the
face of inflation.

"From 1926 to 1968 as the price of electricity declined
from an average of 2.17 cents per kilowatt-hour to 1.55
cents, the Consumer Price Index doubled. In terms of

*E.g., Energy Report, supra at 82 and f.n. No. 1.
**Remarks of Charles F. Luce, entitled "Our Polluted Environment:
Business Searches for Solutions" at Indiana University of Pennsyl-
vania (Oct. 19, 1970).

constant dollars, the price of electricity in 1968 was
less than one-third that of 1926. During this period,
the per capita use increased about eight times, and the
total revenues of the electric power industry about nine-
fold."*

In manufacturing industries, the cost of electric power has
actually decreased in terms of percentage of product value. Between 1939 and 1963, electricity consumption by manufacturing industries increased from 70,870,000,000 Kwh to 408,000,000,000 Kwh, while
cost of purchased power as a per cent of product value decreased from
1.41 per cent to .86 per cent.** Further, taking 1939 as a base
year, the United States Census of Manufacturers indicates that
the industry's 1963 dollar received only 21 cents of labor value,
20 cents in construction and 42 cents in raw materials. With respect to electric power, however, industry received $1.21 on its
1939 dollar.

Second, in order to promote increased use of electric power,
New York utilities employ a promotional rate structure: they reduce the price per Kwh charged to customers as the total amount
of electricity purchased increases.*** In addition, utilities
often offer special rates to large potential customers to deter
installation of competitive energy systems. For example, a few
years ago, Con Ed offered special rates to the owners of Co-op

---

*Energy Report, supra at 84.
**U.S. Census of Manufacturers, 1939 and 1963.
***For example, Con Ed's monthly rates (effective September 17, 1970)
for small users are: $2.40 for 10 Kwh or less; $.05 per Kwh for the
next 290 Kwh; $.04 per Kwh for the next 600 Kwh; $.036 per Kwh for
the next 1,200 Kwh; and $.0325 per Kwh for excess of 2,100 Kwh.
Rates for large users range from $4.50 per Kw for 100 Kw of maximum
demand to $2.35 per Kw for excess over 25,000 Kwh of maximum demand;
and from $.021 per Kwh for the next 3,000 Kwh to $.01 per Kwh for
excess over 3,000,000.

City, a 15,000 resident cooperative apartment development in the
Bronx. The project had decided to install its own total energy
system because Con Ed's then-existing rates were higher than the
project's cost of generating its own power. From the standpoint
of environmental planning, the total energy system may have been
preferable. Such systems can operate at up to 75 per cent efficiency
in terms of converting fuel to useful energy (compared to 34-36 per
cent efficiency of supplying electricity from a central power station)
thus conserving fuel and producing less pollution.* Such units
may also serve to lessen the total environmental impact of electric
power by dispersing (as opposed to concentrating) sources of
pollution** and by eliminating probable energy losses involved in
transmission and distribution. Co-op City accepted Con Ed's special
rate.***

Con Ed's offer of special rates also deterred installation of
an on-site total energy system at the World Trade Center which,
when complete, will demand about 80,000 kilowatts of electric power -
more than a city of about 100,000 population (about the size of
Schenectady).

Third, the public is bombarded with advertisements which urge
either directly or indirectly more consumption,and utilities which
cannot guarantee to supply existing demand continue to engage in
aggressive, promotional activities. Sales bonuses to distributors,
cooperative advertising, financing assistance (especially for conversion to electric heating), equipment and appliance rental programs,

---

*The excess heat generated by on-site production of electricity can
be converted to use for heating during winter, air conditioning during
summer and for making hot water.
**This possible advantage may be offset, however, by the use of tall
stacks at central power stations which may serve to disperse pollutants.
***C. Girard Davidson, The City and Electric Power, a Report to
New York City's Consumer Council, p. 43-44 (Jan. 1968).

and concessions to builders to persuade them to use electricity
are some of the other methods by which the industry encourages
consumption.

Last year, the Edison Electric Institute (EEI), the national
trade association of investor-owned power companies, announced

the biggest advertising program in its history. The "Live Better Electrically" advertising campaign, intended to promote the use of electricity, including the "all-electric home," will cost about $1,500,000, most of which will come from equipment suppliers.

Con Ed's income statements illustrate the substantial reliance of utilities on sales promotion to increase the use of electric power. In 1969, the Company had advertising expenses of about $2,201,660 (equal to $0.008/Kwh sold) and demonstrating and selling expenses of about $3,869,730 (equal to $0.014/Kwh sold).*

According to the Company's 1969 Annual Report "intensive sales efforts combined with normal load growth" enabled Con Ed to sell more electricity in 1969 than ever before. The Report states proudly that (1) "new sales policies in 1969 helped to produce record new sales;" (2) a lighting campaign "contributed significantly" to a 7.8 per cent increase in average residential usage of electricity over 1968; and (3) a low-cost customer financing plan for appliances and wiring "no doubt contributed" to the record number of 23,000 private homes rewired in its service area in 1969.

The utilities' shrewd and relentless efforts to promote electricity is evidenced by Con Ed's recent "environmental" advertising. In a flyer recently sent to residential customers, the company states:

---

*Con Ed's advertising expenses (not including institutional advertising) for the previous three years were:

Year	Dollar Amount	Amount/Kwh Sold
1968	1,881,068	$0.006
1967	1,225,807	0.005
1966	1,163,741	0.005

"Electricity is the <u>cleanest</u> form of energy used by man. But even electricity causes some damage to the environment - to air, water, and the landscape. We therefore urge that everyone conserve electricity at all seasons of the year. By "conserve" we mean: <u>use what you need for healthful, safe and pleasant living, but do not waste</u>." (emphasis added).

The characterization of electricity as "the cleanest form of energy used by man" is grossly misleading, if not an outright lie. It focuses on the lack of pollution at the point of consumption, totally ignoring the substantial environmental damage caused by electric power generation and transmission. Moreover, the company's notion of conserving resources is nothing more than a self-serving request to continue consuming all the electricity one wants.*

The majority of a utility's advertising and promotional costs, plus dues to trade and lobbying associations, qualify as operating expenses recoverable by the utility in the rates charged customers.**

Regulatory agencies allow the coverage of these costs on the theory that increasing demand for power will require building larger plants, which will realize economies of scale and lower unit costs of power generation. Such costs can then be passed on as lower unit prices to the consumer. But, this view totally ignores the environmental costs of electric power - of which the public has not been adequately informed by industry or government - and

*Con Ed recently announced that it has suspended sales promotion of electricity and natural gas for 1971. While builder incentives to install electric heat will no longer be offered, Con Ed <u>will</u> maintain a winter-time electric heat differential that encourages electric heat, and will from time to time encourage the use of off-peak night lighting. It will also advertise in areas of "energy policy, environmental programs and public service". According to Mr. Luce, the decision is not necessarily a binding decision for future years, but will be reviewed from time to time. <u>Around the Con Ed System</u> (March 1971), p. 4.
**Several of these activities have been challenged by competing suppliers, but their use is generally upheld as long as they are granted uniformly.

which have not been factored into the current rate structure. There is no countervailing public interest advertising that points out the relative waste of resources and environmental harm caused by increased use of electricity; nor, have federal or state authorities with responsibility for environmental protection or power made a meaningful effort to bring these problems to the public's attention. Witness, for example, the manner in which the PSC and FPC dismissed the undisputed air pollution problems posed by Con Ed's proposal to expand its Astoria facility in New York City last summer.*

In sum, the utilities, as well as other members of the electrical industry, are engaged in aggressive efforts to manage and develop demands which will serve _their_ needs for increased consumption of electricity. The concept of "consumer sovereignty" bears little resemblance to reality since initiative lies largely with industry, not with the individual. Moreover, the individual is generally not informed concerning the social costs of producing, as well as utilizing, the continuous stream of new and upgraded electrical products.

The need to control and manage individual wants is inherent in the large, modern business complex.** The need to insure a continuous growth in electric power is as vital to the capital-intensive, electric utility industry as the need to plan and manage consumer

---

*See discussion of Con Ed Astoria in Section III. C.(a), _infra_.
**Professor John Kenneth Galbraith, _The New Industrial State_ (1967) p. 201. It is also interesting to note, as Professor Galbraith does, that the more a person's wants are removed from basic, physical needs, e.g., food, shelter, the more susceptible he is to persuasion or management as to what he purchases. This distinction between physical and psychologically based wants has great significance for an increasingly affluent society, like ours, in which a diminishing number of goods and services are designed to satisfy elementary physical needs.

behavior is to other large, modern industries. For example, Long Island Lighting Company states in its 1970 Annual Report (p. 17) that:

> "Increased sales to existing customers now account for the most significant annual revenue gains. Such increased sales to existing customers are being encouraged through planned efforts.... Marketing surveys are an essential part of such efforts. The sales organization then follows through on contacting customers who vary from individuals to corporate and national chain representatives and government authorities."

Moreover, projections of sizeable increases in demand for electric power provide a necessary and convenient justification for the large capital expenditures required to sustain the industry's rapid growth, which provides increasing returns for the utilities. Once having made the projections and the expenditures based thereon, the industry is then committed to promote increased consumption. Also, the more dependent utility customers become on electricity, the greater become the "responsibilities" of the utilities to provide electric power.

The industry and the regulatory agencies are, of course, well aware of the environmental damage associated with their promotional efforts. And yet, notwithstanding the utilities' present inability to guarantee an uninterrupted supply of electric power, the regulatory agencies have refused to limit promotional efforts or to attempt to curb peak demand by, for example, imposing a surcharge for peak use; instead, the utilities are permitted to balance their peak loads by creating more demand.

3. Major Components of Projected Demand

- 173 -

(a) <u>In the Nation</u>*

By 1985, the electric utility industry hopes to treble its total sales. The major areas of projected growth are in electric heating and air conditioning; electric processes in conversion industries, e.g., steel, petroleum, aluminum; and, use of additional and upgraded appliances.

*Most of the information herein is from the 21st Annual Electrical Industry Forecast, <u>supra</u>.

Industrial use is expected to grow rapidly, at about 8 per
cent annually through 1985, although its percentage of total electric sales is expected to decline gradually from about 43 per cent
in 1970 to 38 per cent. Major components of industrial demand will
be new electric processing techniques for minerals and metals, and
increasing use of air conditioners and electric heating in factories.
Use of electricity to produce aluminum and magnesium will slightly
more than triple by 1985, rising from 70.2 billion Kwh in 1970 to
220 billion Kwh.

The commercial sector is also expected to continue to grow
at about 8 per cent annually through 1985 and to increase its share
of total electricity sales slightly from 22 per cent in 1970 to 23
per cent. Major sources of growth are expected to be increased use
of electric heat and air conditioning in schools, hospitals, shopping
centers, churches, and office buildings.

The most rapid growth projected is in the residential market,
which by 1985 is expected to almost equal industrial use.

If industry's promotional efforts are successful, the largest
component of increased residential consumption will be electric
heating of residential dwellings. The forecast growth in electric
heating, together with the planned proliferation of staple and "fad"
appliances, and a raft of new families entering the housing market,
is expected to result in an average residential use of 10,000 Kwh
in 1975. This represents a per capita increase of over 100 per
cent from the 1965 level. By 1985, average residential use is expected to increase to 15,000 Kwh.*

*21st Annual Electrical Industry Forecast, supra at 40.

(b) New York State

Increasing per capita use of electricity is a major factor
in growth in demand in New York State, as well as the Nation. For
example, from 1958 to 1968, electricity use per customer in the
State rose 75 per cent. The number of customers served increased
by only 11 per cent.*

According to the 1967 Report of the Governor's Electric
Power Committee, a large portion of increased demand in New York
State over the next two decades will be in the industrial sector.
The Committee pointed out that many of the fastest-growing manufacturing industries are "major consumers of electric power." It
also maintained that demand would rapidly increase in other sectors:
"current and anticipated technological developments should sharply
expand electric power requirements of households,businesses and
the public sector."

Industrial and commercial customers now account for the
majority of electricity sales in New York state - about 59 per
cent in 1969. Although they represent only about 12 per cent of
total customers, industrial and commercial customers account for
51 per cent of total electric utility revenues (about $875,000,000
out of total revenues of $1.7 billion).**

These statistics underscore the importance to the utilities
of industrial and commercial consumption and the success which the
utilities' promotional rates (which of course mean the most to the
largest users of power) have had in developing business in the in-

*Public Service Commission Annual Report (1968).
**Statistical Year Book of the Electric Utility Industry for 1969
(Edison Electric Institute, Sept. 1970) p. 45.

- 176

industrial and commercial sectors. Governor Rockefeller has recently mounted a large-scale program to provide up to 6,000 MW of additional low-cost power to large industrial users through the New York State Power Authority. This program is intended to and will have the effect of encouraging further consumption by existing and new industrial users.*

Although largest in number (about 85 per cent of total), residential customers now account for only about 29 per cent of total sales and 38 per cent of total electric utility revenues ($654,000,000 in 1969).** Increases in New York State's residential demand are, however, expected to parallel the national trend and gain in the share of total sales and revenues.

(c) New York City

Growth in demand in New York City during the next decade is expected to be derived largely (i) from the construction of new office and apartment buildings, as well as replacement of older buildings with modern facilities that use more electrical energy; (ii) from increases in per capita consumption of electricity resulting from incremental demands in air conditioning; (iii) from added and "upgraded" appliances (i.e., appliances that require more electricity); and (iv) if Con Ed's sales strategy of encouraging "use of electricity during the winter (electric heat)" is successful,*** from expanded use of electric heating.

Population growth is a negligible factor in growing demand for electricity in Con Ed's service area. Also industrial loads

---

*The Governor's program for encouraging increased electric power consumption by large industrial users is discussed in detail in Section V.C. infra.
**Statistical Yearbook of the Electrical Utility Industry, supra at 38-45.
***1969 Annual Report, p.5.

are relatively small, accounting for only about 8 per cent of total sales of electricity.

Since 1959, annual peak load on Con Ed's system has occurred during the summer, between June and September. Due to the rapid growth in air conditioning loads, summer peaks exceed winter peaks by about 25 per cent.

Loads are also influenced by one-time major construction projects such as the World Trade Center.

Currently, no regulatory control is exercised over the addition of major new sources of demand to Con Ed's system or the manner in which their energy requirements are to be met. Neither the utility nor the potential customer is required to justify the need for the additional demand or to make certain that the energy system adopted is environmentally acceptable.

Average electric use per residential customer in New York City is relatively low. In 1969, average residential use by Con Ed's customers was 2,950 Kwh compared to a national average of about 6,570. This is due mainly to the large number of multiple dwellings in the City - apartment dwellers tend to use less electricity than homeowners. They tend to own less energy-consuming appliances than homeowners. Largely as a result of agressive advertising by Con Ed and other members of the electric industry, however, average use per residential customer is rapidly rising: 7.8 per cent in 1969, and 8.5 per cent in 1970. Residential sales increased by 11.3 per cent in 1970 over 1969.

The major electric users in the City are as follows: Commercial - about 44%; residential - about 25%; industrial - about 7.5%; transportation - about 9%.

(d) Electric Heating

Now, about 4.7 million housing units are electrically heated and account for over 15 per cent of total, national residential usage. The utilities project that over 19 million residential units will be electrically heated by 1980 and 25 million by 1985 - an increase of over 400 per cent. If this occurs, and all such units go total electric, they will account for 500 billion Kwh or 45 per cent of total residential use in 1985.*

The intensive sales efforts of utilities to promote electric heating are well illustrated by the "Sunny Comfort" campaign recently launched by LILCO. According to the company's 1970 Annual Report, the campaign

> "was initiated after marketing surveys confirmed that many existing homeowners would install such heating systems in connection with other home improvements. A total of 155 independent electrical contractors... are receiving additional training as electric heat dealers to aid in sales efforts."

Con Ed also actively promotes electric heating, with considerable success. In 1970, electric heat was installed in 26 per cent of new private houses and 31 per cent of new apartment dwelling units in its service area, compared to 9 per cent in each category in 1969. Moreover, conversions of existing homes and apartments to electric heat were up 150 per cent in 1970 from 1969.**

The basic reason utilities promote electric heating is to offset summer peak loads and lower the per unit cost of generating electricity. As explained in Con Ed's 1969 Annual Report: "increas-

---

*21st Annual Electrical Industry Forecast, Electrical World (9/15/70), p. 40.
**1970 Annual Report, p.4.

ing off-peak consumption does not require additional investment in new plant facilities. Instead, it enables us to make better use of existing facilities, and to produce additional revenues at... small incremental cost...."* The "balancing load" argument would tend to support any increased use of reasonably new machinery; and, of course, in the long run, might be counterproductive in that, by balancing one peak load the utility may create another, which in turn would require balancing, etc. In fact, Con Ed was a winter peak system until 1959. The widespread promotion and rapid increase in use of air conditioning has created a summer peak load, which now exceeds previous winter peaks by about 25 per cent (or 1500 MW).**

---

*In 1969, Con Ed installed electric heat in 2,059 new dwelling units (twice as many as in 1968), which represented 9 per cent of new housing starts; and, converted 740 dwelling units to electric heat (3 times as many as in 1968). 1969 Annual Report, p. 6.
**FPC Review of Con Ed 1969 Power Supply Problems and 10-Year Expansion Plans, p. 11 (Dec. 1969).

Another attractive aspect of electric heating - as far as
the utilities are concerned - is its effectiveness as a promotional
tool for the "total electric home." Virtually every electrically
heated home has electric cooling, water heating and clothes dry-
ing. The electrically heated home generally consumes about 23,000
Kwh per year - three to four times the average consumption in a
home which employs an alternate heating system.

In this connection, we note that eleven major utilities (including Con Ed) recently joined together to form a promotional
group called the Utilities Housing Council to promote and assist
in financing low and moderate-income housing.* Support for this
effort has come in large part from the United States Department
of Housing and Urban Development which has urged utilities to
assist in financing construction of 26 million dwelling units in the
next decade. According to G. Richard Dunnells, special assistant
to the Under Secretary of Housing and Urban Development, the Department has specifically set aside $1 million to encourage utility
efforts. He also recently noted that the utilities have an "en-
ourmously high" stake in remodelling rundown urban areas.** The
federal plan makes no apparent attempt, however, to reflect or
avoid the additional environmental costs which would result from
significant incremental demands for electricity and a possible proliferation of all-electric homes arising out of new housing con-

*A. Ripley, Utilities Enter Housing Field to Protect Their Markets
in Decaying Areas of Cities, New York Times, (Nov. 22, 1970).
**Riply, N.Y. Times (Nov. 22, 1970), supra.

- 181 -

struction.

The PSC has recently endorsed the project primarily because
it will enable utilities to protect existing, as well as create
new markets. On August 18, 1970, the PSC granted a request by
New York State Gas and Electric Corp. to spend $1,000,000 to fi-
nance low and moderate income housing and "supporting commercial
facilities" within its service area.* The utility maintained that
there was a critical shortage of housing in its service area - which
includes the New York State Appalachian Area - which adversely affected the economic growth of the service area. While, in approving the petition, the hearing examiner alluded to the need to
solve housing shortages, his opinion makes clear that the underlying basis for approval was that better housing "would redound
to the benefit of petitioner and its utility business." He reasoned that:

> "Privately owned utility companies must be concerned
> with such social problems within their own service dis-
> trict, particularly housing shortages which directly affect
> both consumers and consumption of the services provided
> by them. The petitioner's proposal to participate in
> the furnishing of housing is socially desirable and does
> have some relation to its business obligations."**

In our judgment, utilities should be expressly prohibited
from taking any action to promote the use of electricity in any
housing they finance. In its recent approval of New York State Gas
and Electric Corporation's plan to finance low and moderate income

---

*Niagara Mohawk Power Company has sponsored similar projects in
Rome and Troy, New York. Id.
**Re New York State Electric & Gas Corporation, 85 P.U.R. 3d 494,
496-97 (August 18, 1970).

housing, the PSC should have included a restriction on promotional
activities. The utility will secure a return at least equivalent
to its cost of capital on the project; an additional "promotional"
incentive is thus unnecessary to make the project economically feasible.

Moreover, from a public policy standpoint, it makes no sense
to attempt to solve a housing problem by means which may create a
serious public health problem.

(e) Individual Air Conditioners

The appliance that has had the most immediate effect on many
utilities' load, including that of Con Ed, is the room air condi-
tioner, national sales of which increased from 1.5 million units
$434.5 million) in 1960 to 5.5 million units ($1.12 billion) in
1969. 250,000 room air conditioners were sold in Con Ed's service area in 1969.* Westinghouse and General Electric (the major
suppliers of electric generating equipment) are also major suppliers
of components for air conditioners, as well as many other appliances, and engage in a substantial amount of promotion for such
products.

Individual electric room air conditioners are probably the
least efficient means for cooling. For example, central air conditioning utilizing distributed steam would be about twice as efficient, i.e., utilize 50 per cent less fuel and contribute much
less air and thermal pollution,** and if natural gas were used on

---

*Merchandising Week (A Billboard Publication), Feb. 23, 1970.
**This assumes production of steam at an electric plant and distri-
bution to the user. Of course, if steam were produced on the premises
of the user, losses in distribution would be eliminated and overall
efficiency increased.

the premises, pollution would be reduced even more.

(f) Incandescent Lighting

Incandescent lighting in buildings is another example of extremely inefficient utilization of energy. Flourescent lighting is more than three times as efficient. Elimination of incandescent lighting in large buildings could considerably reduce per capita consumption of electric energy, with a concomitant reduction in environmental harm.*

(g) Other Appliances

Many of the new major appliances on sale now consume considerably more electricity than the ones they would replace. For example, color television sets require two to three times the amount of current used by black and white models they replace. Also, 9 cubic foot refrigerators in wide use today require about 350 Kwh per year. New 14 cubic foot frost-free models replacing the 9 foot models require about 1,200 Kwh per year, and 25 cubic foot combination units require 2,400 Kwh per year.

Another impetus to increased consumption of electricity is the seemingless endless trend toward "fad" appliances (e.g., electric cornpoppers, coffee grinders, carving knives) most of which do not even purport to be "necessities," - their principal appeal is the gimmick involved. Despite a general economic slump, manufacturers predict that sales will continue to grow by 5-10 per cent a year.

*Jaske, R. T., Fletcher, J.F., Wise, K.R., Heat Rejection Requirements of the U.S., in Chemical Engineering Progress (Nov. 1970) p. 18.

In 1969, consumers spent $2.4 billion on electric housewares - half a billion more than was spent on the war on poverty and 60 times more than the utilities spent on research and development. Since coming on the market in 1963, 19 million electric toothbrushes, and 22 million electric carving knives have been sold.

Many utilities in New York State play an active role in promoting appliances. Three run cooperative advertising and promotional programs; together they have at least 600 dealers who tie-in to their programs.*

Consumers, however, are not being adequately advised by labelling or public interest advertising of the increased electric energy requirements needed to operate these "improved" appliances; nor is any action being taken to assure that these appliances are designed to achieve maximum efficiency in terms of energy consumption.

---

*Central Hudson has about 115 dealers; New York State Gas & Electric Co. has about 350; and Rochester Gas & Electric Co. has about 125. The utilities pay a percentage, e.g., 25 per cent of advertising costs, for dealers who "tie-in." Merchandising Week (A Billboard Publication), Feb. 23, 1970, p. 50-51.

B. Suggested Methods for Assessing and Reflecting the
Social Costs of Electrical Energy Production

By assessing the social costs of the production and consumption of electric energy and, by factoring such costs into
the rate and pricing structure of the utility industry, it may
be possible to achieve a reduction in the current growth trend
in electric energy consumption with a consequent reduction in
environmental degradation. The underlying rationale for such
an assessment is to calculate external costs, i.e., social costs
attributable to production, supply and consumption of electric energy,
and to impose such costs on those firms and persons who are
primarily responsible for creating them.

The problem of quantifying social costs attributable to
power generation and distribution is a difficult one. Among the
many factors to be considered are:

(a) dollar cost of pollution-related illnesses in terms
of medical costs and loss of work;

(b) property damage associated with air pollution;

(c) loss of commercial fishing resources owing to thermal
pollution;

(d) loss of recreational land and water;

(e) fixing a dollar cost on aesthetic harm associated with
power generation and transmission facilities;

(f) calculating the cost of genetic damage resulting from
radiation exposure;

(g) the economic cost to a particular locality of businesses
or industries relocating in another area as a result of
environmental degradation;

(h) should social costs be predicted on the harm caused by
power generation and distribution or the funds necessary
to prevent or eliminate environmental harm;

*See Electrical Energy Organization Chart, attached as Appendix A.

(i) should the harmful effects of power generation be
evaluated from the standpoint of marginal impact on
the population, assuming a certain fixed level of
    pollution from other sources, or should all forms
of pollution share an agreed-upon cost of harm.

We feel at least the following methods for reflecting social

costs should be studied:

(1) Disclose the amount of electricity necessary to utilize
consumer products through mandatory labeling by the
manufacturer.

(2) Institute a non-promotional rate structure which would
eliminate the practice of offering a lower unit cost
as consumption increases.

(3) Institute a peak demand surcharge to discourage use
of electricity at peak hours.

(4) Establish an electricity use tax to reflect the social
costs of power generation, supply and use.

(5) Impose legal restrictions on electrical product
manufacturers and distributors with respect to
advertising and promotional activities that encourage
the use of electricity. (We propose an outright
ban on such activities on the part of utilities.)

(6) Establish legal restrictions on load increases and/or
institute outright per diem rationing of electricity
consumption.

1.   Disclose Amount of Electricity Necessary to Utilize
Consumer Products

The amount of electricity necessary to operate consumer

products should be calculated and consumers should be fully

advised of such electric energy requirements, via mandatory

labeling of products by manufacturers.

Together with a program designed to include social costs

in the price of electricity, such disclosure should serve to alert

consumers to the inefficiency of current methods of electric
power generation and the economic implications of excessive
electric energy use attributable to specific appliances. It
may also be desirable to institute some form of public interest
advertising designed to further educate the public regarding the
adverse health, economic and environmental consequences associated
with increased utilization of electrical products.

2. Institute a Non-Promotional Rate Structure

Utility companies are generally able to realize economies
of scale and therefore lower unit costs with successive units
of output. Thus, the block method of rate determination is by
far the dominant one and consists of an initial charge combined
with a reduction in the charge per kilowatt-hour for successive
blocks of energy consumed. Consequently, there has been
a strong incentive both on the part of the utilities to encourage increased use of, and large users to consume more,
electric power. In the past, promotional rates seemed rational
since customer needs were regarded as controlling. This policy
must now be re-evaluated in view of the serious threat to the
environment and public health posed by power generation and
distribution.

In establishing a non-promotional rate structure, it must
be determined whether social costs would (1) bear a linear relation to kilowatt hours; or, (2) increase more than proportion-
ately to increases in kilowatt hours, or vice versa; or (3) experience minimum "fixed costs of pollution" and beyond a threshold be subject to (1) or (2). Whatever rate restructuring is

- 188 -

ultimately required, the current promotional structure should be modified to remove incentives for increased consumption.

An increased price may serve to moderate demand, as well as promote more efficient use of electricity, e.g., better insulation of homes, use of more efficient consumption devices such as flourescent lighting. Any rate change should, however, be implemented in a manner which ensures that basic needs for electric power are not denied to those least able to bear increased costs. It may be necessary to allocate a larger proportionate percentage of total social costs to non-essential uses and industrial or commercial users, as opposed to the basic needs of residential users and public services, such as mass transportation and hospitals.

Additionally, in order to minimize short-run economic hardships, e.g., industries committed to large consumption of low-cost power are likely to be somewhat disadvantaged by a non-promotional rate structure, guidelines must be developed to separate essential from non-essential uses of electric power and to take account of other possible inequities which may result from rate revisions.

3. Institute A Peak Demand Surcharge

Since electric energy is generally not able to be stored, the total capacity of an electric utility system is geared to handle the peak demand. It is therefore rational to charge more for energy consumed at peak hours since the marginal cost to the system is greatest at that time. Failure to impose a peak demand surcharge actually results in a price subsidy to those who use power at peak periods, which is paid by off-peak users.

Some questions which must be considered in devising a peak demand surcharge are: For what period or periods during the winter and/or summer would a surcharge be levied? Would it be levied on a monthly or hourly basis? At what level would the surcharge be set and should it reflect the marginal cost on the system of above-"normal" (however that is measured) use? Who should impose and collect the surcharge (e.g. utilities, state or local government)? What should be done with the funds generated thereby?

Administrative and technical constraints may limit current ability to structure a surcharge. For example, the technology of metering electricity by the hour requires computerization which may be somewhat more difficult to effect on an hourly basis than, for instance, current telephone billing procedures.

Shorter term solutions may be to bill on a monthly basis, (i.e., raise the current bills for given months by a specified percentage).

Further, should the surcharge cover commercial and industrial as well as residential users? The traditional rationale for rate differentials is that different classes of users exert varying demands on the system and that the cost of supplying those demands varies. For instance, bulk quantities of power are cheaper to deliver to a single industrial customer than the same quantity of power delivered to widely dispersed residential users. Also, since some large industrial users have the option of generating their own power, their demand may be relatively more elastic and therefore their rates are generally set lower. Users who do not have this alternative may be subject to higher rates if their demand is relatively inelastic.

In New York City, commercial and residential users impose the greatest burden on Con Ed's system. Moreover, the greatest load on the system usually occurs between the hours of 1 and 4:30 PM during hot summer months. It may be necessary to utilize monthly, if not hourly, differentials for normal peak loads and widespread commercial and residential peak demand surcharges to diminish significantly peak demands on the New York City system.

4. Establish An Electricity Use Tax

An electricity use tax could serve as a complementary or alternative method to those mentioned above for reflecting social costs of electric power production and distribution. The tax could be levied by the State as either a flat rate, a percentage of the total electric bill or as a rate which would increase as consumption increased.

Receipts from a use tax could be segregated from general revenues and channeled into a fund for research and development into environmentally sound and more efficient methods of energy production.

5. Regulating Promotional Activity Which Serves to Encourage The Use of Electricity

When the rationale for increasing demand for electricity was based on lowering the unit costs to the customer (i.e., the more consumption, the lower the unit cost), it appeared reasonable to allow utilities to recover promotional costs as operating expenses. That policy, however, is no longer warranted since utilities are failing to satisfy pressing demands which they are encouraging, in part, through their own promotional activities. Recent brown and black outs have imposed a range of burdensome social costs on the public.

It is clearly contrary to the public interest to permit the utilities to engage in activities which will exacerbate power shortages and environmental problems, particularly when the customer ultimately bears the cost of the industry's promotional efforts. Accordingly, the utilities should be prohibited from engaging in any activities, which serve directly or indirectly to encourage or promote the use of electricity.

Moreover, the advertising and promotional activities carried out by manufacturers and distributors of electrical products, which are likely to have a greater impact upon system demand than those of utilities, should be promptly reviewed with a view to imposing legal restrictions thereon. Measures should be devised to ensure that those promotional activities are (a) consistent with sound environmental objectives and (b) do not mislead the public concerning the adverse environmental consequences of electric power production, distribution or use.

6. <u>Legal Restrictions on Load Increases and Rationing of Electricity</u>

Because a substantial segment of the demand for electricity may be relatively inelastic, it is not clear that the preceeding suggestions would effectively reduce long term consumption consistent with environmental needs. It may be necessary, therefore, to consider the imposition of legal restrictions on load increases. For example, a schedule of maximum increases in electricity growth in a given service area might be established.

As a last resort, an environmentally sound plan and system for rationing the use of electricity might be required. In any event, from an environmental standpoint, it is essential to develop some regulatory control over the addition to utility systems of new sources of demand such as, for example, the World Trade Center. Appropriate governmental authorities might be empowered to determine whether specific development plans are consistent with rational environmental, energy and land use policies and to compel, subject to judicial review, necessary planning changes to accomplish such consistency.

The owners of sizeable new industrial and commercial establishments, as well as existing establishments which will be expanded significantly, might be required to submit a report to appropriate authorities, well in advance of the commencement of operations or expansion, detailing the amount of electricity expected to be consumed on a daily basis; the expected uses of such electricity; the periods of peak demand; the estimated cost; expected source of electric power; alternative sources of electric power, e.g., installation of own generating equipment; alternative sources of energy, e.g., natural gas; and the reasons for rejecting such alternatives. Such an environmental report would hopefully bring some measure of environmental

planning into the private sector, and further would provide
government with a fairly comprehensive view of energy use in
the state.

C. Possible Methods for Reducing Social Costs Associated With Electric Power and Encouraging Sound Environmental Planning

Several practices of electric utilities, as well as inadequacies in the current regulatory framework, appear to hinder sound environmental planning and must be reexamined in the course of developing a rational energy utilization policy and environmental action plan for this state. The major problems that must be addressed are:

(1) the lack of any effective mechanism for subjecting the fundamental questions of whether specific power facilities are in fact needed, and whether they represent the best possible alternative in terms of reliability, efficiency and environmental impact, to meaningful review by regulatory authorities or the public;

(2) the failure of utilities to engage in advance, consultative planning with the public or regulatory authorities responsible for power supply and environmental protection, regarding changes in or expansion of their facilities or regarding contingency plans for dealing with power shortages;

(3) the utilities' present practice of constructing their own power plants in close proximity to their load centers, rather than building them in remote, less populated areas or purchasing power from outside sources;

(4) the present trend toward building fewer, but larger, plants and establishing power complexes which may undermine reliability, increase reserve requirements and aggravate already serious environmental problems; and,

(5) management inefficiencies, including the lack of adequate control over the quality and delivery of purchased equipment.

Prior to discussing these problems, it will be useful to set forth briefly the way in which electric utilities'profits are determined, including the calculation of their rate base.

Utility Rates - Components and Calculation

The regulatory process attempts to guarantee a utility company a certain fair rate of return on its investment, plus ensure recovery of necessary and reasonable operating expenses, while stabilizing the rates which the company is allowed to charge the public. Such stabilization is necessary considering that utility companies are allowed to operate as monopolies in their respective service areas. The rationale for allowing monopolies is the assumed need to avoid duplication of essential equipment in order to achieve economies of scale and, thus, achieve lower unit costs of production which are passed on to customers as lower unit prices.

The rates a utility can charge are based on the following formulae:

$$TR = O + (V-D) \ r \quad *$$

where TR = total revenues allowed

      O = operating expenses

      V = value of the tangible and intangible property, theoretically used and useful in the production of the service

      D = accrued depreciation of the tangible and reproducible property

      r = the fixed rate of return allowed

(V-D) = the rate base

and PQ = TR

where P = price of kilowatts provided

      Q = quantity of kilowatts provided

     TR = total revenues

The profit which an electric utility company realizes is illustrated by the equation:

$$NP = TR - O - T - C$$

*Charles F. Phillips, Jr., The Economics of Regulation,(Richard D. Irwin, 1969, Illinois), p. 131

where   NP = net profit after taxes and charges to income

TR = total revenues

O = operating expenses

T = income taxes

C = charges to after-tax net income, such as interest
on debt, dividends to stockholders, etc.

In the above equations, operating expenses include costs
which are determined either by normal competitive factors (such as
wages, salaries, fuel supplies and maintanance costs), by various
governmental actions (such as taxes) and by the company itself
(such as research and development costs, the current year's depreciation expense, expenditures for promotion and advertising and
certain salaries of executives).

The net or depreciated value of the tangible assets is called
the rate base (V-D in the above equation).
Valuation of tangible property is a major source of controversy
between the regulated companies and the regulatory authorities.
The authorities value the assets either on original cost basis,
reproduction cost basis or on some compromise between the
two.* The assets basically include (1) tangible assets such as
"used and useful" land, buildings and equipment; (2) overhead construction costs, i.e., incidental costs incurred during construction
of a facility, such as administration, brokerage, legal and promotional fees, interest, insurance, taxes and contingencies; (3)
working capital, i.e., funds representing necessary investment in
materials and supplies, and cash required to meet current obligations and to maintain minimum bank balances (included in the rate

*The acceptable definition of assets varies with each State Public
Service Commission.

base to compensate investors for capital they have supplied to a company); and (4) intangibles, including franchise value, water rights, leaseholds, etc.

In order to obtain a change in rates, a utility must ordinarily file a formal application with a state public service commission which, thereafter, holds a hearing and makes a decision. In New York State the process can take up to ten months.*

In its application, the utility company attempts to project its costs ahead, since the time lag between application and action is so long that a new rate application is usually filed immediately after the ruling on the old application. Utility companies may overestimate their projected costs, especially the more volatile operating expenses, and then attempt to reduce expenses after the new rates come into effect. Since a range of permissible rates of return is actually acceptable, and since the time lag between rate changes can be great, utility companies can for short periods realize profits which exceed the allowable rate of return plus the coverage of operating expenses. Of course, they are subject to having their rates reduced if their profits exceed reasonable levels and regulatory authorities have occasionally "urged" companies to reduce rates or have ignored requests for rate increases. However, in such cases, the initiative rests with the regulators to discover abuses and correct them.

---

*A significant exception in New York State is that the PSC allows immediate monthly rate adjustments for increases in fuel costs without a hearing.

(1) Utility Assertions Regarding the Need, as well as
    the Best Means, for Meeting Power Needs Can No
    Longer Remain Unchallenged By the Public or Regu-
    latory Authorities.

The fundamental questions of whether specific power plants
are in fact needed, and whether they represent the best possible
alternative in terms of reliability, efficiency and environmental
impact have not been subject to meaningful review by regulatory
authorities or the public.*

As noted above, utilities have traditionally developed and
executed expansion plans in isolation without meaningful participation by the public or challenge by regulatory authorities.
The general practice has been for a small number of executives,
whose primary concern has been the size of the rate base, economies of scale and low unit costs, to make major decisions in private which are then announced in the manner and at the time which
they determine will best serve the company's interests. In the
case of new power plants, this has often been on the eve of construction.

To date, the public has been denied access to reliable and
complete information concerning the industry's operations. With
the exception of a small number of academicians and public officials, few people - either in or outside of government - have an
adequate understanding of the industry and its problems.

Moreover, neither the power-oriented regulatory agencies nor
the utilities have the requisite public credibility effectively to
carry out their responsibility for providing necessary and reliable power, consistent with adequate environmental protection.

*E.g., Intergovernmental Coordination of Power Development and Environ-
mental Protection Act, Hearings on S.2752 Before the Subcommittee on
Intergovernmental Relations of the Committee on Government Operations
U.S. Senate, 91st Cong., 2d Sess., Pt. 1 , pp. 1-3, (1970).

Joseph C. Swidler, PSC Chairman, has recently acknowledged that

"the power industry now suffers from ... a credibility gap.

> "The public is suspicious of the disinterestedness
> of the industry's conclusions as they relate to en-
> vironmental matters. The suspicion persists that in
> conflicts between environmental protection and econ-
> omic considerations in the location of power supply
> facilities, the latter takes a subordinate position.
> This is unfortunate but perhaps natural, considering
> the general awareness that company managements, like
> all businessmen, are under continual economic stress.
> Nothing can be more unfortunate than to have this
> credibility gap extended to the governing agencies
> responsible for making the decisions which shape the
> environment in which we live."*

We can no longer afford to rely solely upon the Public Ser-

vice Commission (or any other regulatory agency) to oversee elec-

tric utilities - much less can we afford to expand the Commission's

powers (as the Governor has proposed) regarding the need for and

location of electric power facilities.

Clothed in their legal monopolies and responsible for supply-

ing power, the utilities have gone essentially unregulated by

government, the marketplace or the public.

The shortcomings of the current regulatory framework and poli-

cies, as well as utility practices, in terms of providing for a

meaningful review and public participation in utility expan-

sion plans; and the present lack of an adequate means and criteria for

reconciling the competing public interests in securing adequate

---

*Remarks entitled "The New York Program for Reconciling the Ex-
pansion of Energy Supply Facilities with Environmental Protection," Atomic Industrial Forum (March 17, 1970).

electric power and environmental protection are well illustrated
by the controversy which surrounded the recent proposal by
Con Ed to install an additional 1600 MW of fossil-fueled generating capacity in New York, and the company's proposal to
place a 2000 MW pumped storage facility on Storm King Mountain
on the Hudson River.

(a) Con Ed - Astoria

In 1966, Con Ed entered into a Memorandum of Understanding
with the Office of the Mayor of the City of New York in which
the company accepted "the principle that, to the fullest possible
extent, power from coal and oil-fueled plants should be generated
outside City limits and brought into New York City by transmission
lines." Con Ed made this commitment because all the concerned
parties knew that another large coal or oil-fueled generating plant
within New York City would significantly aggravate the City's already serious and growing air pollution problems.

However, in July of 1969, Con Ed suddenly proclaimed its intention to construct an additional 1600 MW of fossil-fueled capacity
at its existing site in Astoria, Queens. The company claimed that,
unless the proposal was approved in its entirety, a power crisis
would develop in 1974, adding that the proposal would also improve
the quality of the City's air by enabling it to retire 1100 MW of
old plants. The Company urged that the additional capacity was
necessary to maintain an adequate reserve capacity, i.e., power
available in case of plant breakdowns or delays in placing planned
units in service, not power to satisfy projected daily needs.

Con Ed maintained that it was essential to utilize the developed
Astoria site because time would not permit construction of a facility at a new site outside the City for service in 1974, and that
there was no feasible, alternative source of power. In effect,
the company presented the City with a _fait accompli_: neither City
officials nor the public participated in the decision-making process which gave rise to the Astoria proposal - even though the
proposal involved a clear breach of a commitment designed to protect the health and welfare of the City's inhabitants.

Permits were required at the federal, state and local levels
but only three related primarily to environmental protection: a
work permit required from the City's Department of Air Resources
and two permits within the jurisdiction of the State Department of
Environmental Conservation (DEC), one relating to thermal discharges
and the other to air pollution.*

Oddly enough, no specific approval of the actual need for
the additional generating capacity was required by either the FPC,**

---

*The regulations of the DEC relating to air pollution control re-
quire any person intending to construct a facility that will "contribute to air pollution" to submit plans and specifications to
the Commissioner for approval prior to initiation of construction.
In lieu of the latter approval, the Commissioner is authorized to
accept approvals granted by selected City agencies (including New
York City's Environmental Protection Administration) in accordance
with standards acceptable to the Commissioner. 10 NYCRR pt. 176.
(To date, we are unaware of any legal action taken by the DEC with
respect to the Astoria facility.)

**FPC jurisdiction regarding construction of power plants extends
only to hydroelectric power systems.

PSC,* or local governmental agency.

In view of the company's 1966 commitment to build no more fossil-fuel plants in the City and the adverse effect additional capacity would have on the quality of the City's air, the City had a right and obligation to demand from Con Ed a full explanation and clear and convincing justification for the proposal, as well as to impose on the facility certain conditions in an attempt to protect the public health and welfare. The company was reluctant, however, to provide extensive documentation to support its proposal; rather, the company portrayed the need for the facility as unassailable and inevitable. The proposal appeared as a small item in a ten-year expansion plan submitted by the company to the City, the Federal Power Commission and the Public Service Commission for comments and review.

Moreover, while Con Ed claimed that the Astoria proposal would benefit the City's air, it failed entirely to mention that the new facility would emit substantial quantities of nitrogen oxide, a dangerous pollutant which can cause chronic respiratory

---

*Last spring the PSC was granted a planning responsibility regarding the formulation and effectuation of the electric utilities' power programs (Public Service Law, § 5). This essentially provides a means for the PSC to promote, not limit, the growth of electric power. It provides that: "The Commission shall encourage all persons and corporations subject to its jurisdiction to formulate and carry out long-range programs, individually or cooperatively, for the performance of their public service responsibilities with economy, efficiency, and care for the public safety, the preservation of environmental values and the conservation of natural resources."

diseases and contribute to formation of Los Angeles type smog.
This omission has been described as "a classic example of a
common form of corporate deceit; define the problem so narrowly
as to exclude all matters about which no action is planned."*

Con Ed - Astoria immediately became the subject of considerable controversy and the Mayor received a variety of opin-
ions as to how to proceed. During the fall of 1969, the then
Commissioner of the City's Department of Air Resources, Austin
N. Heller, recommended against the plant, concluding that it was
"a most inadvisable step in the effort to achieve clean air in
New York City" and would produce "serious deterioration of air
quality in New York City." Shortly thereafter, David E. Lilienthal,
former head of the Atomic Energy Commission, advised the Mayor in
the course of a study of New York City's power supply that the
Heller Report "convinces us that a new, large oil-burning plant,
within the City should not be built unless there is simply no
workable alternative."** Mr. Lilienthal concluded, however, that
no such alternative appeared to be available for 1974.

In November 1969, the PSC issued an opinion stating that
the ten-year plan "would appear to be adequate to meet the demands

---

*The Ralph Nader Study Group Report on Air Pollution, Vanishing Air
(Grossman Publishers, New York, 1970), p. 217.

**New York City's Power Supply, prepared by Development and Re-
sources Corporation (October 1969), p. 21.

of its customers for power...."* The opinion contained no separate
analysis of the Astoria proposal.

In December, 1969, the FPC expressed general approval of the
ten-year plan. With respect to the Astoria proposal, the FPC concluded that the need for the plan arose "primarily as a result of
unforseen delays in the construction of scheduled nuclear units"
and stated that "no other viable alternatives seem to be available
to the company or neighboring systems for constructing or accelerat-
ing the construction of comparable capacity for 1974."** The FPC
briefly analyzed the air pollution problems associated with the
plant, concluding (with no adequate evidence) that the company could
operate it in conformance with City and State requirements. This
conclusion turned out, however, to be entirely erroneous and misleading.

In the spring of 1970, the Mayor created an Interdepartmental
Committee on Public Utilities (ICPU) to study the proposal and submit recommendations for action. The ICPU was chaired by the Administrator of the Municipal Services Administration and included
the Corporation Counsel, Deputy Mayor Timothy Costello, and the
heads of the Environmental Protection Administration (EPA), the
Economic Development Administration, and the Department of Consumer
Affairs.

One of the first actions taken by the ICPU was to request Con
Ed to submit a brief in support of the proposal, setting forth

*In re Consolidated Edison Company of New York, Inc., Case No. 25293
(Nov. 7, 1969), p. 38.
**A Review of Consolidated Edison Company 1969 Power Supply Problems
and Ten-Year Expansion Plans, Bureau of Power, FPC (December 1969),
pp. 40,71.

in detail all the alternatives which were explored and the reasons each was rejected. The company responded with a 12-page letter, consisting primarily of undocumented, conclusory statements such as we "explored all alternatives exhaustively before concluding....that Astoria was the only feasible site...for 1974."* Needless to say, this response provided little assistance to the ICPU in its effort to evaluate the Astoria proposal.

After carefully considering the proposal and all available material, the ICPU reached a split decision, voting 3-2 in favor of expansion. The majority, led by Milton Musicus, Municipal Services Administrator, concluded that there were no feasible alternatives available to meet the City's power needs in 1974.

The minority, led by Jerome Kretchmer, Administrator of EPA, concluded that the proposed expansion would result in serious adverse effects on the public health which could not be overcome and that, in any event, the additional facility was not necessary to provide the company with adequate reserve capacity for 1974. With respect to the need for the new units in 1974, EPA pointed out that, without the Astoria addition, the company's reserve margin for 1974 (36%) would substantially exceed the reserve margin recommended by the FPC and PSC (20%), and compared favorably to the company's reserve margins for 1971-73.

EPA also found unconvincing the company's claim that it had "exhaustively" explored all alternatives (Astoria, located in the company's load center, was the cheapest and easiest alternative)

*Letter from Louis H. Roddis, President, Con Ed to Milton Musicus, Administrator, Municipal Services Administration, dated June 12, 1970.

and maintained that viable alternatives did exist, the most promising of which was the purchase of power from members of the New England and/or New York State Interconnected Systems.*

The majority of the ICPU agreed with EPA's view that the new units posed a grave risk for the City's health and welfare, but felt it would be possible to minimize the risk by requiring Con Ed to burn low-sulfur fuel oil in, and install the latest pollution-control equipment on, all its plants in the City.** The majority also argued that if, after the facility were built and operating, it posed a health hazard to New Yorkers, the City could have the plant shut down.

Faced with a sharp division of opinion among the members of his administration and the need to inform adequately the public of the environmental costs involved in the installation of a 1600 MW facility in Astoria, the Mayor decided to open the critical issue to public debate and, at the same time, solicited the views of federal and state agencies with expertise in environmental and power problems. In so doing, he noted that the split decision of the ICPU "underscores the dilemma of reconciling the City's critical need for power and the threat pollution poses to the health and well-being of all New Yorkers."

Predictably, the power-oriented agencies reported favorably on the expansion proposal and the environmental protection agencies opposed it.

Federal air pollution control officials concluded that the Astoria expansion was "inconsistent with the drive to meet

*Report to ICPU from Jerome Kretchmer, dated July 31, 1970.
**Report of the ICPU to Mayor John V. Lindsay, dated Aug. 1, 1970.

reasonable air quality standards "in New York City, as well as
New Jersey. It advised that all additional generating capacity
should be placed outside the City.* The Commissioner of the DEC
submitted an analysis in which he noted that implementation of the
proposal would "seriously jeopardize plans to meet air quality standards" and recommended that alternative sites be sought.**

The PSC argued that the plant should be built in order to
avoid the prospect of "recurrent summer brownouts." It took
notice of the pollution problem but asserted that "rapidly developing technology" should be able to solve much of the problem "a
few years after the plant was in operation."*** (emphasis added).

The FPC - noting at the outset that "there is no good answer
to the problem" - observed in rather quarded language that the
Astoria expansion was "the most practical means and perhaps the
only hope for providing the added power supply facilities which
are needed to meet the 1974 summer peak loads and provide an
acceptable level of reserves." The FPC rationalized away the
pollution issue with the observation that "a sincere effort on
the part of Con Ed can permit operation of the new Astoria units
without creating an untenable air pollution problem."**** Unfortunately, "sincerity" had little to do with it.

In addition, both the FPC and PSC concluded that it was unrealistic to expect that Con Ed could burn natural gas at the

*Correspondence from Kenneth L. Johnson, Regional Air Pollution
Control Director, APCO, to Jerome Kretchmer, dated July 20 and
July 22, 1970.
**Letter from Henry L. Diamond, Commissioner, DEC, to Mayor John
V. Lindsay, dated August 18, 1970.
***Letter from Joseph C. Swidler, Chairman, PSC, to Mayor John V.
Lindsay, dated August 18, 1970.
****Comments by FPC Bureau of Power on ICPU Reports on Astoria Plant,

new units, as the majority of the ICPU had recommended. Since the FPC controls the allocation of natural gas throughout the country, its statement was more than an opinion - it was a decision.

Governor Rockefeller took no part in the public debate despite the statewide, as well as national, implications of the Con Ed-Astoria controvery, and his assertion in a book, entitled "Our Environment Can Be Saved", published during his reelection campaign last fall that he has "frequently criticized power companies which have insisted on locating their facilities in the midst of cities...."*

On August 22, 1970, the Mayor announced that he would only allow one-half of the proposed Astoria expansion - 800 MW rather than 1600 MW, noting that this would provide the reserve urged by all power officials for 1974 and cut in half potential pollution from that source.

The Mayor conditioned his approval on the signing of a new Memorandum of Understanding in which Con Ed agreed, inter alia, that (1) it shall not place any additional fossil-fuel plants in the City; (2) it must make every reasonable effort to obtain natural gas for use in the new unit and its other plants; (3) when natural gas is unavailable, it must use low sulfur fuel in its entire system, or fuel of a low sulfur content, if required generally of persons who burn fuel oil in the City; (4) it must add stack gas processes and other emission controls to the new unit to reduce noxious emissions to levels consistent with emission

---

Attached to letter from John N. Nassikas, Chairman, FPC, to Mayor John V. Lindsay, dated August 14, 1970.
*Nelson A. Rockefeller, "Our Environment Can Be Saved" (Doubleday & Company, Inc., 1970), p. 79.

standards established by the City; (5) it must close down at least
1,100 MW of old units in the City by 1974; (6) it must develop
additional, jointly owned power plants outside the City and enter
into additional contracts for purchase of power from outside
sources; (7) it must spend $4 million for, and devote a site for
use in, a joint project to develop a process for removal of
noxious emissions resulting from combustion of fossil fuels; and
(8) it must develop long-range plans for power supply for a period
of 20 to 25 years and develop a mechanism for joint planning
and review with the City.

    (b)   Con Ed - Storm King

Just three days before the Mayor announced the Astoria decision,
the FPC approved Con Ed's plan to build a 2000 MW pumped storage
hydroelectric plant at Sorm King Mountain, on the Hudson River
near the town of Cornwall.* The Storm King facility, which is
intended to supply power to New York City during periods of peak
demand, will consist primarily of an upper reservoir on top of the
mountain, a power station on the Hudson and a tunnel which would
convey water between the reservoir and the power station. Off-peak
power from other Con Ed plants would be used to pump water up
the mountain into the reservoir.

Incredibly, the FPC's decision was in part based on a finding
that the facility would contribute to abatement of air pollution
in New York City. This finding, however, is clearly wrong because
Con Ed can and undoubtedly will use plants in the City to pump
the project.

If plants in the City are used to provide pumping energy

---

*In RE Consolidated Edison Company of New York, Inc., Project N o. 2338,
Opinion No. 584 (issued August 19, 1970).

for the plant - the total effect on the quality of the City's air would be worse than the installation of another fossil-fuel plant in the City. This is so because, for every kilowatt of power generated at the Storm King plant, it takes 1.4 kilowatts to pump water up the mountain. Also the use of in-City fossil-fueled plants to supply Storm King's need would result in the release of a significant amount of additional pollutants into the City's heavily polluted atmosphere at a very bad time from an air pollution standpoint, i.e., late night and early morning when the general stillness of the night air and frequency of early morning stagnations decrease considerably the likelihood of dispersion of the pollutants.

Significantly, on October 12, 1970, the FPC rejected the City's request that Con Ed be precluded from using in-City plants to pump the Storm King project. The City is appealing the decision to the federal courts on this, and other grounds.

(c) AEC Review of Utility Proposals

While the AEC licenses nuclear power plants, its review of utility proposals has - until passage of the National Environmental Policy Act of 1969 (P.L. 91-190) - been limited entirely to the radiological effects of nuclear plants; the need for plants has not been examined.

The National Environmental Policy Act of 1969 (effective January 1, 1970)(NEPA) requires the AEC, as well as other federal agencies, to consider the total environmental impact of major nuclear facilities licensed by it; whether particular facilities are actually needed ; and, possible alternatives to such facilities. In a recently issued statement outlining how it proposes

- 212 -

to implement its obligations under NEPA, the AEC indicated prefer-

ence for more power at the expense of the environment.*

Under the proposed procedure, parties to licensing proceed-

ings regarding nuclear power reactors and fuel reprocessing plants

may raise as an issue whether issuance of a permit or license

would be likely to result in a significant adverse effect on

the environment. If such a result were indicated, the AEC will

then consider

> "the need for the imposition of requirements for the
> preservation of environmental values consistent with
> other essential considerations of national policy, in-
> cluding the need to meet on a timely basis the growing
> national requirements for electric power."**

Moreover, the AEC ruled that the requirements of NEPA would not

be applied to already licensed facilities and that environmental

challenges could only be made with respect to license applications

filed after March 4, 1971. It argued that this ruling was required

> "to avoid unreasonable delays in the construction and
> operation of nuclear power plants urgently needed to
> meet the national requirements for electric power...."

Further, the Commission rejected a suggestion to require

"backfitting" of facilities, i.e., addition, elimination or modifi-

cation of structures, systems or components of facilities that

have received a construction permit, or that are in operation, de-

signed to provide substantial additional protection of the environ-

ment.

The AEC proposed no standards or criteria for assessing the

---

*35 Fed. Regis. No. 235 (December 4, 1970), Revised Appendix D to
10 C.F.R. Pt. 50.
**10 C.F.R. Pt. 50, Revised Appendix D, §11(a).

actual need for more facilities. It has no expertise in this area. We understand that it intends to rely heavily on FPC projections of demand in deciding the question of need. In other words, the AEC does not intend independently to examine the issue but, rather, will pass along the responsibility to the FPC.

(d) The Need for Advance, Consultative Planning

Utilities must be required to inform the public fully of their plans, possible alternatives, and the basis for the alleged need to expand well in advance of construction,and to involve public officials concerned with power and environmental protection in the planning process at the earliest possible date. This requirement, together with substantial advance planning, i.e., preparation and discussion with governmental officials and the public of five, ten, fifteen and twenty year plans, should serve to assist in resolving environmental, as well as power, problems and avoiding unnecessary delays. Utilities would be required to justify to the public and governmental officials the actual need for more power, as well as fully investigate all possible alternative means for meeting established power needs.

Moreover, advance planning, accompanied by public participation, must extend to contingency plans for dealing with power short-ages. During New York City's power crisis last summer, Con Ed reduced the supply of electric power to the subway system with the result that subway speeds were reduced to as low as 18 mph. Tens of thousands of commuters were inconvenienced; some may even have suffered adverse health effects. The following day Mayor Lindsay personally requested Mr. Luce to maintain subway service and to re-order the company's emergency priorities to accomplish this end.

During this same period, the City suffered seriously high levels of air pollution. The Mayor requested all citizens to avoid driving their private passenger vehicles into Manhattan, thereby increasing the City's reliance upon mass transit. Clearly, to the extent that the subway system was implicated and did not offer a reasonable alternative to the passenger vehicle, Con Ed's emergency priorities for curtailing service were inconsistent with the environmental needs of the city.

The circumstances surrounding the City's air pollution and power crises last summer, as well as the power crisis this winter which resulted in heat being shut off in subway stations during sub-freezing weather, illustrate the necessity for advance planning by the utilities in consultation with relevant governmental agencies. It is not enough for public officials merely to be given the opportunity to comment on plans previously prepared by utilities. Utility representatives should be required to consult with public officials prior to the preparation of contingency plans so that public policy considerations are focused upon at the earliest possible stage.

The seriousness of the problems encountered in rationing power during shortages has recently been acknowledged by the PSC. It has recently held public hearings to review the nature of and need for utility load shedding practices.

(2) The Practice of Building Power Plants In Close Proximity To Load Centers Should Be Reviewed

In the past, utilities have generally met demands by constructing their own plants as close to their load centers as possible, particularly when this approach would serve to minimize unit costs of producing power. For example, according to the FPC, Con Ed

> "in an endeavor to hold its bulk power supply cost to a minimum ... has developed all of its generating resources within its service area and in close proximity to the high load demand localities.... Alternatives for securing power from sources beyond the boundaries of its service area have proven ... to be less favorable, economically, than in-system generation..."*

From an environmental standpoint, however, it may be preferable (at least as regards persons in or near the load center) to have plants built in remote, less populated areas and to have a utility transmit power from such areas or to purchase power from, outside sources Moreover, if and when social costs of electric power are factored into the production costs, the incentive to build plants near load centers may be significantly decreased.

Several factors may enter into a utility's decision as to whether to build a plant near the load center or to buy power from outside sources, e.g., the availability and reliability of purchased power; the cost of transmission lines; potential loss of power during transmission. Trade-offs must be made between the environmental degradation and adverse health effects resulting from locating power plants in densely populated areas and additional costs that may result from obtaining power from outside sources. It should be noted, however, that the present method for computing a utility's profits

---

*FPC Review of Con Ed 10-year Expansion Plans, supra at 68.

discourages utilities from purchasing power from outside sources. Given the present system for calculating permissible rates of return, there is little incentive, except perhaps interest rates, for a utility to minimize costs of construction.* As opposed to construction of a plant, only the cost of transmission facilities required to import power from outside sources is included in the rate base. Moreover, the costs of purchasing power are only recoverable as operating expenses, which, of course are not subject to the allowable rate of return. Also, since a prime objective of utilities is to reduce operating costs, particularly below those projected in rate proceedings, purchased power (which increases cost) is not likely to be favored in utility planning.

There is also not likely to be any significant incentive to build plants in areas remote from load centers, at least in the case of Con Ed. The additional costs for transmission lines, particularly if required to be placed underground, may raise the unit cost of electricity to unacceptable levels. On the other hand, land, labor and materials may be cheaper in other areas of the state.

In sum, utilities should be encouraged to coordinate planning with a view toward developing an interconnected power system designed to provide reliable power with the least possible harm to the environment. In this connection, the current method of calculating permissible rates should be reevaluated in order to eliminate any disincentives therein to purchasing power from outside sources or locating plants in the most environmentally preferable areas.

---

*Capital costs are included in the rate base; the cost of purchased power, however, is only recoverable as an operating expense. (footnote continued following page.)

The current method of calculating the permissible rate which
a utility company can charge encourages capital concentration
to the extent that the cost of borrowing money to finance capital
expansion is less than the permissible rate of return. Since the
rate of return is calculated on the basis of the net plant (the
value of the tangible and intangible property minus the accrued
depreciation on that property) increases in property accounts
allow the company to earn a certain percentage return. Balanced
against this allowable rate of return is the expense of the interest on the debt used to finance the capital expansion, which
is not covered as an operating expense.

   For example, if a company has a net plant of
   $1 million, and is allowed 5% return, it will be al-
   lowed $50,000 in revenues and operating expenses. An
   additional $50,000 to the net plant would be accompanied
   by an allowed 5% return or an additional $2,500 in rev-
   enues. If, however, the cost of borrowing the $50,000
   were 7%, the company would subtract from net profits
   $3,500 since interest on debt comes out of net profits,
   thus the net result would be a decrease of $1000 in
   profits. If, however, the interest rate were only
   4%, the expansion would result in a net gain of $500
   ($2,500 which is 5%, or allowable return on $50,000
   minus 4% x $50,000 or $2,000 = $500). Interest rates
   recently have been just about equal to the general range
   of allowable returns. However, normal interest rate
   fluctuations may shift the balance at any time.

In addition, since operating expenses such as depreciation
are covered, even though not subject to a rate of return, a utility
company with a large depreciation is allowed to recoup these non-
cash operating expenses. A utility company is constantly balancing the positive factors of having (1) a high rate base with larger
allowable revenue (the rate of return) and (2) of realizing economies of scale through increased plant size, with the negative
factors of (1) removing from that rate base depreciation, even though
the costs of depreciation are covered, and (2), the cost of interest payments on the money borrowed to finance capital expansion
of the rate base.

3. The Utilities' Purchase of Larger Units and the Establishment of Power Complexes Aggravates Already Serious Environmental Problems and May Undermine Reliability of Power Supply.

The present practice in the utility industry is to build
fewer, but larger, plants to achieve economies of scale and lower
unit costs of production. Large plants are particularly desirable for nuclear power, according to utilities, because of the
relatively low operating costs of nuclear plants.

In the late 1950's, 300 MW was considered a maximum size. In
1968, however there were 145 plants of 500 MW or larger, with 45
over 1,000 MW. Much of the new generating capacity installed in
the next 20 years will come in the form of about 250 power plants
of 2000 MW to 3000 MW.* There are about 3400 power plants in the
country today.

As size of individual units has increased, so has the tendency to locate the larger units at single sites. Power complexes
of 5000 MW are expected to become common over the next twenty
years, with the largest reaching 10,000 MW.

From an environmental standpoint, the trend toward larger
units and power complexes raises serious problems. Some argue that
larger plants offer an environmental benefit "because less pollution
per kilowatt-hour can be produced in a large and more efficient
power plant"**and emissions from such plants are easier to control
than emissions from several smaller energy systems. The former
argument ignores the fact that concentration of large amounts of

---

*EPE Report, supra at 25.
**Statement of Dr. Lee A. DuBridge, Hearings before Subcommittee on
Intergovernmental Operations of the Committee on Government Operations, U. S. Senate, 91st Cong., 2d Sess. on S.2752 (Pt. 1), p. 40
(1970).

generating capacity at one place, as noted above, intensifies the impact of power generation on the local environment and, "if un-controlled, could overwhelm the surrounding environment."* For example, a 3200 MW facility burning low sulfur fuel oil, i.e., 0.37 per cent sulfur, would emit 60,000,000 pounds of sulfur ox-ides, 108,000,000 pounds of nitrogen oxides and 6,800,000 pounds of particulate matter per year, operating at a 55 per cent load factor.

Increasing the size of individual plants will also intensify the thermal pollution problem, especially for nuclear plants, which discharge 50 per cent more hot water than fossil-fueled plants.

> "Although the total amount of heat disposed of to the environment may not increase when a single plant replaces two, and the generating capacity is the same, the impact is far greater because the amount of dilution immediately available is decreased greatly and heat losses to the atmos-phere between sites do not occur."**

When Con Ed completes nuclear units 2 and 3 at Indian Point (about 2,200 MW including #1), over 2 million gallons of heated water per minute will be discharged into one of the narrowest, as well as the best spawning, portions of the Hudson.

The potential radiation hazards associated with nuclear plants - particularly in the event of an accident - also increase with the size of the reactor.

The ease of emissions control argument in favor of large power plants ignores entirely the relative inefficiency of current methods

*Energy Report, supra at 90.
**S. C. Bloom, Heat - A Growing Water Pollution Problem, Environ-ment Reporter (Monograph No. 4 - May 1, 1970), p. 2.

of electric power generation and transmission (and consequent increase in pollutants, waste heat and wasted fuel) as compared to
direct conversion of fuel to useful energy on the user's premises.

Larger Unit Sizes Increase Risk of Breakdown and Raise Reserve Requirements.

The trend to increasing unit size, itself a function of increasing _per capita_ consumption of electric energy, has a number
of implications regarding reserve requirements of utilities that
deserve mention. All electric power systems maintain a reserve
capacity designed to protect against scheduled and unscheduled
outages of equipment, errors in estimating local growth and delays
in meeting schedules (so-called planning reserve). A significant
portion of the additional generating capacity planned to be installed by utilities in the next decade will be reserve capacity,
not designed to meet daily load requirements. To the extent that
reserve requirements can be reduced by, for example, increased
system inter-connections, or regional coordination of maintenance
schedules, some of the environmental problems associated with
power generation may also be reduced.

As a general rule, when units are added to a power system
which have capacities larger than the system average, the required
generation reserve is also increased. Initial installation of a
large unit to a system composed of smaller sized units will cause
a sharp increase in reserve requirements, i.e., a requirement for
the utility to add more generating capacity to the system to insure against the loss of the increasingly larger units. For example, Con Ed's reserve formula is that it needs enough extra ca-

pacity at any one time to cover the <u>loss of its largest unit</u> (now 1000 MW), plus the loss of a medium size unit, plus a miscellaneous contingency of 500 MW. Larger units thus perpetuate additional need for more units.

A related problem posed by larger units is that they increase the risk of a single breakdown causing a massive power shortage. In the past few years, New York City has experienced severe power shortages attributable to the breakdown of larger and newer units. For example, in the summer of 1969, Con Ed reduced voltage by as much as 8 per cent owing to the breakdown of its 1000 MW Ravenswood unit.

Again, last summer, the breakdown of the same unit (which has been out of service intermittently since it was placed in service in 1965) has contributed to a continuing power crisis which has necessitated voltage reductions and selective blackouts in New York City.* If two 500 MW units rather than a single 1,000 MW unit had been constructed, the risk of a total loss of power would have been materially reduced and this summer's power crisis possibly avoided. For example, if the chance of failure of one machine at any one time is one in a thousand, the chance of two such machines failing simultaneously is one in one million.**

Charles Luce, Chairman of Con Ed, recently acknowledged the problem posed regarding system stability by larger power units:

"I do not think the industry is quite as sanguine as it was a couple of years ago about the rate at which we are going to build these large units, because we are running into too many problems of reliability with these

*Con Ed's nuclear unit at Indian Point has also broken down during the last two summers.
**See Victor Wouk, founder of the Reliability Committee of the Institute of Electrical & Electronic Engineers, letter to Editor, New York Times (Feb. 10, 1971).

big units. When you drop 1 million kilowatts, as right
now can happen, you impose serious questions of system
stability, and when you drop two or three of them, very
serious problems."*

Moreover, it appears that larger units, which are increasingly
complex and are operated at higher pressures, are less reliable
than traditional smaller units, i.e., they experience a higher rate
of forced outages.**Jack Busby, President of Pennsylvania Power
& Light Co., had the following to say as to the poor performance of the new 600 - 1000 MW units: "We hoped the new machines
would run just like the old ones we're familiar with, but they sure
as hell don't."

A recent FPC staff report tends to confirm Busby's observation:

"There has been a tendency to blame the forced outage
emergencies on the obsolete units, but the overall effect of outages of the older units is debatable. Many
of the most modern large thermal units throughout the
country have also experienced high forced-outage rates,
and Consolidated Edison might have had similar experiences if new thermal units had become available on an
earlier schedule. The older Consolidated Edison units
are generally small and do not represent the loss of a
large block of capacity when forced outages do occur."***

The trend toward larger units and the concentration of generating capacity at single locations must be reexamined with a view
toward ensuring system stability and reliability of power supply,
and encouraging sound environmental planning of utility facilities.

*Hearings before the Subcommittee on Intergovernmental Relations
of the Committee on Government Operations, U.S. Senate, 91st Cong.,
2d Sess., on S. 2752, Pt. 1, p. 85 (1970).
**The FPC has estimated forced outage rates as follows:
(1) existing fossil-fueled units: 300-500 MW - 5.5%
(2) future fossil-fueled units: 600 MW - 5.8 - 7.8%
                                800 MW - 6.7 - 9.4%
                               1000 MW - 7.4 - 10.7%
(3) future nuclear units: 1000 MW - 6.5% - 10.9%
                          2000 MW - 10% - 16%
***FPC Review of Con Ed's 1969 Power Supply Problems and 10-Year
Expansion Plans, p. 32 (Dec. 1969).

4. The Increasing Inability of Electric Utilities to Pro-
    vide a Reliable Supply of Electric Power is in Part
    the Result of Poor Management and Inadequate Control
    Over the Quality and Delivery of Equipment.

The increasing failure of the electric utility industry
to provide reliable electric power is partly the result of
extremely poor planning, and inadequate control over the quality
and delivery of equipment.*

Traditionally, the utility industry has perhaps been the
most complacent and poorly managed industry in the United States.
This judgment is not only shared by environmentalists and utility
customers; it is a judgment held by industry executives themselves.

> "The trouble is that the utility business is too good ...
> and when you don't have to hustle you get lazy."
>
> Donald Cook, President
> American Electric Power

> "We failed to forecast that it is going to take longer
> to get these (new) ... facilities built. We failed to
> forecast the outage rate of new facilities would be as
> high as it has been."
>
> A. H. Aymond, President
> Edison Electric Institute

The November, 1969 issue of Fortune Magazine summarized
the problem as follows:

> "In a time of trouble the utilities badly need resource-
> ful management. But utility executives are generally
> unimaginative men, grown complacent on private monopoly
> and regulated profits. Nor are they spurned to improve-
> ment by the state regulatory commissions, which seem
> neither willing nor able to prod the utilities into
> action."**

---

*E.g., AEC Authorizing Legislation,Fiscal year 1971 (pt.3), supra at 1156,
1181 .
**Main, A Peak Load of Trouble for the Utilities, Fortune
(November, 1969) p. 118.

The Edison Electric Institute recently surveyed 85 generating plants installed during the two-year period 1966-1968.
All plants included in the survey were of the 200 MW size or
larger. Four nuclear units were delayed for periods ranging
from 3 to 12 months. 51 fossil-fueled units were delayed up
to six months. No delays were attributed to public opposition based on environmental concerns. The most significant
causes of delay (over 80 per cent) were due to equipment failure, labor shortages, construction labor strikes and late delivery of equipment.

The Edison Electric Institute analysis also indicated that
late delivery of equipment would be the prime reason for delay
during the period 1969-1971.*

The following excerpt from a special report on the utilities issued by Business Week is also revealing:

> "Utilities can only wring their hands over construc-
> tion delays. Most do not keep large work forces;
> they hire contractors to handle construction. But
> they often aggravate the problem by scheduling plants
> all at the same time. The classic case of this was
> the recent nuclear plant binge. Within 23 months,
> from February, 1965 through December, 1967, 47 util-
> ities ordered a total of 67 units, the earliest of
> which are now coming into service. Before 1965,
> back to the infancy of nuclear power, there were
> only 21 atomic plants ordered or operating. And in
> the 23 months since January, 1968, only 23 have been
> announced.
>
> "The reason for the rush was simple enough: General
> Electric and Westinghouse were selling 'turnkey'
> plants at what looked like bargain-basement prices,
> and nuclear plants were the 'in' thing.
>
> "A few years from now, when all these plants are
> operating and while demand continues to grow, the
> same utilities will be shopping for new capacity and
> will probably order in rapid succession again. And
> when the next generation of nuclear plants, the breeder
> reactors, becomes commercial sometime in the 1980's,

---

*Energy Report, supra at 22.

another stampede is likely. For years, manufacturers and contractors have tried to break utilities of this habit, with little success. Says J.J. William Brown, general manager of the atomic power equipment department at GE: 'Cyclical buying is a fact of life in selling to the electric utilities. I don't know of any mechanism we could employ to keep them from buying like individuals.'"*

As noted above, large new units are breaking down with alarming frequency. For example, the 1,000 MW Ravenswood unit which Con Ed purchased from Allis-Chalmers Manufacturing Company has been out of service constantly since placed in service in 1965. Most recently it broke down in July of last year and is still out of service.

Industry executives concede their failure to exercise adequate quality control. For example, William G. Kuhns, President of General Public Utilities Corporation, has recently stated:

"We are finding more problems with equipment now than ever before. Things happen that simply should not have happened. We are going to have to develop a level of quality control that has been applied to nuclear equipment."**

Moreover, PSC Chairman Joseph Swidler has remarked that:

"quality control in the new large generating units, both fossil fuel and nuclear, leaves much to be desired..."***

Currently, however, no regulatory body (including the PSC****) exercises any direct control over the quality of equipment purchased by utilities or the terms of equipment supply contracts.

*Why Utilities Can't Meet Demand, Business Week (11/29/69).
**Main, Fortune (Nov., 1969) supra.
***Statement before the Subcommittee on Intergovernmental Relations of the Senate Committee on Government Operations on S.2752 (Aug. 3, 1970).
****The only power now exercised by the PSC relates to whether supply contracts should be let for public bidding. Each utility is now required to file with the PSC proposed cost-plus contracts in excess of $25,000 for construction, improvement or extension of its plant, works or system. Such contracts become effective 45 days after filing, unless the Commission determines that "the public interest" requires that the contract shall be let after public bidding. The Commission can waive this requirement upon a showing by the utility that compliance "would be impracticable or unduly burdensome." 16 NYCRR pt. 215; Public Service Law, §115.

The poor quality of equipment may in part be attributable to a lack of any meaningful competition in the equipment supply market. Only a few companies supply electric power equipment to the utilities. Con Ed's 1000 MW Ravenswood unit was the last unit produced by Allis-Chalmers before dropping out of the steam-turbine generator business.* General Electric Company and Westinghouse Electric Corp. account for over 90 per cent of the sales of steam-turbine generators and associated equipment, with a few foreign companies accounting for the remainder.

The gas turbine-generator market is similarly concentrated. General Electric and Westinghouse occupy about 60 per cent of the market, with Pratt & Whitney and the Worthington Company sharing most of the remaining 40 per cent.

Moreover, there are only four major domestic suppliers of equipment for nuclear power plants. They are Westinghouse, General Electric, Combustion Engineering and Babcock & Wilcox.

An additional utility practice that requires close scrutiny by regulatory officials and the public is the adequacy and basis for utility maintenance programs. Generally, equipment is taken out of service during off-peak periods for maintenance. Equipment failures, such as those recently experienced by Con Ed, require upgrading of traditional maintenance scheduling.

Moreover, it appears that nuclear facilities, because of their unique fuel cycles and the hazards of radiation, will require utilities to reexamine normal maintenance methods used for fossil-

*Allis-Chalmers has recently re-entered the market.

fueled plants and to develop procedures suitable for nuclear facilities.* One example of the special problems caused by nuclear
plants is the extreme delay experienced by Con Ed in placing its
275 MW Indian Point 1 unit back in service after it broke down in
May of last year. The unit was finally returned to service this
February. Much of the delay was the result of the existence of
radioactivity in the piping being repaired (which allowed repair-
men to work only 15 minutes some times, and up to an hour at others),
and the need to design a novel piece of equipment for the repair.
According to Richard H. Freyberg, Assistant Vice President for
Power Engineering, Con Ed and its equipment suppliers experienced
a "'gross inability to determine how much time to do a job' like
this."**

Despite the evidence of poor management, inadequate quality
control and late deliveries of equipment, there has been a growing
tendency on the part of utiliites, the FPC and PSC, to blame the
opposition of environmentalists for current difficulties. For example, PSC Chairman Joseph Swidler recently told a Congressional
Committee that the principal reason that nuclear plants have not
been coming on line as scheduled was "protracted licensing procedures resulting from objections on environmental grounds....
Abandonments have all been due, I believe, to opposition based on
environmental grounds."***

David Freeman, Director of the Energy Policy staff of the

*See, e.g., AEC Authorizing Legislation, Fiscal Year 1971 (Pt. 3),
supra at 1181.
**Khiss, Con Ed Puts Indian Point Unit Back in Service (N.Y. Times
2/10/71).
***Statement of Joseph C. Swidler, Chairman of PSC, before the Sub-
committee on Intergovernmental Relations of the Senate Committee
on Government Operation on S. 2752 (Aug. 3, 1970).

Federal Office of Science and Technology, has a different view:

> "The conservationists have been receiving more than
> their fair share of the blame for the present tight
> power supply situation. After all, the generating
> facilities coming on the line this year and next were
> ordered five or more years ago, before the general
> opposition to power plants became so intense.... Maybe
> the environmentalists will cause the brownouts of 1973
> and beyond, but I do not think they are the primary
> cause of our present situation."*

According to W. Donham Crawford, Vice President and Managing

Director of Edison Electric Institute, "the elimination of environ-

mental obstacles cannot, in itself, alter drastically the current

difficulties we (i.e., the utilities) ... are experiencing."**

Efficiency Incentives or Inefficiency Disincentives

Utilities have traditionally been allowed a specific rate of

return on the theory that to deny them this would amount to a con-

fiscation of property without due process of law. The ability of

a company to attract new capital depends in large part on its earn-

ings pattern and the risk (or lack thereof) of investing in that

company and the potential returns on such investment. When a com-

pany's earnings are fixed through regulation, all companies - those

that are well managed and those that are not - can earn roughly the

same return. The incentive for management efficiency and to develop

ways to reduce costs in order to maximize profits and increase sales

is largely removed. There is no stimulus for efficiency comparable

to the stimulus of competition. Of course, regulatory lag in ruling

on rate changes, as well as the allowance of a range of permissible

---

*168 Science 1554, 1555 (6/29/70).
**Hearings, pt. 2 (Vol. 1), supra at 1810.

returns on capital investment, can create some incentive for operating efficiency in order to secure the highest permissible returns. However, knowledge that virtually all operating costs will be recovered, regardless of inefficient operations is likely to decrease the incentive to minimize costs.

What can be done to encourage increased efficiency on the part of utility management? As a first step, quality control standards should be prepared in the immediate future by appropriate governmental bodies with the assistance of utilities, and enforced via advance contract review procedures. Manufacturer's guarantees with respect to emissions, safety and equipment reliability must reflect the most advanced technology; and, strict penalties should be contained in each contract for failure to complete and deliver equipment on time, as well as failure to meet performance guarantees.

Moreover, measures must be devised which will make utilities more responsive to the need for quality control. It may be necessary to impose economic sanctions on utilities in the event of equipment breakdowns. At the least, if a breakdown occurs owing to the negligence of a utility's supplier, or the negligence of the utility in selecting or maintaining its equipment, the utility should be precluded from passing on any additional costs attributable to the breakdown (e.g., repairs, purchased power) to its customers.* The utility's rate base includes capital equipment

---

*According to Con Ed, the outages of its Ravenswood No. 3 and Indian Point No. 1 units last year and this year have resulted in additional costs of about $15,700,000, which includes maintenance and repair costs, plus the cost of purchased power required by loss of those units. Con Ed Press Release re request for new rate increase, dated 3/31/71.

which the utility operates to serve the public. If such equipment
is forced out of service owing to poor or negligent management,
the investor rather than the customer should bear the loss.   It
may also be desirable to require the removal of broken down equipment from the rate base where it is out of service for a substantial
period.

Further, it may be necessary to impose outright penalties
on utilities for inefficient operations, once an acceptable method
for determining "efficiencies" is established. Such penalties
could be deducted from either allowable operating costs or from the
net plant account in the form of a negative goodwill account (thus
reducing the rate base and producing the greatest impact).   In
either of these two instances, the rates to customers would be reduced, an equitable action considering that customers bear the
major burden of management inefficiencies in terms of inconvenience
and increased costs. Penalties could be assessed on the basis of
power reductions (deducting a comparable percentage of the monthly
bill) or as a flat "damages" rate.

In establishing a penalty system, it should be recognized that
penalties may adversely affect the ability of a utility to attract
and retain capital investment, which could conceivably have an adverse effect on the company's efficiency. Any penalty which reduced
the net income of a utility or the allowable rate of return would
affect the potential stockholders and bondholders, and may force
interest rates on debt equity higher owing to increased "risk."
Utility companies may, however, have been immune too long from the
usual risks encountered in competitive markets.

V. The Governor's Electric Power Program

A. Maximum Growth of Electric Power

Notwithstanding an efficient public relations campaign to
persuade the public of his concern for the environment,* Governor
Rockefeller is committed to the ever-increasing growth of electric
power in this state. Moreover, the Governor is committed to meeting
all demands for power - primarily with nuclear generating capacity -
even though satisfaction of such demands would result in serious
environmental damage.

According to the Governor, "keeping pace with electrical power
demands is indispensible.... When power stops, modern living
stops. We have an instant reversion to the dark ages.   We must
double our power output over the next 10 years."** Thus the Governor -
as do the investor-owned utilities - seeks to characterize those
who raise environmental objections to the rapid expansion of power
facilities as neanderthals whose objective is to return modern
society to the "dark ages." Clearly, the issue is not "no power"
or doubling our power output." As pointed out above, the fundamental issues underlying the growing use of electric power and its
adverse environmental impact are far more complex. They cannot
be disposed of by simplistic declarations for more power.

---

*E.g., Nelson Rockefeller, "Our Environment Can Be Saved," supra.
**"Power," A Program Paper by Nelson A. Rockefeller (October 24,
1970).

Last spring the Governor unveiled a program to regulate the siting of major utility and transmission facilities.* In essence, the Governor proposes to vest exclusive authority for approving sites in the Public Service Commission. A community wherein the plant - nuclear or otherwise - is proposed to be located would have no authority to reject it if the Public Service Commission approved the location.

Power Politics

In an apparent attempt to avoid the widespread public opposition likely to be occasioned by his siting proposal, the Governor introduced his legislative package during the closing days of the legislative session - on or about April 13, 1970 - thereby precluding any serious, detailed study or debate of the critical issues involved. The portion of the proposal dealing with siting of transmission facilities was enacted and quickly signed into law by the Governor on April 20, 1970 (Chap. 272, Laws of 1970).

Objections raised by concerned environmental groups, as well as legislators, resulted in the withdrawal of the portion of the legislation regulating power plant siting. In its place, the

---

*Major utility facility includes: (a) a thermal electric generating facility with 10 MW or more capacity; (b) a facility for the production of steam for distribution, or distillation or purification of water for distribution, designed to produce 75,000 lbs. steam per hour or more; (c) a fuel gas storage facility of 250 million cubic feet or more capacity.

Major utility transmission facility includes: (a) a 125 KV or larger electric transmission line extending 1 mile or more, or a line of 100KV to 125 KV capacity extending more than 10 miles, including associated equipment; but   does not include any such transmission line approved by the FPC for a hydro-electric facility; (b) a fuel gas transmission facility extending 1,000 feet or more, used to transport fuel gas at pressure exceeding 125 lbs. per square inch.

legislature established a nine-member Temporary Commission on
the Environmental Impact of Major Utility Facilities (Temporary
Commission) to perform the narrowly defined task of proposing
legislation to the 1971 legislature to establish "appropriate
state procedures...to regulate and determine the siting of
(major public utility) facilities."

Power Demands Must be Met Regardless Of Environmental Impact

The selection of the PSC as the siting authority provides
compelling evidence of the Governor's desire to give top priority to
the satisfaction of all demands for power whatever the environmental
cost. Traditionally, the PSC has been primarily concerned with the
economics of supplying adequate power. Moreover, it has been
regarded as the captive of the utilities it is responsible for
regulating. While the Governor, during the early days of his
election campaign last year, successfully proposed certain overdue
reforms of the PSC,* the fact remains that the PSC is institutionally
committed to, and has a basic responsibility for assuring that,
all demands for electric power are met. According to the recently
appointed Chairman of the PSC, Joseph C. Swidler,** a former chairman

---

*Amendments to the Public Service Law enacted last spring provide
that: No more than three members of the PSC can be from the same
political party, and authorize the agency to encourage utilities,
individually or collectively to develop plans designed to supply
power with efficiency, economy and care for preservation of environmental values. Public Service Law, §§ 4.1, 5.2.
**As a result of last year's amendments to the Public Service Law,
the Chairman of the PSC now serves "at the pleasure" of the Governor
and has very substantial executive powers to run and organize the
agency. Thus, while the Governor "relinquished" the right to appoint
all members from his own party, he greatly enhanced his ability to
control the daily activities and policies of the PSC by increasing
the powers of the Chairman, while at the same time, placing the
Chairman entirely under his own control.

of the FPC and lawyer for the electric utilities, a major reason for
lodging siting responsibility in the PSC is that:

> [A]s the agency with general responsibility for reviewing
> the services of electric utilities of the state, the Commission
> is in the best position to insure that the supply respon-
> sibilities of the utilities are given recognition and that the
> utilities will be directed into channels of growth which are
> compatible with environmental consideration. To fragment the
> responsibility for review of power supply programs might
> invite collapse of the ability of the power industry to
> respond to demands for power service."*

The standards which govern the granting of transmission line

approvals by the PSC are designed to meet the objectives of "more

power" while minimizing environmental concerns. Under the Gov-

ernor's transmission facility law (Chap. 272, Laws of 1970), the

PSC is required, prior to approving a site, to determine the basis

of the need for the facility, the nature of the probably environ-

mental impact of the facility, and that it represents the minimum

adverse environmental impact, considering"available technology" and

"economics of alternatives." This standard clearly assumes that the

facility will be built - whether or not it adversely affects the

environment. Any finding of the probable environmental impact by

the PSC is meaningless since, whatever the impact, the utilities will

be able to build the cheapest line using whatever technology is

available - regardless of whether the technology will serve to

lessen the environmental impact.

The basic standard governing the PSC's decision whether to

approve a power plant site in the proposed siting legislation

(S.9360) is one of "acceptability."** The key section provides

that:

---

*Address entitled "The New York Program for Reconciling the
Expansion of Energy Supply Facilities with Environmental Protection,"
before Senior Management Forum, Atomic Industrial Forum (March 17, 1970).
**Additional objections to S.9360 are set forth in Exhibit C hereto.

- 235 -

"In making such decision, the Commission shall consider whether
the effect of the facility on the public and on the environment
when considered with other environmental conditions man-made
or natural, is acceptalbe, considering the total cost to the
society as a whole, possible alternate methods of power
generation, power or gas transmission of water or steam supply,
as the case may be, and the immediacy and totality of the
needs of the people of the state for the facility proposed.
The Commission may limit the alternatives to be subject to
consideration to those which in its judgement are most
appropriate."

By its terms, therefore, this legislation would empower the

Commission to make a finding of "acceptability," notwithstanding a

seriously adverse environmental impact associated with the construction

or operation of the facility. In fact, this was precisely the

Commission's stand in the recent Con Ed - Astoria case.

Suppose, for example environmental considerations were

equally weighted with respect to alternative sites under study,

i.e., wherever the utility sought to locate its power plant, the

impact on air and water quality would be seriously damaging. Would

the Commission then refuse to issue a certificate for either site,

or would it instead choose among equally poor alternatives that

site which offered the cheapest source of power, compromising

the issue in favor of satisfying power demands?* Undoubtedly, it

would take the latter course since, in effect, the proposed

legislation specifically empowers the PSC to override legitimate

environmental concerns in order to sarisfy any and all power demands.

*The more specific standards to be employed in determining acceptability
deal with alternate means of supplying power. There are no specific
environmental standards contained in the bill. Section 126(c) requires
consideration of "the public interest, convenience and necessity." With
the exception of this boiler plate phrase, the assumption that we must
continue to meet all energy demands in some manner - a principle which
underlies our present crisis - remains essentially unchallenged.

B. Maximize Development of Nuclear Generating and Fuel
   Processing Capacity

In 1968, Governor Rockefeller launched a major State Electric
Power Program the primary objective of which was to assist the
utilities in promoting and developing nuclear power in New York
State. The underlying purposes of the program were economic - viz.,
(1) to encourage high-load industrial users to locate in New
York State by insuring an adequate and cheap power supply, and
(2) to provide an impetus to the development of large scale industry
engaged in production and reprocessing of nuclear fuel, as well
as radioactive waste storage facilities, able to serve utilities
on a nationwide basis. In promoting this program, the Governor
stressed that minimization of air pollution would be a beneficial
effect of maximizing nuclear power. As shown earlier in the report,
however, nuclear power plants and nuclear fuel reprocessing plants
create serious environmental hazards - including air pollution in the
form of radioactive gases. However, according to the Governor
"it is perfectly possible to locate and design nuclear power
plants with minimum hazard to the environment. The agitation
against these plants has obscured the technological possibilities."[*]

The State Electric Power Program was a logical extension of
the Governor's ongoing plans to make New York State the No. 1
nuclear state in the nation. During his first year in office, he
announced his intention to encourage development of atomic
energy for power and industry in New York State.

[*]Nelson A. Rockefeller, Our Environment Can Be Saved, supra at 84.

- 237 -

The "1959 Atomic Development Plan for the State of New York,"
submitted to the Governor by an advisory committee, cited "the
potentially very large market represented by domestic atomic power
reactors" and the high costs of producing electricity from conventional fuels in New York and New England as compelling reasons
for this state to develop a nuclear fuel reprocessing industry
and promote nuclear power. A year later, the State's seven major
private utilities established a research corporation named Empire
State Atomic Development Associates, Inc. (ESAD) to foster research
in nuclear technology.

In order to carry out the program, the utilities need fuel
reprocessing and waste storage facilities and so in 1962, the
Governor proposed the creation of the New York Atomic and Space
Development Authority (NYASD), a so-called public benefit corporation, "to encourage and cooperate in the maximum development
and use of atomic energy for peaceful and productive purposes
within the State...."* The legislature adopted the Governor's
program and NYASD was authorized to undertake construction and
operation of major nuclear fuel reprocessing and waste storage
facilities in cooperation with private industry.

NYASD consists of five members, appointed by the Governor
with the advice and consent of the Senate. Every action taken
by NYASD, however, is subject to the Governor's approval.**

---

*Public Authorities' Law, § 1854.
**Public Authorities' Law, § 1853.

NYASD's efforts led to the establishment of the Western
New York Nuclear Service Center (WNSC), a site of approximately
3,345 acres owned by NYASD located at West Valley in Cattaraugus
County about 30 miles south of Buffalo. This site now houses the
first and only commercial, nuclear fuel reprocessing plant in the
country and is generally available as a radioactive waste storage
site serving the entire Northeast. The site was touted by the
Governor during his election campaign last fall as "the nation's
first state-owned atomic-industrial reservation."

Nuclear Fuel Reprocessing in New York State

The nuclear fuel reprocessing plant is owned and operated by
Nuclear Fuel SErvices, Inc.,* (NFS), a subsidiary of Getty Oil
Company, with Skelly Oil Company, a Getty subsidiary, holding a
minority interest. The plant was placed in operation in 1966,
after receipt of the requisite AEC operating license which contains
standards for emission of radioactive effluents. This was the first
facility license issued by the AEC to a nonreactor installation.
The plant cost about $32 million of which NFS put up $22 million,
NYASD $8 million, and the major investor-owned utilities in the
state $2 million (through ESAD).

To date, although the plant has never operated in excess of
50 per cent of its annual capacity of 300 tons of spent fuel,** it
has processed about 530 tons of uranium and 1300 kilograms of
plutonium received from a variety of sources outside of the state,

---

*Corporate headquarters are located at Wheaton, Maryland. The Company
operates facilities for the production of nuclear materials, e.g.,
uranium, thorium, plutonium oxides, pellates, fuel rods, naval reactor
fuels, in Erwin, Tennessee.
**About 30 tons of fuel is discharged annually for reprocessing from
a 1000 MW plant.

e.g., Commonwealth Edison Company of Chicago, Con Ed, Pacific
Gas & Electric Company (California), Puerto Rico Water Resources
Authority, Yankee Atomic Electric Company (Mass.)

During its first few years of operation, discharges of radioactivity from the facility - particularly in liquid effluents -
often substantially exceeded allowable limits. Liquid effluent
from the plant is discharged into Buttermilk Creek, which flows
by the facility. Buttermilk is a tributary of Cattaraugus Creek -
also on the site - which forms a reservoir at Springville, New
York and flows on to Lake Erie. There are over 350 dairy herds
within 10 miles of NFS and much of the nearby land is used as
a source of public water supply.

Since early 1968, Strontium 90 activity has been increasing
in Cattaraugus Creek, downstream of the facility. Between October
1969 and March 1970 the levels were about 38 per cent of the
AEC's maximum permissible concentrations on an annual basis.* In
a letter dated May 31, 1968 the AEC warned NFS that "release from
the NFS plant should be significantly reduced...."**

The principal radioactive gases discharged from NFS stacks
at the facility are krypton and iodine. In 1968, a process filter
failed resulting in emissions of radioactive particulates in excess
of allowable amounts - which required the plant to be shutdown.

In June of last year, NFS announced a $12 million program to
triple the capacity of the reprocessing plant by mid-1963. According
to Mr. T.C.Runion, President of NFS, the company's target for radioactive

*Radioactivity Bull. of N.Y.S. Dept. of Health, 2/27/70 (69-4),
6/26/70 (70-170).
**Quoted in The Nuclear Threat Inside America, Look (12/15/70).

emissions is "something of the order of less than 5 per cent of the limit." He concedes, however, that

> The operating characteristics of the plant, the practical problems we ran into, have all pushed us above those limits. Fortunately, the plant has not operated at a level above 50 per cent of its capacity. So as we contemplate future heavier production loads we have to take steps to make sure we do bring the plant back down to these target levels we are talking about.*

The amount of radioactivity produced at the plant will increase considerably as the plant throughput and radiation levels of spent fuel increase. For example, when the plant is expanded, "tritium releases to the surface waters may increase from the present high discharge of 1,200 curies per month to 20,000 curies per month."** According to Mr. Runion, this has prompted NGS to spend $3 million of the $12 million on improved methods of pollution and radiation control. One NFS proposal for dealing with tritium, for which a license application has been filed with the AEC (but no public hearing has been held) is to drill a 7,000 foot deep disposal well designed to put the tritium solution below the level of ground water into a layer of sandstone.

Krypton emissions will not be reduced by the new control devices. According to Mr. Runion, air dispersion is "more than sufficient" to reduce emissions "to below offsite permissble limits."***

As noted above (p. 122), Mr. Runion in his testimony before the Joint Congressional Committee on Atomic Energy, has conceded that the ability to achieve zero or near-zero radioactive emissions is an economic and not a technological problem. The economic factor is

*Hearings, pt. 2 (Vol. 1), supra at 1710.
**Hearings, pt. 2 (Vol.1), supra at 1726. This would be about 30 per cent of the allowable concentrations.
***Id. at 1727.

- 241 -

particularly important to the fuel reprocessor because his business depends largely on marketing a fuel which is competitive in cost with other nuclear and fossil-fuels. Mr. Runion stated before the Committee that "we recognize that our continued chemical operations rest on the economic implications of cost versus fuel values to the utility company."*·

Storage of High Level Radioactive Wastes in New York

At the WNSC, high-level radioactive wastes are stored in liquid form in two 750,000 gallon carbon steel tanks and two 15,000 gallon, stainless steel tanks, installed in concrete, underground vaults, owned by NYASD. Currently, about 510,000 gallons of wastes are contained in the large tanks and about 12,000 gallons in the 2 smaller tanks. NYASD intends to change the tanks about every 20 years to protect against leakage owing to deterioration of protective materials.

The site is also used for permanent storage of solid radioactive wastes generated at nuclear facilities throughout the Northeast. Since activation as a nuclear waste storage site in 1963, WNSC has received at least 1,000,000 cubic feet of solid nuclear wastes, which are buried in underground trenches.

Governor's Electric Power Committee

The State Electric Power Program is for the most part based on recommendations contained in the Report of the Governor's Electric Power Committee, dated December 15, 1967.

Many of the members of the Governor's eighteen-member Electric Power Committee were the same individuals who benefited from the

*Hearings, pt. 2 (Vol. I), supra at 1705.

1968 Power Program, i.e., James A. Fitzpatrick, Chairman of PASNY,
Oliver Townsend, Chairman of NYASD, Ernest P. Acker, President of
Empire State Atomic Development Associates, Inc., Errol L. Doebler,
Chariman of Long Island Lighting Co., Ronald R. Peterson, State
Commissioner of Commerce, Minot H. Pratt, Vice President of
Niagara Mohawk Power Corp., Peter J. Brennan, President of
Building & Construction Trades Council, and Arthur Jamieson,
President Ostego Electric Corporation, Inc. Neither environmental
interests nor New York City were represented on the Committee.

The Committee recommended that the "optimum methods of
providing for state needs" were, inter alia "by relying upon
nuclear energy as the most promising source of future economic
power...; by expediting and fully implementing the plans of the
investor-owned utilities to construct large scale nuclear generating
plants....;"and by expanding NYASD's power to cooperate with
private utilities in the development of nuclear power. In support
of nuclear power, the Committee cited high costs of fossil fuels
to New York State utilities relative to nuclear fuel reprocessed
here; "safety and reliability" of nuclear plants, plus freedom
from "combustion" products; economic development arising out of the
creation of nuclear fuel cycle industries; and, generation of low-
cost electric power. The Committee further urged that, although
potential sites were available for nuclear plants, they should
be obtained "in time to prevent their preemption for other purposes.
The full accomodation at such sites of the public interest in
health, safety, conservation, esthetics and recreation must be
assured at minimum cost to the electricity consuming public." (emphasis
added). Thus, the Committee clearly intended to downgrade the

environmental costs of producing electric power in favor of encouraging its use by keeping costs to a minimum.

To implement the Committee's recommendations, the Governor
successfully proposed to the legislature substantial new powers
for NYASD which were principally designed to assist electric
utilities (a) in carrying out nuclear research and development and
(b) in keeping their costs as low as possible. The legislature
granted NYASD the power (a) to participate with private power
companies in the construction and operation of experimental or
developmental nuclear power facilities within the state; (b) to
develop, prepare and furnish land by sale or lease to private
utilities for use in construction and operation of nuclear power
plants and related facilities;* and (c) to acquire and lease or
otherwise make available nuclear fuel for use in the production
of power.

NYASD's $30 million debt limit was also removed, as was
virtually all regulatory control. No meaningful safeguards were
included, however, to ensure that the funds raised by NYASD would
be spent in the public interest. NYASD can (a) establish fees,
rentals and charges for use of any property or facility under its
jurisdiction, or sell any product or service it provides

---

*As regards sites for nuclear plants, NYASD has the power to "enter
into any lands, waters or premises for the purposes of making bor-
ings, soundings, surveys or other investigations necessary to the
purposes of the authority...." Public Authorities Law §1855.9
NYASD also has the power to acquire any real property it deems
necessary for its corporate purposes in the name of the state by
dedication, agreement, condemnation or appropriation. Public
Authorities Law, §1856. Appropriation merely involves preparation
of a map of the land by the Department of Public Works and filing
the map with the clerk of the county where the land is located and
the Secretary of State. Once the map is filed, title to the land
vests in NYASD. The former owner is entitled to fair compensation
for the property. See Highway Law §30.
The 3,345 acre site for the Western New York Nuclear Service Center
was acquired by appropriation.

"to provide funds for such...corporate purposes as the
authority may deem appropriate;"* and (b) issue bonds and notes
"in such principal amounts as, in the opinion of the authority,
shall be necessary to provide sufficient moneys for achieving"
its corporate purposes.**

According to Governor Rockefeller, removal of NYASD's debt
limit and its coincident ability to own fuel "will greatly enhance
the development of nuclear support industries in the state, such
as the reprocessing industry already established through the
private-state cooperation in Cattaraugus County." (1968 Special
Message to the Legislature on Electric Power.)

Nuclear Power Siting Committee

To date, NYASD has not acquired a site for a nuclear
generating facility.*** However, with the aid of a six-member
Interdepartmental Nuclear Power Siting Committee, approved and
appointed by the Governor, it is compiling an inventory of
"candidate sites" and the Governor has recently declared that
NYASD "will acquire the sites."**** According to
James G. Cline, Chairman of the NYASD, the Authority plans to
acquire "suitable sites" as soon as possible"to prevent their
being put, over the next few years, to less vital land uses."*****

---

*Public Authorities Law, §1855.9.
**Public Authorities Law, §1860.1.
***NYASD has identified two areas in the State, one on Lake Ontario,
the other on the St. Lawrence River, as appropriate for location of
a 350 MW demonstration, breeder reactor.
****Power-A Program Paper, by Nelson A. Rockefeller (Oct. 24, 1970) p.5.
*****Letter to the Editor of the New York Times from James G. Cline,
dated August 13, 1970.

The Committee is heavily weighted in favor of commercial and power interests. Four of the six members are Joseph Swidler, PSC Chairman (added by the Governor in Feb., 1970); Dr. William E. Seymour, Deputy Commissioner of Industrial Services and Technologies of the State Department of Commerce; Dr. John Dunning, Chairman of the Nuclear Program of ESAD; and Charles Bolz, Chairman, Planning Committee of the New York Power Pool. The remaining two member are Dwight F. Metzler and Dr. W. Mason Lawrence of the DEC.

According to its Eighth Annual Report (4/1/69 - 3/31/70), NYASD plans to consult with local officials, conservation groups, etc., and hold public hearings. Whether such hearings will provide an opportunity for effective community participation in nuclear power plant siting decisions is highly questionable. Since there is no legal requirement for NYASD to hold a public hearing, it will exercise full control over hearing procedures: more importantly, however, whatever objections are raised at such a hearing, the ultimate power to determine the location of a nuclear site rests with the Governor. Significantly, there is no comparable siting committee exploring sites for fossil fueled or other type of power generation within the State.

Other NYASD Activities to Carry Out the Governor's Power Program

Other activites of NYASD designed to carry out the State Electric Power Program include: (1) opening of a $400,000 Plutonium Storage Facility last year at the WNSC, which now stores about 340 kilograms of plutonium under contracts with Yankee Atomic Electric Co. (Mass.), Con Ed and Commonwealth Edison Company of Chicago -

this is viewed as the first step toward establishment of a plutonium
fuel fabrication complex by private industry; (2) participation
in the $12 million expansion of NFS's reprocessing facility; (3)
arrangements to lease nuclear fuel to Con Ed, Niagara Mohawk,
Rochester Gas & Electric (4) contract with United Nuclear Corporation
and PASNY to supply $9 million of uranium for first core of PASNY's
800 MW plant; (5) participation, with General Electric and ESAD, in
the development and siting of a 350 MW demonstration breeder
reactor in New York State.

Atomic Energy Council

To further promote nuclear power, in the same year that he
launched the State Electric Power Program the Governor introduced
legislation creating the Atomic Energy Council within the State
Department of Commerce. Significantly, no similar step has been
taken to create an Energy Council; the sole emphasis is on "Atomic"
power.

All members of the Atomic Energy Council are appointed by the
Governor. The Deputy Commissioner of Commerce serves as executive
secretary, overseeing the daily operations of the Council.

The Council is charged with the duties of, inter alia:

(1) advising the Governor and legislature with respect to
programs for the regulation and control of atomic energy activities;

(2) coordinating regulatory programs of state and local agencies
affecting atomic energy activities and correlating them with the
federal government and other states; and,

(3) developing a coordinated position regarding federal programs
affecting atomic energy activities and coordinating presentation of
views of all state and local bodies concerning such regulatory

programs.

All state and local agencies must keep the council "fully and currently informed" as to their activities relating to atomic energy; and, no rule, regulation or ordinance relating to atomic energy can become effective until 90 days after it has been submitted to the Council. (Commerce Law, §104).

The Council devotes a large portion of time to reviewing and commenting on amendments to the AEC's rules and regulations, as well as federal legislation affecting atomic energy activities. Also the Council - in the person of the assistant general counsel of the Commerce Department -formally represents the state in AEC hearings regarding nuclear facilities, including nuclear power plants proposed to be located in the State. The Council has supported all applications for nuclear facilities to date. Reportedly, in each case it sought merely to have the utility agree to keep radioactive emissions "as low as practicable."

The Commerce Department's utlimate responsibility is to promote and protect the "interests and welfare of New York business, industry and commerce" (Commerce Law §100.1).

Even the Committee on Public Utilities of the New York State Senate has questioned the propriety of authorizing the Commerce Department to oversee the regulation of nuclear power, concluding that: "the attraction of industry should not be intermingled with the serious problems of the careful use and development of nuclear power."* Moreover, the failure of the Governor to recommend the

*Second Interim Report of New York State Senate Committee on Public Utilities (September, 1969), p.31.

creation of an overall State Energy Council, rather than simply

a myopic Atomic Energy Council, serves to underscore - along with

NYASD - the tremendous imbalance in this state in favor of nuclear

power.

C. Low Cost Power for Large Industrial Users

PASNY* was established as a public benefit corporation in
1931 to develop hydroelectric power using the Niagra and St.
Lawrence Rivers primarily "for the benefit of the people of the
state as a whole and particularly the domestic and rural consumers
to whom the power can economically be made available...." PASNY
was required to ensure that municipalities and political sub-
divisions in the state "secure a reasonable share of power generated"
by its projects. Sales to and use by industry was ostensibly a
secondary purpose, i.e., to secure revenues so that domestic and
rural use would be at the lowest possible costs.**

A major objective of the Governor's Power Program, however,
is to assist large industrial users of electricity, particularly
the electrochemical and electrometallurgical industries.***
Thus the Governor, through PASNY, has made available 6,000 MW of
additional, low cost power to industry.

In furtherance of his power program and to push the development
of nuclear power, the Governor in 1968 successfully proposed
legislation which authorized PASNY (a) to construct and operate
base load nuclear generating and hydroelectric, pumped storage
facilities, and (b) to contract with private utilities for power
needed to enable PASNY to supply additional low-cost power to high-

---

*PASNY is run by five trustees appointed by the Governor.
**Public Authorities Law   § 1005(5).
***Governor's 1968 Special Message to the Legislature on Electric
Power.

load factor industry pending completion of new generating capacity. Power generated at PASNY's new facilities will be available to industries that purchase blocks of 5,000 KW or more and have load factors of 75 per cent or better. The cost of power must also represent at least 7.5 per cent of the value of products produced through its use.

PASNY has never sold more than 7% of its power to municipal and cooperative users in the state. In 1969, 43% of its power (9.6 billion Kwh) went to industrial users (19% by direct sales from PASNY; 24% through private power companies) and 44% (9.7 billion Kwh) went to private power companies, who in turn, resold the power to domestic and rural users at a profit.*

As a result of the 1968 amendments, a larger share of PASNY's power will undoubtedly go to industry. Power generated at its new facilities must be used initially to firm the capacity of the Authority's hydro plants, to supply high-load factor industry and to meet requirements of its existing municipal and cooperative customers. Any excess power must be sold to private utilities, for resale at a profit to their customers.** Potential municipal customers - such as New York City - are precluded from buying any power generated by PASNY's new facilities directly from PASNY - they must buy it instead from private utilities. This is an unwarranted scheme to benefit the private utilities at the expense of the public.

In addition to the direct environmental damage which will result from expanding PASNY's electric power facilities, encouraging industry to maximize its use of electricity appears to undermine sound environmental planning in New York State. For example,

*PASNY 1969 Annual Report, p. 28.
**Public Authorities Law §1001, 1005.

promoting aluminum production by making available low-cost power
is environmentally unsound. Aluminum is made from a process that
uses about 10 Kwh of energy per pound just to recover the metal
from ore. Remelting used aluminum requires significantly less
electric energy. Also, it has been estimated that, while an
energy equivalent of 2700 Kwh is required to produce a ton of
steel from ore, an energy expenditure of only 700 Kwh is needed
to produce the same ton from reclaimed steel.*

While recycling aluminum and steel would, therefore, reduce
the need for electric power (and also cut down on solid wastes)
the availability of low-cost power reduces the manufacturer's
incentive to cut down on power and thus, his incentive to turn to
recycling.

The Governor's remodeling of PASNY stands as an excellent
example of his preference for power and lack of a sincere commitment to environmental protection.

D. The Governor Has Ceded to the AEC Exclusive Regulatory Authority
    Regarding Radiation Hazards of Major Nuclear Facilities.

The investor-owned utilities have made a substantial effort
to promote nuclear power, largely through ESAD, which has invested
at least $20,000,000 to develop nuclear technology since 1960.
ESAD recently committed $5,000,000 to assist General Electric
to develop a breeder reactor to be located somewhere in New York
State.**

_____
*D.R. Anthrop, Environmental Side Effects of Energy Production, supra
at 41.
**NYASD Eighth Annual Report, supra at 18.

- 252 -

The utilities find New York State a particularly comfortable area for the promotion of nuclear power: no state or local body exercises any regulatory authority over the radiological effects or safety features of nuclear power plants, reprocessing facilities, or nuclear fuel fabrication plants in this state. The Governor in 1962 and again in 1965 entered into formal agreements with the AEC which commit the State to refrain from regulating the radiation hazards associated with such facilities.

At the time the 1962 Agreement was entered into, there were three agencies within the State with primary regulatory responsibility regarding the health and safety aspects of the possession and use of radiation sources: The State Department of Health, responsible for public and medical health throughout the State, except New York City, in which the New York City Department of Health is so responsible; and the State Department of Labor, responsible for industrial health and safety throughout the State, including New York City. Article VII of the Agreement required the state to obtain and maintain in effect modifications of the rules and regulations administered by these agencies:

> "so as to exempt (except for registration; notification; inspection, not including operational testing but including sampling which would not substantially interfere with or interrupt any Commission licensed activities; and routing and scheduling of material in transit) licensees of the Commission from so much of such (rules and regulations)....as pertain to protection against radiation hazards arising out of...(licensed) activities (i.e., power plants, nuclear fuel reprocessing facilities)...."

The State Sanitary Code, the State Industrial Code and the New York City Health Code were all revised as of October 15, 1962, to conform with the requirements of Article VII of the 1962 Agreement.*

*E.g. New York City Health Code, Section 175, pp.456-57 (Introductory Note)

In 1965, the Governor entered into a Memorandum of Understanding with the AEC to supplement the 1962 Agreement. Paragraph 4 of the Memorandum provides that:

"(4) It is a mutual objective of the Commission and the State to avoid dual regulation for purposes of protection against radiation hazards of activities licensed by either party within the State. Accordingly, and in view of paragraph (5) and the other provisions of this Memorandum of Understanding:

(a) the State will use its best efforts to exempt activities licensed by the Commission (e.g., construction and operation of nuclear power reactors, fuel reprocessing plants)...from State regulations which are directed toward protection against radiation hazards from those radiation sources which are regulated by the Commission; (exception for such matters as access to records and facilities, sampling and measuring, routing and scheduling of material in transit)...."

Through these agreements, the Governor has assured utilities and those engaged in nuclear fuel reprocessing that they will be free from any state or local regulation regarding the radiation hazards posed by nuclear facilities.

New York State continues to rely on the AEC despite the increasing criticism of the AEC's standards by several scientists as unsafe; its failure to set limits specifically for nuclear power facilities; the clear conflict of interest between the AEC's roles as regulator and promotor of nuclear power; the AEC's failure to fully inform the public of the risks and consequences of major reactor accidents involving large reactors now being planned for service; and the drastic reduction in federal safety research and development regarding such reactors.

Other states have ordered utilities planning nuclear power plants to restrict their emissions of radiation to levels well below the AEC's allowable emissions. For example, Maryland author-

ities recently issued a construction permit to the Baltimore Gas
& Electric Company to build a nuclear plant on Chesapeake Bay which
limits permissible radioactivity levels in liquid discharges to
one percent of AEC standards.

The Minnesota Pollution Control Agency has refused to issue
a permit to Northern States' Power Company for a nuclear power
reactor unless it restricts radioactive discharges into the
Mississippi River to 2 percent of AEC standards. The Company
has brought an action in the United States District Court in
Minnesota seeking a determination that the State has no authority
to regulate the radiological health and safety effects of its
plant. The power company claims that the Congress has vested
exclusive authority to set radiological health and safety standards
in the AEC under the Atomic Energy Act of 1954, as amended (42
U.S.C. Sec. 2011, et. seq.). Minnesota contends, on the other hand,
that the regulation of radiation hazards is not preempted to the
federal government and that, in any event, it has a constitutional
right and obligation to protect the safety, health and welfare of
its citizens by regulating radioactive waste releases to the
environment. The Attorneys General of seven states* - and attorneys
for certain members of the Southern Governor's Conference -
filed briefs in support of Minnesota's position. New York State
has declined to support the suit.

The District Court recently upheld the company's position
and ruled that it need not comply with Minnesota's radiation
emission standards. This decision will be appealed and the issue

*Pennsylvania, Michigan, Maryland, Wisconsin, Vermont, Missouri,
Virginia

will most likely be resolved by the United States Supreme
Court.

Whether or not the federal government has preempted the regulation of radiological effects of major nuclear facilities, the
critical question now is whether there is any justification for
continuing to exclude state and local authorities from regulating
radiation hazards by imposing standards stricter than federal
standards in accordance with their respective police powers?
Should the Atomic Energy Act of 1954 be amended explicitly
to permit state and local governments to impose stricter standards?
In our view, the answer is clearly yes. Commenting on the Minnesota
case, a recent editorial in the New York Times concluded

> "It is a perversion of the Federal system to forbid states to
> take additional measures to safeguard the health and welfare
> of their citizens. Indeed, encouragement of such local
> initiatives in pollution control will make for a more
> livable America."*

New York State's refusal to support Minnesota's effort to
exert regulatory authority over radiation hazards caused by
nuclear power plants is further evidence of this Administration's
preference for power over the environment.

Sound public health and environmental policy require that
state and local agencies with responsibility in these areas have
the option to establish more rigid standards than federal authorities
regarding all radiation hazards associated with nuclear power
development. It is clear, however, that the Governor and the
nuclear industry feel otherwise. As noted above, the Governor has
formally agreed with the AEC to refrain from regulating radiological
effects of power plants and nuclear fuel facilities. In fact,

*New York Times (12/12/71)William D. Ruckelshaus Administrator of
the federal EPA has also recently expressed the view that states should
be permitted to set stricter standards for radiation exposure than the
AEC. Environmental Reporter (Current Developments) p.1074 (2/5/71) - 256-

in 1969 he <u>vetoed</u> a law which would have set limits on radioactivity in liquid effluents discharged by power plants into the State's waters.*   The proposal was triggered by citizens protesting New York State Gas and Electric's proposal to build a 820 MW nuclear plant on Lake Cayuga, a small lake located a few miles from Cornell.

There is no question that radioactivity poses a serious threat to human health. Thus, regulation of radiological effects of nuclear facilities presents a classic case for the exercise of traditional local police powers - reserved by the 10th Amendment - to protect the health and welfare of local inhabitants.

The AEC's refusal to recognize a legitimate interest on the part of states and localities to regulate radiation hazards appears entirely inconsistent with its willingness to accept and be bound by state and local determination of all other environmental impacts, including thermal pollution, of a proposed plant.   Under its proposed policy for complying with the National Environmental Policy Act of 1969, the AEC states it will consider certification by state authorities of reasonable assurance of compliance with state standards as dispositive of the environmental issues covered thereby.**

The principal arguments advanced in favor of exclusive federal legislation are: (a) that the AEC has access to "the experts" in radiation control, the implication being either that these experts are the exclusive property of the AEC or that expertise can not be developed elsewhere; (b) the safety record of nuclear plants, i.e., the fact that they generally emit only a small portion

*Governor's Veto Memorandum No. 323, dated May 26, 1969, disapproving Assembly Bill No. 5857, Senate Reprint No. 15,010.
**10 C.F.R. pt.50, Revised Appendix D, §11(b).

of permissible limits of radiation under normal operation; (c) that, if a major accident occurs, it will probably result in interstate damage.

The argument regarding access to experts is hardly credible. A substantial number of governmental and university personnel around the country are well qualified to assess radiation hazards associated with major nuclear facilities. A major obstacle to AEC support for state regulation is, of course, its own desire to avoid outside regulation plus its clear intention to promote nuclear power. The AEC operates and promotes many nuclear projects, e.g., nuclear weapons tests, nuclear waste storage facilities, test reactors, which may also be subject to state regulation. Any additional regulation of power facilities - which is likely to be stricter than AEC regulations - poses a threat to the rapid expansion of nuclear power.

One of the most compelling arguments in support of the need for state and local regulation is the AEC's frequent claim of good operating results from nuclear facilities to date. The AEC constantly reminds its critics that most power plants (not fuel reprocessing plants) generally emit only a small percentage of allowable radiation limits. Why then doesn't the AEC lower its standards to reflect the clearly available technology and operating results and also to induce equipment suppliers to develop "cleaner" equipment? The usual response to this suggestion is that plant operators need "flexibility", i.e., a few days a year a plant will exceed this "good" operating result and should not be penalized therefore.* This "protective" attitude is in our view

*See discussion in Section III.E.2, supra at 117.

wholly unjustified and in reality is nothing more than a "license"
to pollute. Clearly what ought to occur is that the standards
should be dramtically reduced and rigid sanctions in the form of
civil penalties, or temporary shutdown of the plant, imposed when
the standards are exceeded. Only in this way will plant owners
and operators feel compelled to conduct operations as safely as
possible.

Moreover, there can be no sound reason for denying those
persons most directly threatened by radiaition hazards the
right to determine the level and kind of risks to which they are
to be exposed.

E. Exclusive Authority for PSC to Approve Sites for Electric
   Power Facilities

The Governor, his newly appointed Chairman of the PSC Joseph
C. Swidler, and the power companies are determined to establish
a mechanism for lodging exclusive authority to approve sites for
electric power facilities in a state body - preferably the power
oriented PSC - without the authorization of those communities within
which the facilities are proposed to be located.

Those closely associated with power interests take this position
because such a regulatory scheme will greatly assist utilities in
locating plants throughout the state and, thereby, promote the
growth of electric power.

The state legislature also appears to have (temporarily at
any rate) accepted this position. During the closing days of last
year's legislative session, the legislature enacted the transmission
facility siting law (Chap. 272, Laws of 1970). This law authorizes
the PSC in approving a site for transmission facilities to reject

any applicable local law or requirement which the PSC finds "is
unreasonably restrictive in view of the existing technology; or
of factors of cost or economics; or of the needs of consumers
whether located inside or outside of the locality."

The legislation proposed by the Governor with regard to
regulating the siting of electric power plants (S.9360) grants
the PSC the identical authority to disregard applicable local
requirements in approving such plants. The grounds upon which the
PSC can reject a local requirement as "unreasonably restrictive,"
i.e., technology is unavailable, it will cost the utility or
consumer too much money, the plant is needed to meet demands of
consumers in other areas of the state, are obviously designed
to keep utility and power costs low in order to promote power
consumption. These standards are tantamount to a blanket authorization
to ignore legitimate and well-founded community opposition to a
power plant in favor of satisfying the demand for electricity
anywhere in the state at the cheapest prices, without adequate
consideration of environmental costs.

Suppose, for example, a utility company submitted an application
to the Commission requesting authorization to construct a large,
fossil-fueled generating plant within New York City. Clearly the
plant would impose a serious environmental burden on the quality
of New York City's air. The Commission could decide that the"...
total cost to society as a whole" or "...the totality of the needs
of the people of the state" required the location of the facility
within New York City. Such a decision would subject a given community to an environmental hazard in order to achieve a claimed

- 260 -

economic benefit to "society as a whole."

This legislation would, in effect, compel local governments to accept power generating plants that fail to meet reasonable environmental standards. For example, it would allow the PSC to overrule New York City's recent decision to deny Con Ed's request to install an additional 1600 MW of fossil-fueled generating capacity in the city because it would contribute significantly to the already serious air pollution problems facing the City and to limit the expansion to only 800 MW under certain condition designed to minimize its air pollution effects. The PSC could order New York to accept not only another 800 MW plant, but any additional plants - fossil or nuclear - which it approves.

The legislation could also serve to undermine the City's ability to enforce a fundamental condition to its issuance of a permit to Con Ed authorizing 800 MW - namely that the Company will retire at least 1,100 MW of old, in-city generating facilities by 1974. From the City's standpoint, the purpose of the agreed trade-off was to ameliorate the effect the new facility will have on the quality of the City's air .

The proposed siting bill authorizes the PSC to exert jurisdiction over any new plant intended to replace an existing plant, if in the Commission's view, the new facility is not a "like replacement" for the existing plant. Con Ed could, if it chose to do so, seek the PSC's approval to replace the old units slated for retirement with other larger, perhaps more polluting plants. The City would be powerless 'to prevent such replacement if the PSC deemed the plants "acceptable."

The underlying assumption of those who favor exclusive state control of siting is that a locality where a power plant is proposed to be located has no right to determine whether or not to accept a plant in its environs, and that localities, if left to their own devices, will irrationally reject all plants. According to Chairman Swidler:

> "parochial interests should not prevent the location of utility facilities...required on the basis of a broad state-wide interest and which are well located in relation to statewide siting opportunities."*(emphasis added)

> "There are many people who fly the environmental banner with no better justification than their desire to keep all utility facilities out of their own parishes, and have them located somewhere else...."**

Increased local opposition to power plants largely reflects increased awareness on the part of the general public of the clear and substantial environmental hazards associated with such plants. Moreover, many responsible people believe that it is time to ask why we need more plants and to examine critically the costs and benefits of current policies that encourage rapid growth in demand.

Also, it is not without significance that local communities have often favored power plants for economic reasons: a large plant contributes substantially to the tax base and may attract industry. According to Louis Roddis, Jr., President of Con Ed, "ad valorem taxes on the plant...(are)often the deter-minative factor in determining acceptability in a small community, and has often been so demonstrated."***

*Address entitled "Power System Planning and Land Use," before the Conference on the Revision of the States'Land Development Laws (Oct. 5, 1970).
**Address entitled "The New York Program for Reconciling the Expansion of Energy Supply Facilities'with Environmental Protection," before Senior Management Forum, Atomic Industrial Forum (March 17.1970)
***Roddis, Metropolitan Siting, supra p. 13.

Under the proposed legislation, the local community seeking
to enforce its own environmental standards is accorded only the
opportunity to present its case to the PSC. The burden of establishing the reasonableness of local laws is placed upon the local governments that have enacted them. This is a radical departure
from the well established rules of law that extend a presumption
of validity to the duly enacted laws of local governments. Moreover, the Governor's bill undermines the presumption in the very
area in which it has been and should be accorded the greatest
weight, viz., the exercise of the police power to protect the public
health and welfare.

Should a utility be prevented from installing a facility owing
to local law, the utility can and should seek prompt judicial
review to overturn that law as arbitrary or unreasonable. Neither
the PSC nor any other administrative body is an appropriate forum
for the resolution of that issue. Indeed, we regard any proposal
to empower a regulatory body to decide whether a local law is
reasonable as an unjustified attempt to centralize political
power and to prevent local communities directly affected by
electric power facilities from having an effective voice in the
decision making process.

VI. Basic Conclusions and Recommendations

A. Temporary State Commission on Energy Needs, the Public
    Interest and the Environment

We recommend the establishment of a fifteen-member Temporary
State Commission on Energy Needs, the Public Interest and the Environment. Based on a full examination of the societal costs and
benefits of continuing or decreasing growth in demand for electric
power, the Commission would critically review the industry, governmental and regulatory policies that encourage such growth and the
policies and practices that have encouraged inefficient production,
supply and usage of electric power. The Commission's ultimate responsibility would be to formulate a rational energy policy and
environmental action plan for the state, within approximately two
years after its initial working meeting.

Composition of Temporary Commission

The Temporary Commission must comprise   persons from
the private sector with expertise in the areas of power supply,
consumer affairs, environmental protection, natural resource management, public health, economics, and community planning and who
are fully qualified to make an independent objective analysis of the
problems before the Commission. The members should be appointed
by a task force including the Commissioner of the Department
of Environmental Conservation, the Chairman of the State
Public Service Commission, the Chairman of the New York City
Interdepartmental Committee on Public Utilities and the
Chief Judge of the New York State Court of Appeals, with

the advice and consent of the Senate.

In the course of developing a rational energy policy and environmental action plan for the State, the Temporary Commission would be required to:

(a) assess the relative environmental impact and societal costs of all possible, alternative sources of energy, and determine the role electric power should play in satisfying energy needs.

(b) critically examine all components of existing and projected demand for electric power and formulate criteria for identifying essential and non-essential uses of electric power; thereafter, the Commission should determine the actual need for the replacement, expansion and installation of new electric power plants, associated equipment and transmission facilities and the environmental impact thereof.

(c) re-examine all industry and governmental policies, as well as laws, rules and regulations which may promote demand for electricity or growth of electric power; develop methods for quantifying the social and environmental costs of producing and supplying electric power; and recommend methods for factoring those costs into the price of electricity, including but not limited to:

i. disclosing to the customer the amount of electricity necessary to utilize electrical products, and requiring manufacturers to provide such information through labelling;

ii. instituting a non-promotional rate structure which would eliminate the practice of offering a lower price per unit as use increases, adequately reflect the social costs of the generation and

supply of electric power, but, which would be designed so as not
to inhibit satisfaction of essential needs for electric power;

iii. instituting a peak demand surcharge to discourage use
of electricity by industrial, commercial and residential users
during periods of peak demand;

iv. establishing an electricity use tax to reflect the
social costs of power production and use;

v. imposing legal restrictions on activities on the part
of electrical product manufacturers and distributors that serve
directly or indirectly to encourage or promote the use of electricity;

vi. establishing legal restrictions on load increases and/
or instituting per diem rationing of electricity use;

vii. developing methods for monitoring, measuring and evaluating the impact of the above-listed, and other recommended,
measures on patterns of electricity use.

(d) formulate standards of efficiency for production, transmission and use of energy in general and electric power in particular.

(e) investigate methods for encouraging environmentally
sound planning, as well as increasing the reliability and efficiency of electric power supply, including but not limited to:

i. establishing priorities for power supply during shortages, designed to minimize environmental harm while meeting essential electric power needs;

ii. critically examine the current methods for calculating
utility rates with a view toward making revisions therein which
will create economic incentives for utilities to construct electric

power generation and transmission facilities at locations and in
a manner which involves the least possible overall environmental
harm, to utilize the most efficient methods for producing and supplying electric power, and which will encourage the maximum use of
system interconnections for supplying power;

iii. investigate the social and environmental costs and
benefits of combination gas and electric companies to determine
whether it is in the public interest to permit a single utility
to engage in distribution of gas and electricity, considering the
different environmental consequences involved in the use of each
form of energy;

iv. examine the environmental, as well as power reliability
implications, of large generating units, and formulate environmental
and reliability criteria for the design and size of generating
units;

v. formulate quality control standards for equipment acquired by electric utilities, including standards for liquid and
gaseous emissions, safety and equipment reliability, and in this
connection, examine and recommend possible economic and/or other
sanctions to be imposed on utilities and/or equipment suppliers in
the event of equipment breakdowns, including removal of damaged
equipment from the rate base when it is out of service for a substantial period and measures to preclude utilities from passing
along to customers additional costs attributate to equipment breakdowns,

e.g., repairs, purchased power, etc;

vi. examine the environmental and economic impact of precluding utilities from purchasing land for power plant sites and,
instead, requiring the locality within which a plant has been approved   to acquire the site (perhaps with some state financial assistance) and lease the site to the utility;

vii. study and recommend state and federal legislation to
mandate construction of intra-state and interstate interconnections
among utility systems.

(f) establish priorities and recommend methods for financing
research and development, as well as make recommendations concerning the type and degree of participation required from private and
public sources, e.g., electric utilities and/or their suppliers,
government, colleges and universities; and, examine the need to
provide economic incentives for research and development, as well
as recommend methods for so doing, such as including a utility's
research and development expenditures unrelated to specific equipment, which have been approved by the appropriate environmental
authorities, in the utility's rate base.

(g) consider whether water cooled, burner power reactors
should be located in the state in view of their failure to conserve
resources, substantial cuts in federal safety research programs regarding such facilities, and the environmental, as well as safety,
problems they pose.

(h) formulate criteria for siting electric power generation
and transmission facilities in the state; should the Commission
determine that additional nuclear power, fuel reprocessing or new

fuel fabrication facilities may be placed in the state consistent
with environmental, health and safety needs, it should formulate
criteria for siting such facilities; in developing siting criteria,
the Commission should give consideration to underground construction, as well as other siting methods which minimize environmental
impact and other hazards .

(i) propose standards for the emission of radioactive effluents from existing major nuclear facilities within the State, including power plants, fuel reprocessing and fuel fabrication facilities; in this connection, the Commission should publicize in
full the biological and non-biological data underlying the proposed
standards, as against possible alternatives thereto, and propose
a mechanism for periodic review of such standards.

(j) reexamine the State Electric Power Program to determine
what changes, if any, are necessary to protect adequately the environment and to conform to a rational energy policy for the state. In
its study of this program, the Commission should:

i. review the state's commitment to the promotion and
development of nuclear power plants, nuclear fuel reprocessing, fuel
fabrication, and radioactive waste disposal facilities to determine
whether such commitment is consistent with sound public health, energy utilization and environmental standards;

ii. evaluate the environmental consequences of encouraging
electric power consumption by large industrial users and the alternatives thereto;

iii. critically review the need for, and functions, policies

and practices of the Power Authority of the State of New York
and the New York State Atomic and Space Development Authority
to determine what changes therein are necessary or appropriate.

(k) formulate detailed safety standards for water-cooled
power reactors, as well as guidelines for design and engineering
safeguards for such reactors; in this connection, estimate and
publicize the risks and possible consequences of accidents involving large reactors, i.e., 1000 MW, 3000 MW, 5000 MW, 10,000 MW.

(l) examine the technological feasibility of establishing
a zero release standard for noxious emissions from fossil-fuel
plants and for radioactive effluents from major nuclear facilities, and recommend measures necessary to achieve zero-release
or releases as near-zero as possible, including an estimate of
the cost of such measures.

(m) consider whether the storage of liquid and solid radioactive wastes should be banned in this state; if and to the extent the Commission determines such wastes can be stored in this
state consistent with adequate protection of the public health and
the environment, it should develop criteria for storage of liquid
and solid radioactive wastes at fuel reprocessing, as well as
power plant, sites; formulate safety standards, including design
and engineering safeguards, for storage facilities and waste
solidification plants; and, prepare a report setting forth the
risks and possible consequences of leaks or spills of radioactive
wastes in storage, as well as in transit.

(n) critically review the functions, policies and practices of the Public Service Commission and recommend revisions therein designed to restrict the agency to performing an economic regulatory function, and to remove it from performing any significant role in environmental planning. In this connection, the Commission should recommend creation of an appropriate multi-interest body (or bodies) to exercise primary responsibility for effectuating a rational energy utilization and environmental action plan for the state, including, if appropriate, a body (or bodies) with basic responsibility for siting major utility facilities within the state.

B. Regulation of Power Plant Siting

1. We are opposed to the Governor's power plant siting program and any other legislation regarding the siting of electric power plants and associated equipment which:

(a) favors power over environmental needs;

(b) prevents communities wherein such facilities are proposed to be located from rejecting them;

(c) vests the exclusive power to approve sites in any governmental agency;

(d) fails to vest ultimate responsibility for site approval in an elected official, or officials; and

(e) fails to address the fundamental policy questions raised by electric power and its impact on the environment before establishing a procedural framework limited to power facility siting decisions.

2. Electric power plants and associated equipment are a major source of health hazards and environmental degradation in this state, e.g., air pollution, water pollution, despoilation of landscape, radioactive wastes. Any siting proposal which enables a state-wide body to override legitimate environmental opposition to the location of a generating plant offers no meaningful solution to such environmental problems; in fact, such a proposal is likely to be counter-productive. By enabling utilities more easily to overcome environmental objections, it may well eliminate the industry's chief incentive to put its own house in order.

3. The most severe health and environmental damage resulting from the construction and operation of a power plant is within the community where the plant is located and, as yet, no adequate means have been developed for controlling such damage. That community must therefore maintain the right to apply its laws and regulations with respect to such facilities, provided they constitute a proper exercise of the local police power, as determined in the first instance by a court of competent jurisdiction; and, any community wherein a plant is proposed to be located must have the right to reject it, consistent with the requirements of due process.

4. No single-interest regulatory agency is an appropriate body for regulating the siting of major utility facilities. Proper resolution of siting issues requires an objective balancing of health, environmental and power need consistent with the total

public interest. Ultimate responsibility for resolving contro-
versies involving these competing needs should be lodged in elected
officials, who are most readily and directly accountable to the
public. Moreover, members of communities within which facilities
are proposed to be located, as well as non-governmental representatives, must play an active and effective role in evaluating utility
proposals to alter or expand their facilities.

5. While we regard as irrational and contrary to the public
interest any attempt to develop a regulatory framework for power
plant siting prior to formulation of a comprehensive energy policy
and environmental action plan for the state, we propose the following interim procedure.*

We recommend the creation of a State Power Facility Siting
Committee to evaluate and make recommendations concerning proposals to expand existing or install new power facilities to the
governing body of the locality, i.e., city, town or village, wherein the facility is or would be located; and, a requirement for a
Site Approval Certificate from such governing body before commencement of a proposed expansion or acquisition of a site for installation of additional facilities.

The State Power Facility Siting Committee would comprise
the following persons:

---

*The siting procedure recommended herein would apply to major
utility facilities as defined in S.9360, attached hereto as Appendix B.

1. Commissioner of the Department of Environmental Conservation.

2. Chairman of Public Service Commission.

3. Commissioner of the State Department of Health.

4. Commissioner of Parks and Recreation.

5. Chairman of the County Environmental Management Council for the county within which a facility is or would be located, or alternatively located.

6. The Chief Executive Officer of the locality (i.e., city, village or town) within which a facility is or would be located, or alternatively located.

7. The head of any agency or department of any such locality which has responsibility for environmental protection and, in the case of New York City, the Chairman of the Interdepartmental Committee on Public Utilities.

8. Each member of the State Legislature in whose district a facility is or would be located, or alternatively located.

9. Three members, who are not governmental officials or employees, and who have no direct or indirect interest in public utilities, their suppliers, or the manufacture, sale, or distribution of consumer products. Of these three members, one shall be a recognized expert in the field of public health, one in the field of natural resource management and one in the fields of economics and community planning. These members would be selected by other members of the Committee upon receipt of utility proposals.

The Chairman of the DEC and Chief Executive Officer of each locality involved would serve as co-Chairmen. Members representing a locality involved would serve as full voting members at such times as the Committee considers matters concerning facilities located, or which would be located, or alternatively located in their locality.

After receiving a site proposal, the Siting Committee would hold a public hearing in the locality within which a facility is,

or would be, located. Upon completion of the hearing and study
of the proposal, the Siting Committee would be required to submit
a report and recommendations regarding the proposal to the governing body of the locality in which the facility is or would be located, or alternatively located. The Committee's Report would include (but not necessarily be limited to) an assessment of the
actual need for the facility; the nature of the probable environmental impact of the facility, including a specification of every
adverse effect on, and conflict with, governmental policies concerning the public health, safety and the environment; possible
alternatives to the facility, e.g., fossil-fueled as opposed to
nuclear plant, importation of power; possible alternative sites;
and, the adverse health, safety and environmental effects that
cannot be avoided, as well as the reasons why such effects constitute sufficient or insufficient grounds for rejecting the facility. In making any recommendations, the Siting Committee would
be bound by all applicable federal, state and local laws or regulations.

The governing body of any locality receiving a report and
recommendations from the Siting Committee would be required promptly
to approve or disapprove of the proposal, or accept or modify the
Siting Committee's recommendations in the same manner as provided
for passage of a local law. If the body approves the facility, it
would issue a Site Approval Certificate containing any conditions
the body deems necessary or appropriate.

form to a long-range plan for development of an electric power grid
by the electric power systems serving the state and interconnected
systems, serve the interests of electric system economy, efficiency
and reliability, and conform to a plan for elimination of all overhead lines; and whether the facility would pose an undue hazard to
persons or property along the area it traverses.

All local requirements would apply to each transmission facility except that county governing bodies would be authorized to
set aside local requirements which are found, after a public hearing, to be unreasonably restrictive under the circumstances. The
urgent need for a vastly improved inter-connected systems (not only
from a power supply standpoint, but on environmental grounds), as
well as the large number of permits that might be required for a
single line from numerous local jurisdictions, warrant this approach.

2. We further recommend that utilities be required to develop
an orderly program, consistent with environmental and safety needs,
for placing proposed and existing transmission lines underground,
as well as to establish a fund therefor.

3. Increasing demands being made on our limited land resources by utilities and all other sources require that the Siting
Committee, with the assistance of the PSC, DEC and Department of
Transportation, must make every possible effort to have public services
within the state engage in multiple use of rights-of-way.

D. Measures Which Require Immediate Implementation

1. Immediate Measure to Reduce Growth in Demand

As an initial step toward reducing growth in demand for electric power, we recommend an immediate prohibition against any and all activities on the part of electric utilities which serve directly or indirectly to promote or encourage the use of electricity.

2. Immediate Measures to Encourage Research and Development

To obtain a substantial commitment by industry and government to engage in research and development aimed at improving the efficiency of existing methods for generating and transmitting electricity; developing alternative sources of power which are more efficient and less polluting, technology for controlling radioactive discharges and other pollutants emitted from power plants,and environmentally sound and safe underground transmission and distribution facilities, and to study further the short and long-term effects on ecological systems, human health, plant, animal and aquatic life of effluents from nuclear and fossil-fueled plants, we recommend:

(a) That utilities be required to commit a fixed percentage of gross revenues to research and development (subject to prior approval by the DEC and appropriate local authorities) and that no future increases in rates be granted unless (i) a significant percentage thereof is spent on research and development designed to eliminate adverse environmental effects and maximize efficiency of electric power production and supply; (ii) the utility involved agrees to install the most advanced technology for the control of harmful emissions on all of its present and proposed facilities; (iii) the utility agrees to establish a fund and program for placement of existing and future transmission lines underground (or water), which program shall be subject to annual review by appropriate local and state authorities; and (iv) the utility agrees to establish a fund and a program (in consultation with appropriate governmental agencies) to ensure that adequate emergency power facilities are available for essential public services, such as hospitals, mass transit, sewage treatment, street lighting. Since utilities are legally obligated to furnish a reliable power supply, they should have the ultimate responsibility for supplying auxiliary power facilities for use in the event of a power failure within their service area.

The size and nature of research and development expenditures should be subject to the approval and supervision of representatives of the DEC, as well as environmental authorities within a particular utility's service area.

(b) The establishment of a public benefit corporation, to be called the Environmental Energy Systems and Resources Corporation, with power to contract with utilities, private parties or municipalities to conduct research regarding, or to provide, environmentally sound energy systems or low-polluting fuels consistent with the energy policy and environmental action plan formulated by

the Temporary Commission. The corporation would not have the power
to purchase land, except to establish research facilities. Its members would be appointed by the Governor, with the advice and consent of the Senate, from a list of qualified candidates initially
submitted by the Temporary Commission and, thereafter, to be submitted by a nominating committee of the corporation.

(c) Creation of an Environmental Energy Systems and Resources Fund, to be administered (on an interim basis) jointly be
the PSC and DEC, to provide up to 50 per cent state aid to utilities, private parties or municipalities for demonstration projects
designed to develop more efficient and environmentally acceptable
energy systems, low-polluting fuels; for construction of underground
transmission and distribution lines; and, to assist local governments in the purchase and/or construction of sites for power generating facilities.

(d) Withdrawal from the New York Atomic and Space Development
Authority of the power to acquire interests in land, except for
research facilities.

(e) That the federal government vastly increase research and
development funding for (i) the development of magnetohydro-
cynamics, thermionics and other methods for increasing the efficiency
of generating electric power, (ii) the development of technology
for   controlling noxious emissions from fossil-fueled plants, (iii)
the production of low-polluting fossil fuels, particularly the desulfurization of oil and coal, and (iv) the development of nuclear
fusion and solar power as sources of energy which offer the
possibility of substantially conserving other less-abundant, energy resources, and may decrease environmental problems and health hazards

associated with current and other projected methods of electric
power generation. Additional research and development must also
be conducted to determine the public health, safety and environmental impact of fusion and solar power.

3. Immediate Measures to Improve Quality Control

Since the electric utilities have failed to exercise meaningful quality control over new equipment, as evidenced by the recur-
ring breakdown of new, large generating units, and since no regulatory body (including the PSC) now exercises any direct control
over the quality of equipment purchased by utilities or the terms of
equipment supply contracts, we recommend as interim measures that:

(a) The PSC be authorized (in consultation with the DEC and appropriate local authorities) to review the terms of proposed contracts for construction, improvement or extension of a utility's plants, works or systems (over $25,000) and grant approval only upon finding that (i) such contracts satisfy reasonable quality control standards; (ii) contain manufacturer's guarantees with respect to harmful emissions, safety and equipment reliability which reflect the most advanced technology; (iii) contain strict penalties for failure to complete and deliver equipment on time, as well as for failure to meet performance guarantees.

(b) Penalties for failure to perform equipment supply contracts must be strictly enforced. The Attorney General and the public should be accorded the right to seek appropriate judicial relief if the utility companies or regulatory agencies fail to enforce significant contract provisions.

(c) Measures must also be devised which will make utilities more responsive to the need for quality control. We have requested the Temporary Commission to formulate sanctions to be imposed on utilities in the event of equipment breakdowns. At the least, if a breakdown occurs owing to the negligence of a utility's supplier, or the negligence of the utility in selecting or maintaining its equipment, the utility should be precluded from passing on any additional cost attributable to the outage (e.g., repairs, purchased power) to the customer. The utility's rate

base includes capital equipment which the utility operates to
serve the public. If such equipment is taken out of service because
of poor or negligent management, the investor rather than the customer should bear the loss. Moreover, it may be desirable to require
the removal of damaged equipment from the rate base when it is out
of service for a substantial period.

(d) Utilities must be required to shut down facilities
that fail to meet applicable emission standards; and, together
with appropriate public agencies, to develop contingency plans designed to prevent a shut-down from curtailing essential public
services.

(e) An appropriate legislative committee should examine
and issue a report regarding the kind of legal actions which might
be created (a) to compensate the public for damages suffered owing
to equipment outages, lack of low-polluting fuels, failures to
develop and/or install adequate pollution control devices; and
(b) to require industry to take action necessary to eliminate adverse environmental consequences resulting from power production
and supply.

E. Comprehensive Long Range Planning and Citizen Involvement

1. To date, neither the public nor governmental officials
have been involved in a meaningful way in the utility planning process. Moreover, the public has generally been denied access to reliable and complete information concerning the operations of the
utility industry.

2. The fundamental questions of whether projected rates
of growth are acceptable in terms of environmental degradation, adverse health effects and resource conservation; whether specific
power plants are in fact needed; and,whether they represent the
best possible alternative in terms of reliability, efficiency and
environmental impact have not been subject to meaningful review by
regulatory authorities or the public. Because utilities have been
able to plan in secret without meaningful regulatory control or public participation, their assertions regarding the need for more power and the best means for meeting such needs have gone essentially
unchallenged.

3. Accordingly, we recommend that utilities be required:

(a) to submit annually to the PSC, DEC and appropriate
local agencies, including environmental protection agencies, comprehensive five, ten, twenty and twenty-five-year plans describing
in detail projected peak loads, reserve margins, existing generating
and transmission facilities, scheduled facilities and projected service dates, planned facilities (together with probable location
thereof),a description of steps taken to correct or improve the environmental impact and efficiency of its facilities, steps taken
to coordinate planning and systems with other electric systems, maintenance schedules and the basis therefor·

(b) to submit to appropriate state and local agencies for review and approval proposed agreements with each existing or new industrial and commercial user of electricity expected to add a significant annual demand to its system (e.g., the average commercial use in 1969 was about 38,000 Kwh). A utility should also be required to secure approval prior to adding to its system load large residential developments, e.g., Co-op City (which had the capacity to install an on-site total energy system).

(c) that the DEC be required to publish periodically the environmental impact of existing facilities and project the impact over five and ten year periods based on currently available technology.

4. We need a continuing, critical and independent review of utility planning and management practices. If the energy establishment is to become more responsive to public needs, the principle of meaningful, community participation must be accepted and applied to the utility industry.

We therefore recommend the creation of a five-man Citizens Advisory Board for each investor-owned utility in the state, PASNY, and NYASD. These advisory boards should:

(a) include individuals with experience in public health, environmental, consumer and economic affairs, who are clearly independent, and who reside in the utility's service area;

(b) be appointed by legislators who represent the service areas of the respective utilities in consultation with local authorities responsible for environmental protection;

(c) have full access to the books and records of the utility;

(d) have the right to meet with its board of directors from time to time to review utility practices. The Boards should be authorized to consult with management regarding major decisions (such as the siting of large generating plants or requests for rate changes) as well as to review operating practices and procedures. The Boards should be required to issue an annual public report setting forth the basis for major utility decisions, the Board's position thereon, and recommended action, if any, with respect thereto.

These Boards would serve several essential needs: (a) they would provide a mechanism for meaningful citizen participation in the utility's decision-making process; (b) members would develop an independent expertise which could provide the basis for an intelligent challenge to, and assessment of, industry and regulatory policies; and (c) such boards could assist industry in obtaining public support for and confidence in the difficult decisions that must be made regarding energy needs and the environment.

Operating funds for advisory boards should be provided primarily by the utility involved, with some government assistance.

F. Measures to Eliminate Undue Concentration in the Energy Supply Market

We as well as other public officials are profoundly disturbed at the oil companies' efforts to control all of the nation's energy resources. Such a concentration of economic power not only undermines the effort to structure a sound environmental policy and maintain healthy, interfuel competition; it also creates a dangerous, political force.

The United States Department of Justice has an obligation to institute suits challenging the acquisitions by major oil companies of their actual and potential competitors in the energy market as violative of the antitrust laws.

Congress should also take immediate action to prevent further concentration of energy resources and to compel energy producers to divest themselves of their interests in competing firms and to restrict production to only one source of energy, with the possible exception of oil and natural gas.

G. Measures to Deal with Projected Development of Nuclear Power

1. Evaluation of Additional Nuclear Facilities In This State

(a) The number and size of nuclear power plants is projected to increase dramatically in this state over the next 30 years, to be accompanied by expansion of nuclear fuel reprocessing facilities, a plutonium fuel fabrication complex, more radioactive wastes and increased risk of nuclear accidents.

(b) In our judgment, no proposal to install additional nuclear facilities*, i.e., power plants, fuel reprocessing and fabrication facilities, waste storage and solidification facilities, in this state can be responsibly evaluated, or should be supported, by state and local authorities (particularly those responsible for protecting the public health and environment) and by the public in general until:

i. valid state standards are established with respect to the safety and radiation hazards posed by such facilities; and

ii. federal and state authorities make and publish a comprehensive analysis of the risks and possible consequences attributable to a major reactor accident involving facilities in sizes 1000 MW, 3000 MW, 5000 MW, and 10000 MW, as well as leaks and spills of high-level radioactive wastes, likely to be produced by such facilities, in storage and in transit.

*footnote on next page

There is little doubt that these two conditions, if acted upon
in good faith, could be met in a relatively short period of time,
and should not interfere with the satisfaction of power
needs in this state.

We would also urge the Temporary Commission to determine
whether the additional measures set forth in sub-sections 2 through
5 below to deal with the projected development of nuclear power
must also be satisfied prior to the consideration of additional nuclear
facilities in this state.

2. State and Local Regulation of Safety and Radiation
Hazards

(a) Governor Rockefeller has ceded to the Atomic Energy
Commission exclusive authority to regulate radiation and safety
hazards associated with major nuclear facilities in this state,
including power plants, nuclear fuel reprocessing and nuclear fuel
fabrication facilities.

(b) We recommend immediate termination of those portions
of agreements entered into between Governor Rockefeller and the AEC
in 1962 and 1965 which obligate the state and localities to refrain
from promulgating and enforcing radiological health and safety
standards regarding such facilities. The DEC, together with local
environmental protection and public health authorities, should assist the Temporary Commission in developing design and engineering
guidelines and standards with respect to safety, radiation exposure
and radioactive emissions designed to achieve zero or near zero re-

*By additional facilities we mean facilities which have not (as of
March 1, 1971) received a construction permit from the United States
Atomic Energy Commission. All nuclear plants scheduled for service
between now and 1975, i.e., Con Ed's Units No. 2 (scheduled for this
year) and No. 3 (scheduled for 1973) at Indian Point and PASNY's
(con'd)

lease of radioactivity from nuclear facilities. Such guidelines and standards should also cover liquid and solid waste storage facilities, and waste solidification plants. Further, monitoring and enforcement machinery should be developed which will ensure adequate enforcement of the standards.

Sound public health and environmental policy requires that state and local agencies with responsibility in these areas have the option to establish more rigid standards than federal authorities regarding all radiation and safety hazards associated with nuclear power development.

(c) In order to eliminate any doubt as to whether the federal government has preempted the regulation of radiological health and safety hazards posed by major nuclear facilities, this state should join with other states and localities in a concerted effort to amend the Atomic Energy Act of 1954 expressly to authorize states and local governments to set stricter standards than the federal government regarding these and any other environmental problems associated with such facilities.

3. Abolish State Atomic Energy Council

Responsibility for formulating state policy regarding regulation and control of nuclear power, as well as for representing the state in AEC licensing proceedings, is now lodged in the Atomic Energy Council, a body within the State Commerce Department. The

---

(con'd from previous page)
J. A. Fitzpatrick Unit (scheduled for 1973), would thus be excluded. Our exclusion of these facilities is not, however, intended in any way to indicate approval or disapproval of these facilities.

Atomic Energy Council should be abolished. Responsibility for formulating state policy regarding nuclear power must be placed in the DEC or in a fully independent, multi-interest body capable of analyzing objectively the public health hazards and environmental impact of nuclear power, as well as its possible use to promote industrial development. We have requested the Temporary Commission to make a recommendation covering this point.

4. Repeal Federal Price-Anderson Act of 1957

We recommend repeal of the portions of the Price-Anderson Act of 1957 which limit the liability of owners and suppliers of nuclear power facilities and nuclear fuel reprocessors for harm caused by a nuclear accident or radiation, and imposition of full financial responsibility on them for any such harm. This state, together with other states and interested localities, should make a concerted effort to have such provisions repealed.

5. Transfer of Full Regulatory Authority Regarding Licensing, Safety, Public Health, and Environmental Impact of Nuclear Facilities from the Atomic Energy Commission to the EPA.

The Atomic Energy Commission's history as and legal responsibility to be a promoter of nuclear power renders it unqualified to regulate siting or safety features of major nuclear facilities, including power plants, fuel reprocessing and fabrication facilities, or to enforce radiation standards established by the new Environmental Protection Agency.

Federal legislation should be introduced to withdraw from the AEC all regulatory, enforcement and monitoring authority which pertains in any way to the safety, public health or environmental impact of major nuclear facilities, e.g., siting, reactor safety. Such authority at the federal level should be placed in the Environmental Protection Agency.

6. Federal Radiation Standards for Specific Nuclear Facilities

The federal EPA should review existing AEC standards for radiation exposure and radioactive emissions and publish new standards which set limits explicitly for specific nuclear facilities, e.g., power plants, fuel reprocessing facilities, as opposed to a general limit for   man-made sources of radiation.

STATE OF NEW YORK

9360

IN SENATE

April 13, 1970

Introduced by COMMITTEE ON RULES—read twice and ordered printed, and when printed to be committed to the Committee on Public Utilities

AN ACT

To amend the public service law, the public health law, the condemnation law and the public authorities law, in relation to the siting and operation of major utility facilities and to repeal paragraphs a and b of subdivision three of section one thousand two hundred thirty of the public health law relating thereto

The People of the State of New York, represented in Senate and Assembly, do enact as follows:

1   Section 1. The legislature hereby finds and declares that there is

2   at present and will continue to be a growing need for public utility

3   services including electric, gas, water and steam utilities which will

4   require the construction of major new facilities. It is recognized

5   that such facilities cannot be built without in some way affecting the

6   physical environment where such facilities are located. The legisla-

7   ture further finds that it is essential in the public interest to mini-

EXPLANATION — Matter in *italics* is new; matter in brackets [ ] is old law to be omitted.

1 mize any adverse effect upon the environment and upon the quality
2 of life of the people of the state which such new facilities might
3 cause. The legislature further finds that present practices, proceed-
4 ings and laws relating to the establishment of sites for such utility
5 facilities may be inadequate to protect environmental values and
6 take into account the total cost to society of such facilities, and have
7 resulted in delays in new construction and increases in costs which
8 are eventually passed on to the people of the state in the form of
9 higher utility rates and the possible threat of the inability of the
10 public and investor-owned utilities to meet the needs of the people
11 of the state for economic and reliable utility services. Furthermore,
12 the legislature finds that existing provisions of law do not provide
13 adequate opportunity for individuals, groups interested in conser-
14 vation and the protection of the environment, municipalities and
15 other public bodies to participate in timely fashion in the decision
16 to locate a specific major facility at a specific site. The legislature
17 therefore hereby declares that it shall be the purpose of this act to
18 provide a forum for the expeditious resolution of all matters con-
19 cerning the siting of such facilities presently under the jurisdiction
20 of multiple state and local agencies including the courts of the state,
21 and all matters of state and local law, in a single proceeding to which
22 access will be open to citizens, groups, municipalities and other
23 public agencies to enable them to participate in these most important
24 decisions.

25 § 2. The public service law is hereby amended by adding thereto
26 a new article, to be article seven, to read as follows:

ARTICLE VII

SITING OF MAJOR UTILITY FACILITIES

§ 120. *Definitions. Where used in this article, the following terms, unless the context otherwise requires, shall have the following meanings.*

1. *"Municipality" means a county, city, town or village in the state.*

2. *"Major facility" means: (a) a facility for the production of steam for distribution or for distillation or purification of water for distribution, designed to produce seventy-five thousand pounds of steam per hour or more; (b) a thermal electric generating facility with a generating capacity of ten thousand kilowatts or more; (c) an electric transmission line of a design capacity of one hundred twenty-five kilovolts or more extending a distance of one mile or more, or of one hundred kilovolts or more and less than one hundred twenty-five kilovolts, extending a distance of more than ten miles,*

1 *including associated equipment, but shall not include any such*
2 *transmission line, transformer or substation located underground*
3 *in a city with a population in excess of one hundred twenty-five*
4 *thousand or a primary transmission line approved by the federal*
5 *power commission in connection with a hydro-electric facility; (d)*
6 *a fuel gas transmission facility extending a distance of one thousand*
7 *feet or more, to be used to transport fuel gas at pressures in excess*
8 *of one hundred twenty-five pounds per square inch; or (e) a fuel*
9 *gas storage facility of a capacity of two hundred fifty million cubic*
10 *feet or more at ambient temperature and pressure.*

11 *3. "Person" means any individual, corporation, public benefit*
12 *corporation, political subdivision, governmental agency, munici-*
13 *pality, partnership, co-operative association, trust or estate.*

14 *§ 121. Certificate of environmental compatibility and public need.*
15 *1. No person shall, after July first, nineteen hundred seventy, com-*
16 *mence construction of a major facility in the state without having*
17 *first obtained a certificate of environmental compatibility and public*
18 *need (hereafter in this article called a "certificate") issued with*
19 *respect to such facility by the commission. The replacement of*
20 *existing with like facilities, as determined by the commission, shall*
21 *not constitute the construction of a major facility. Any facility*
22 *with respect to which a certificate is required shall thereafter be*
23 *built, maintained and operated in conformity with such certificate*
24 *and any terms, limitations or conditions contained therein. A certi-*
25 *ficate may only be issued pursuant to this article.*

26 *2. A certificate may be transferred, subject to the approval of the*
27 *commission, to a person who agrees to comply with the terms, limita-*
28 *tions and conditions contained therein.*

1   *3. A certificate issued hereunder may be amended as herein pro-*

2 *vided.*

3   *4. This article shall not apply to any major facility a. for which,*

4 *on or before July first, nineteen hundred seventy an application has*

5 *been made for a license, permit, consent or approval from any fed-*

6 *eral, state or local commission, agency, board or regulatory body, in*

7 *which application the location of the major facility has been desig-*

8 *nated by the applicant; or b. the construction of which has been*

9 *determined upon by a municipality or public benefit corporation*

10 *which has sold bonds or bond anticipation notes on or before July*

11 *first, nineteen hundred seventy, the proceeds or part of the proceeds*

12 *of which are to be used in payment therefor.*

13   *5. Any person intending to construct a major facility excluded*

14 *from this article pursuant to subdivision four may elect to waive*

15 *such exclusion by delivering notice of such waiver to the commission.*

16 *This article shall thereafter apply to each major facility identified*

17 *in such notice from the date of its receipt by the commission.*

18   *§ 122. Application for a certificate. 1. An applicant for a certi-*

19 *ficate shall file with the commission an application in such form as*

20 *the commission may prescribe containing the following information:*

21 *(a) the location of the site or right-of-way; (b) a description of the*

22 *facility to be built thereon; (c) a description of any effluents and*

23 *liquid, solid or gaseous wastes to be produced by such facility*

24 *including estimates of the amount, the composition and in the case*

25 *of liquids the temperature thereof; (d) a description of any studies*

26 *which have been made of the environmental impact of the project*

27 *and the results thereof; (e) a statement explaining the need for the*

28 *facility; (f) a statement of the reasons why the site or right-of-way*

1 *is believed suited for the location of the facility; and (g) such other*

2 *information as the applicant may consider relevant or the commis-*

3 *sion may by regulation require.*

4 *2. Each application shall be accompanied by proof of service of:*

5 *(a) a copy of such application on*

6 *i. each municipality in which any portion of such facility is to be*

7 *located and, with the exception of electric and gas transmission*

8 *lines, to each municipality within two miles of such proposed loca-*

9 *tion. Notice to a municipality shall be addressed to the chief execu-*

10 *tive officer thereof, shall specify the date on or about which the*

11 *application is to be filed;*

12 *ii. the commissioner of health, the commissioner of environmental*

13 *conservation, the commissioner of commerce and the director of the*

14 *office of planning coordination;*

15 *iii. in the event such facility or any portion thereof is located*

16 *within its jurisdiction, the Hudson river valley commission;*

17 *iv. in the event such facility or any portion thereof is located*

18 *within its jurisdiction, the St. Lawrence-eastern Ontario commission.*

19 *(b) a notice of such application on persons residing in municipal-*

20 *ities entitled to receive notice under subparagraph i. of paragraph*

21 *a. Such notice shall be given by the publication of a summary of*

22 *the application and the date on or about which it will be filed, in*

23 *daily newspapers which represent at least fifty percent of the daily*

24 *newspaper circulation in such municipalities.*

25 *3. Inadvertent failure of service on any of the municipalities,*

26 *persons, agencies, bodies or commissions named in subdivision two*

27 *shall not be jurisdictional. Such failure may be cured pursuant to*

1 regulations of the commission designed to afford such persons ade-
2 quate notice to enable them to participate effectively in the proceed-
3 ing. In addition, the commission may, after filing require the
4 applicant to serve notice of the application or copies thereof or both
5 upon such other persons and file proof thereof as the commission may
6 deem appropriate.

7   4. An application for an amendment of a certificate shall be in
8 such form and contain such information as the commission shall
9 prescribe. Notice of intent to file such an application shall be given
10 as set forth in subdivision two.

11   § 123. 1. Hearing on application for certificate. Upon the receipt
12 of an application complying with section one hundred twenty-two,
13 the commission shall promptly fix a date for the commencement of
14 a hearing thereon not less than sixty nor more than ninety days after
15 such receipt, which hearing shall be a public hearing. The testimony
16 presented at such hearing may be presented in writing or orally,
17 provided that the commission may make rules designed to exclude
18 repetitive, redundant or irrelevant testimony. The commission may
19 permit the receipt of sworn testimony from a party in writing, pro-
20 vided that such party makes available during the proceeding an
21 individual or individuals who may be orally examined and cross-
22 examined. The commission shall make a record of all testimony in
23 such hearing.

24   2. On an application for an amendment of a certificate, the com-
25 mission shall hold a hearing in the same manner as a hearing is held
26 on an application for a certificate if the change in the facility to be
27 authorized would result in any material increase in any environ-

1 mental impact of the facility or a substantial change in the location
2 of a portion of such facility or in the case of gas or electric trans-
3 mission lines or in the case of other facilities a change in the basic
4 location of any such facility. In all other applications for an amend-
5 ment, the commission may hold such hearing.

6 § 124. Parties to certification proceedings. 1. The parties to the
7 certification proceedings shall include:

8 (a) the applicant

9 (b) the department of health

10 (c) the department of environmental conservation

11 (d) the department of commerce

12 (e) the office of planning coordination

13 (f) where the facility or any portion thereof is to be located within
14 its jurisdiction, the Hudson river valley commission.

15 (g) where the facility or any portion thereof is to be located
16 within its jurisdiction, the St. Lawrence-eastern Ontario commission.

17 (h) a representative of the commission designated by the com-
18 mission to represent the public interest in such proceedings

19 (i) a municipality entitled to receive notice under paragraph a of
20 subdivision two of section one hundred twenty-two, if it has filed
21 with the commission a notice of intent to be a party, within thirty
22 days after the date given in the notice as the date for filing of the
23 application.

24 (j) any individual resident in a municipality entitled to receive
25 notice under paragraph a of subdivision two of section one hundred
26 twenty-two, if he has filed with the commission a notice of intent to
27 be a party, within thirty days after the date given in the published
28 notice as the date for filing of the application.

1   *(k) any domestic nonprofit corporation or association, formed in*

2   *whole or in part to promote conservation or natural beauty, to pro-*

3   *tect the environment, personal health or other biological values, to*

4   *preserve historical sites, to promote consumer interests, to represent*

5   *commercial and industrial groups or to promote the orderly develop-*

6   *ment of the areas in which the facility is to be located, if it has filed*

7   *with the commission a notice of intent to become a party, within*

8   *thirty days after the date given in the published notice as the date*

9   *for filing of the application.*

10   *(l) such other persons or entities as the commission may at any*

11   *time deem appropriate.*

12   *2. Any person may make a limited appearance in the proceeding,*

13   *entitling such person to file a statement in writing by requesting*

14   *such status and by filing a copy of such statement within thirty*

15   *days after the date given in the published notice as the date for*

16   *filing the application. All papers and matters filed by a person*

17   *making a limited appearance shall become part of the record. No*

18   *person making a limited appearance shall be a party or shall have*

19   *the right to present oral testimony or cross-examine witnesses or*

20   *parties.*

21   *3. The commission may for good cause shown permit to become a*

22   *party, a municipality entitled to become a party under subdivision*

23   *one, but which has failed to file a requisite notice of intent within*

24   *the time required.*

25   *§ 125. Conduct of the hearing. A record shall be made of the*

26   *hearing and of all testimony taken and the cross-examinations*

27   *thereon. The rules of evidence applicable to proceedings before a*

1 *court shall not apply. The commission may provide for the consoli-*
2 *dation of the representation of parties, other than governmental*
3 *bodies or agencies, having similar interests.*

4 *§ 126. The decision. 1. Upon the record the commission shall*
5 *render a decision either granting or denying the application or*
6 *granting it upon such terms, conditions, limitations or modifications*
7 *of construction or operation of the facility as the commission may*
8 *deem appropriate. In making such decision, the commission shall*
9 *consider*

10 *(a) whether the effect of the facility on the public and on the*
11 *environment when considered with other environmental conditions,*
12 *man-made or natural, is acceptable, considering the total cost to the*
13 *society as a whole, possible alternative sites within the state or*
14 *alternate methods of power generation, power or gas transmission*
15 *or water or steam supply, as the case may be, and the immediacy*
16 *and totality of the needs of the people of the state for the facility*
17 *proposed. The commission may limit the alternatives to be subject*
18 *to consideration to those which in its judgment are most appropriate.*

19 *(b) whether the proposed site and the facility to be constructed*
20 *conforms to applicable state and local laws and regulations issued*
21 *thereunder, provided that the commission may refuse to apply any*
22 *local ordinance, law, resolution or other action or any regulation*
23 *issued thereunder or any local standard or requirement which would*
24 *be otherwise applicable if it finds that as applied to the proposed*
25 *facility such is unreasonably restrictive in view of the existing*
26 *technology, or of factors of cost or economics, or of the needs of*
27 *consumers whether located inside or outside of such municipality.*

1   *(c) whether the facility will serve the public interest, convenience,*

2 *and necessity, provided, however, that a determination of necessity*

3 *for a major facility made by the power authority of the state of New*

4 *York pursuant to section ten hundred five of the public authorities*

5 *law shall be conclusive on the commission.*

6   *2. A copy of the order and any opinion issued therewith pursuant*

7 *to section one hundred twenty-seven shall be served upon each party.*

8   *§ 127. Opinion to be issued with decision. In rendering a decision*

9 *on an application for a certificate, the commission may issue an*

10 *opinion stating its reasons for the action taken. If the commission*

11 *has found that any local ordinance, law, resolution, regulation, or*

12 *other action issued thereunder or any other local standard or re-*

13 *quirement which would be otherwise applicable is unreasonably*

14 *restrictive pursuant to paragraph b of subdivision one of section*

15 *one hundred twenty-six, it shall state in its opinion the reasons*

16 *therefor.*

17   *§ 128. Judicial review. 1. Any party aggrieved by any order*

18 *issued on an application for a certificate may apply once for a*

19 *rehearing under section twenty-two within thirty days after issuance*

20 *of the order and thereafter obtain judicial review of such order in a*

21 *proceeding as provided in this section. Such proceeding shall be*

22 *brought in the appellate division of the supreme court of the state*

23 *in the judicial department embracing the county wherein the pro-*

24 *posed facility is located, provided that if such facility is located in*

25 *more than one county and such counties are located in more than*

26 *one judicial department, such proceeding may be brought in any one*

27 *but only one of such departments. Such proceeding shall be initiated*

28 *by the filing of a petition in such court within thirty days after the*

1 *issuance of an order by the commission upon the application for*

2 *rehearing, together with proof of service of a demand on the com-*

3 *mission to file with said court a copy of a written transcript of the*

4 *record of the proceeding before it and a copy of its order and*

5 *opinion, if any. The commission's copy of said transcript, order*

6 *and opinion, if any, shall be available at all reasonable times to all*

7 *parties for examination without cost and for the purposes of con-*

8 *sidering possible judicial review of said order. Upon receipt of such*

9 *petition and demand, the commission shall forthwith deliver to the*

10 *court a copy of the record and a copy of its order and opinion, if*

11 *any. Thereupon the court shall have jurisdiction of the proceeding*

12 *and of the questions determined therein, and shall have power to*

13 *grant such relief as it deems just and proper, and to make and enter*

14 *an order enforcing, modifying, and enforcing as so modified, remand-*

15 *ing for further specific evidence or findings or setting aside in whole*

16 *or in part such order. The appeal shall be heard on the record with-*

17 *out requirement of reproduction. The commission may appear in*

18 *court by one of its attorneys. No objection that has not been urged*

19 *by the party before the commission shall be considered by the court,*

20 *unless the failure or neglect to urge such objection shall be excused*

21 *because of extraordinary circumstances. The findings of fact on*

22 *which such order is based shall be conclusive if supported by*

23 *evidence on the record considered as a whole or by information set*

24 *forth in the opinion. The jurisdiction of the appellate division of*

25 *the supreme court shall be exclusive and its judgment and order*

26 *shall be final, subject to review by the court of appeals in the same*

27 *manner and form and with the same effect as provided for appeals*

28 *in a special proceeding. All such proceedings shall be heard and*

1 determined by the appellate division of the supreme court and by

2 the court of appeals as expeditiously as possible and with lawful

3 precedence over other matters.

4 2. The grounds for and the scope of review of the court shall be

5 limited to whether the order of the commission and opinion, if any is

6 (a) in conformity with the constitution and the laws of the state

7 and the United States.

8 (b) supported by evidence in the record or by information

9 properly considered in the opinion.

10 (c) within the commission's statutory jurisdiction or authority.

11 (d) made in accordance with procedures set forth in this article

12 or established by rule or regulation of the commission.

13 (e) arbitrary, capricious or an abuse of discretion.

14 3. Except as herein provided article seventy-eight of the civil

15 practice law and rules shall apply to appeals taken hereunder.

16 § 129. Jurisdiction of courts. Except as expressly set forth in

17 section one hundred twenty-eight and except for review by the court

18 of appeals of a decision of the appellate division of the supreme

19 court as provided for therein, no court of this state shall have jur-

20 isdiction to hear or determine any matter, case or controversy con-

21 cerning any matter which was or could have been determined in a

22 proceeding under this article or to stop or delay the construction or

23 operation of a major facility except to enforce compliance with this

24 article or the terms and conditions of a certificate issued hereunder.

25 § 130. Powers of municipalities and state agencies. Notwith-

26 standing any other provision of law, no state agency, municipality

27 or any agency thereof may require any approval, consent, permit,

28 certificate or other condition for the construction or operation of a

1 *major facility with respect to which an application for a certificate*

2 *hereunder has been issued, other than those provided by otherwise*

3 *applicable state law for the protection of employees engaged in the*

4 *construction and operation of such facility, and provided that in the*

5 *case of a municipality or an agency thereof, such municipality has*

6 *received notice of the filing of the application therefor.*

7 *Neither the Hudson river valley commission nor the St. Lawrence-*

8 *eastern Ontario commission shall hold public hearings for a major*

9 *facility with respect to which an application hereunder has been*

10 *filed, provided that such commission has received notice of the filing*

11 *of such application.*

12 § 3. Paragraphs (a) and (b) of subdivision three of section one

13 thousand two hundred thirty of the public health law are hereby

14 **repealed.**

15 § 4. Section one thousand two hundred thirty of such law is

16 hereby amended, by adding thereto a new subdivision, to be sub-

17 division seven, to read as follows:

18 *7. In the case of a major facility, as defined in section one hun-*

19 *dred twenty of the public service law, for the construction or opera-*

20 *tion of which a certificate is required under article seven of such*

21 *law, an applicant shall apply for and obtain such certificate in lieu*

22 *of a permit under this section. Any reference in this article to a*

23 *permit under this section shall, in the case of such major facility,*

24 *be deemed for all purposes to refer to such certificate.*

25 § 5. Paragraph (j) of subdivision two of section one thousand two

26 hundred seventy-seven of such law is hereby amended to read as

27 follows:

1 (j) Consider for approval plans or specifications for air cleaning
2 installations or any part thereof submitted to him pursuant to the
3 rules of the board, and inspect the installation for compliance with
4 the plans or specifications, *except that in the case of a major facility,*
5 *as defined in section one hundred twenty of the public service law,*
6 *for which a certificate is required pursuant to article seven of such*
7 *law, such functions shall be performed by the public service com-*
8 *mission.*

9 § 6. Section one thousand fourteen of the public authorities law,
10 as amended by chapter two hundred ninety-four of the laws of nine-
11 teen hundred sixty-eight, is hereby amended to read as follows:

12 § 1014. Public service law not applicable to authority; incon-
13 sistent provisions in other acts superseded. The rates, services and
14 practices relating to the generation, transmission, distribution and
15 sale by the authority, of power to be generated from the projects
16 authorized by this title shall not be subject to the provisions of the
17 public service law nor to regulation by, nor the jurisdiction of the
18 department of public service. [The] *Except to the extent article*
19 *seven of the public service law applies to the siting and operation of*
20 *a major facility as defined therein, the* provisions of the public ser-
21 vice law and of the conservation law and every other law relating to
22 the department of public service or the public service commission
23 or to the conservation department or to the functions, powers or
24 duties assigned to the division of water power and control by chapter
25 six hundred nineteen, of the laws of nineteen hundred twenty-six,
26 shall so far as is necessary to make this title effective in accordance
27 with its terms and purposes be deemed to be superseded, and
28 wherever any provision of law shall be found in conflict with the

1 provisions of this title or inconsistent with the purposes thereof, it
2 shall be deemed to be superseded, modified or repealed as the case
3 may require.

4 § 7. Section eighteen hundred seventy of such law, as added by
5 chapter two hundred ninety-four of the laws of nineteen hundred
6 sixty-eight, is hereby amended to read as follows:

7 § 1870. Public service law not applicable to authority. [The]
8 *Except to the extent article seven of the public service law applies*
9 *to the siting and operation of a major facility, the* authority shall
10 not be subject to the provisions of the public service law or to regu-
11 lation by or the jurisdiction of the department of public service or
12 the public service commission by reason of any contract, agreement
13 or arrangement entered into by the authority with any power com-
14 pany, any water distribution company or agency or the power
15 authority of the state of New York, or more than one of the above,
16 or by reason of any action taken thereunder by the authority.

17 § 8. Subdivision three of section four of the condemnation law is
18 hereby amended to read as follows:

19 3. The public use for which the property is required and *either*:
20 *a.* a concise statement of the facts showing the necessity of its
21 acquisition for such use, *or,*

22 *b. if the property is to be used for the construction of a major*
23 *facility as defined in section one hundred twenty of the public*
24 *service law with respect to which a certificate of environmental*
25 *compatibility and public need has been issued under such law, a*
26 *statement that such certificate relating to such property has been*
27 *issued and is in force.*

28 § 9. This act shall take effect July first, nineteen hundred seventy.

Additional Objections to S.9360

Section 121 (4) excludes from the provisions of this legislation those facilities for which authorization has been
sought elsewhere on or before July 1, 1970, or the construction of which has been decided upon by a municipality or
public benefit corporation if bonds or bond anticipation
notes have been sold to finance the project. However, if
the utility company prefers to proceed under the provisions
of this legislation and would otherwise be excluded there-
from, it may pursuant to Sub. 5 simply elect to waive such
exclusion. This would permit Con Ed to secure approval
for the construction of an additional 800 MW facility in
Astoria, Queens whereas the City has already denied such
approval on air pollution grounds. Presumably, other localities in the state will find themselves in the same position.

Section 123 provides for a public hearing on the application
to be held between 60 and 90 days of its submission. At least
twice as much time should be provided for interested parties to
prepare for a public hearing. Also, the place of the hearing is
not designated. The Commission should be required to hold a hearing
in any county in which any portion of the facility is proposed to
be located.

Section 124 enumerates those parties entitled to be heard in the
certification proceeding. Included therein is a Commission

designee who is charged with representing the "public interest.'
Unfortunately, that term is not defined. It is ██ ██ wrong to
cloak a Commission-designee with the authority to represent the
public without providing some guidelines as to concerns that he
is to advance.

The utility companies are will represented in proceedings
before the Commission. They have access to data and expert
witnesses not easily obtainable by those outside of the energy
establishment. Certainly, then, a "public representative"
should be charged with the responsibility to advocate the environmental cause in any given proceeding; just as clearly, such
a representative should not be appointed by, or in any way be
associated with the Commission. If a governmental official is
to participate as a "public defender," it would be preferable
to appoint a member of the Attorney General's office.

Section 125 authorizes the Commission to consolidate the representation of non-governmental parties having similar interests.
While some administrative inconvenience may result from allowing diverse environmental groups to represent themselves before
the Commission, if the power to consolidate such representation
is granted, it must be circumscribed by standards and limitations
which preclude abusive and arbitrary exercise of such power.

The interests of environmental groups, ranging from
consideration of aesthetic beauty to clean air and water, are
as numerous and complex as are the issues raised by the siting
of a power generating plant. Given the expense and difficulty

of administrative litigation in this area, it seems unlikely
that any environmental group would frivously duplicate the
efforts of another. Should such a problem arise, the Commission
is given ample power to deal with it by the exclusion of irrelevant evidence. It is far more important to insure a full and
adequate record and an airing of all relevant issues than it
is to simplify the administrative procedure.

Section 126 (a) authorizes the Commission to limit its consideration of alternatives to a proposed site to those "...
which in its judgment are most appropriate." This is an ar-
rogant and untenable restriction on the power of the judiciary
to review the Commission's findings. It is also in conflict
with the decision of the United States Court of Appeals for
the Second Circuit in Scenic Hudson Preservation Conference v.
FPC, 354 F.2d 668 (1968) where the court held that administrative agencies must "probe all feasible alternatives" before
granting a license for a power plant.

In order to determine whether the administrative ruling is
arbitrary or capricious, the court must have before it the
alternatives to that decision. Limiting the record made in
the administrative hearing - the only record before the court -
to considerations which the Commission deems appropriate will
wholly emasculate the judicial function.

Section 126 (c) provides that a determination of necessity for
a major facility made by PASNY from the requirement of justi-
fying in a public proceeding the need for additional power
facilities in its area of service, and perhaps having to sub-
stantiate its determination before a court in a review proceeding, is wholly unjustified - particularly in view of the
recent expansion of its power to include construction of nuclear and pumped storage facilities. All utilities - public
or private - must be required to subject their expansion plans
to public scrutiny and judicial review.

Section 127 authorizes but does not require the Commission to
issue an opinion stating the reasons for its decision. In the
event that the Commission rejects a local law as unreasonably
restrictive, the Commission - if it chooses to issue an opinion -
must state its reasons therefor. Apparently, the Governor
feels that, where utilities are involved, neither the courts
nor the public are entitled to know the basis for the actions
taken by public regulatory agencies.

Section 128 provides for a form of judicial review. It permits
an aggrieved party to petition the Commission for a rehearing
and thereafter to petition the Appellate Division for a review
of the Commission's final determination. Curiously, the section precludes the court from reaching a finding of fact contrary to that of the Commission if the latter's finding is sup-

ported by either "... evidence on the record considered as a whole or by information set forth in the opinion." (Emphasis added). Thus the Commission may simply include within its opinion statements which have not been subject to challenge or rebuttal during the administrative hearing. These statements would then constitute evidence which the judiciary would be compelled to accept. This is a radical departure from traditional rules concerning administrative decision-making and judicial review thereof. We find nothing in the bill or the Governor's memorandum in support of it which would justify this procedure.

In the final analysis, this legislation effectively excludes the judiciary from reviewing the decisions of the Public Service Commission with respect to the siting of power plants.

Section 129 forecloses all other access to the judiciary by any party, group or governmental agency seeking review of the utility's proposal.

In essence, therefore, this legislative scheme contemplates virtually unassailable administrative authority, confining the judiciary to the narrowest possible role and local government to virtually none. These vast powers should not be lodged in a single governmental body, whether it be the Public Service Commission or any other administrative agency.

Addendum: Governor's 1971 Power Siting Bill (Program Bill #55)

On April 12, 1971, as this document was going to
press, the Governor introduced his 1971 power plant siting
bill in the legislature. The bill, which is substantially
similar to S.9360 discussed above, amends the transmission
facility siting law (Chap. 272, Laws of 1970) to grant
the Public Service Commission the exclusive authority
to determine the need for and location of power plants
in the state and to override any local law or requirement
it finds "unreasonable." Our analysis of and opposition
to the Governor's power plant siting proposal remain
unchanged.

Selected Authorities
Concerning Power and the Environment*

A. Energy Resources and Power Demands

"An Analysis of the Current Energy Problem," remarks made by
John N. Nassikas, Chairman, Federal Power Commission (FPC),
before Electric World Conference for Utility Executives,
Washington, D.C., January 14, 1971.

"Data on Coordinated Regional Bulk Power Supply Programs,: Northeast
Power Coordinating Council," FPC Order 383-2, Docket R-362,
September 1, 1970.

"East Coast Supply and Demand for Low Sulfur Fuel," by William
Kasper, Associate Economist, Office of Economic Research,
New York State Public Service Commission (PSC), April
1, 1971.

Edison Electric Institute, Statistical Year Book of the Electric
Utility Industry for 1969, September 1970.

"Electric Power Environmental Policy Act of 1970," prepared by
the FPC, together with accompanying Environmental Statement
and transmittal letter from John N. Nassikas, Chairman, to
Spiro T. Agnew, President of the United States Senate,
September 30, 1970.

"Energy Resources for Power Production," by M. King Hubbert,
United States Geological Survey, presented at Symposium on
Environmental Aspects of Nuclear Power Stations, sponsored
by the International Atomic Energy Agency (IAEA Symposium),
August 10-14, 1970.

"Environmental Challenge to Natural Gas," remarks made by Lawrence
J. O'Conner, Jr., Commissioner, FPC, before the Midwest Oil
and Gas Industry Symposium, Society of Petroleum Engineers,
Chicago, Illinois, April 1, 1971.

Federal Power Commission 1970 National Power Survey, 3 vols.

Nassikas, John N., Chairman, FPC, Statement presented to the
Committee on Interior and Insular Affairs, United States
Senate, April 29, 1970, set forth in Hearings on S.3354 to
amend the Water Resources Planning Act to provide for a
National Land Use Policy, 91st Congress, 2nd Session, pt. 1.

"New York City's Power Supply," prepared by Development and Resources
Corporation under the direction of David E. Lilienthal,
October, 1969.

*The materials listed in this Appendix are the documents we have
found particularly helpful in preparing this study and should also be
of assistance to the reader. The list does not claim to include all
available material on the subject of electric power and the environment
or every source of information examined in the course of the study.

"An Outline of National Energy Policy: Some Personal Reflections,"
Remarks made by John N. Nassikas, Chairman, FPC, at the
FPC's 50th Anniversary Conference, June 1970.

"Problems of Energy Supply in a Crowded World," remarks made by
Joseph C. Swidler, Chairman, PSC, at the New York City Bar
Association, New York City, October 15, 1970.

"Regulation of the Electric Utilities in the 1970's," remarks
made by John N. Nassikas, Chairman, FPC, before the Thirty-
Eighth Annual Convention of the Edison Electric Institute,
June 1, 1970.

"Report to Governor Nelson A. Rockefeller from the Governor's
Electric Power Committee," December 15, 1967.

"A Review of Consolidated Edison Company 1969 Power Supply Problems
and Ten-Year Expansion Plans," by the Bureau of Power, FPC,
December, 1969.

"Review of Con Ed's Revised Ten-Year Plan," by PSC, Cas. No. 25293,
November 7, 1969.

"Twenty-First Annual Electrical Industry Forecast," by Leonard M.
Olmstead, Electrical World, September 15, 1970.

The User's Guide to the Protection of the Environment, by Paul
Swatek, (New York: A Friends of the Earth/Ballantine Book, 1970).

"Why the U.S. Is In An 'Energy Crisis'," by Lawrence A. Mayer,
Fortune Magazine, November 1970, p. 74.

B. Electric Utilities

1. Regulation

"The City and Electric Power," report prepared by C. Girard Davidson
for the Consumer Council of the City of New York, March 10,1968.

The Economics of Regulation, by Charles F. Phillips, Jr., (Homewood,
Illinois: Richard D. Irwin, Inc., 1969, revised edition).

Free Enterprise and Economic Organization - Regulation of Entry,
Rates and Discrimination, (Vol. II), by Louis B. Schwartz
(New York City: The Foundation Press, Inc., 1966, 3rd edition).

"Interim Report of the State Joint Legislative Committee on Consumer
Protection concerning the Public Service Commission of the
State of New York and the Utilities Regulated by It,"
December 15, 1968.

"Pricing Utility Services in the 1970's," seminar sponsored by
Committee on Public Utility Law, New York State Bar Association,
January, 1971.

Principles of Public Utility Rates, by James C. Bonbright, (New
York: Columbia University Press, 1961).

*Updating Public Utility Regulation: Assuring Fair Rates and Fair
Returns*, by John Bauer, Public Administration Service,
1966.

Utility Regulation: New Directions in Theory and Policy by W. G.
Shepard, T. G. Gies, eds., (New York: Random House, 1966).

2. Industry Problems

"Energy Crisis: Environmental Issue Exacerbates Power Supply
Problem," by Philip M. Buffey, 168 *Science* 1554, February
24, 1970.

Freeman, S. David, Director, Energy Policy Staff, Office of Science
and Technology, Executive Office of the President, Testimony
before the Subcommittee on Antitrust and Monopoly Legislation
of the Senate Committee on the Judiciary, May 5, 1970.

"A Peak Load of Trouble for the Utilities," by Jeremey Main, *Fortune
Magazine*, November 1969, p. 116.

"Power for Tomorrow: The Siting Dilemma," by Charles F. Luce, 25
Record of the Association of the Bar of the City of New York,
No. 1, January, 1970.

"Public Opposition to Nuclear Power--An Industry Overview," presented
by Harry G. Slater, Atomic Industrial Forum, Inc., at the
IAEA Symposium.

"Special Report: Why the Utilities Can't Meet the Demand," *Business
Week*, November, 1969.

"The Task Ahead for the Power Industry of New York," remarks made
by Joseph C. Swidler, Chairman, PSC, at the New York State
Utilities Executives Conference, September 28, 1970.

White, Lee C., Remarks made before the Annual Meeting of the
Missouri Basin Systems Group, Denver, Colorado, February
4, 1970.

C. Environmental Effects of Electric Power

1. General

"Air Pollution and the Regulated Electric Power and Natural Gas
Industries," FPC Staff Report, September, 1968.

"The Economics of Clean Air," report of the Administrator of the
Environmental Protection Agency to the Congress of the United
States, 92nd Congress, 1st Session (Doc. No. 92-6) (March, 1971).

"Electric Power--Impact on the Environment," remarks made by John
J. Duran, Jr., Director of the Utilities Divison, California
Public Utilities Commission, presented before the American
Power Conference, April 23, 1970.

"Environmental Aspects of Power Plants," by Neimeyer, L.E.,
    McCormick, R. A., and Ludwig, J.H., National Air Pollution
    Control Administration, presented at IAEA Symposium.

"Environmental Cost of Electric Power," by Dean E. Abrahamson,
    Scientists Institute for Public Information, 1970.

"Environmental Effects of Producing Electric Power," Hearings
    before the Joint Committee on Atomic Energy, Congress of
    the United States, 91st Congress, 1st Session and 2nd Session,"
    parts 1 (October-November, 1969) and 2 (January-February,
    1970).

"Environmental Effects of Producing Electric Power," selected
    materials prepared for the use of the Joint Committee on
    Atomic Energy, Congress of the United States, August, 1969.

"Environmental Quality: The First Annual Report of the Council on
    Environmental Quality," August 1970.

"Federal Power Commission Interests in Environmental Concerns
    Affecting the Electric Power and Natural Gas Industries,"
    FPC, 1969.

Man's Impact on the Global Environment: Assessment and Recommend-
    ations for Action, report of the Study of Critical Environ-
    mental Problems, Sponsored by the Massachusetts Institute
    of Technology (Cambridge, Mass.: MIT Press, 1970).

"New Ways to More Power with Less Pollution," by Lawrence Lessing,
    Fortune Magazine, November 1970, p. 78.

2. Thermal Pollution

"Fish and Power Plants," by Albert C. Jensen, The Conservationist,
    December-January, 1969.

"Handling Hot Water, with a Payoff," by Roland Stewart, S.P.
    Mathur, The Conservationist, December-January 1970-71.

"Heat--A Growing Water Pollution Problem," by Sandra C. Bloom,
    Monograph No. 4, Environment Reporter, May 1, 1970.

"A New River," Environment Staff Report, 12 Environment No. 1, p.
    36, January-February, 1970.

"Problems and Opportunities in Waste Heat Disposal," remarks of
    Joseph C. Swidler, Chairman, PSC, before Conference on
    Beneficial Uses of Thermal Discharges, Albany, New York,
    September 18, 1970.

"Problems in Disposal of Waste Heat from Steam-Electric Plants,"
    by the Bureau of Power, FPC, 1969.

"Thermal Effects and Nuclear Power Stations in the USA.," by
    R. E. Nakatani of Batelle Memorial Institute and D. Miller
    and J. V. Tokar of Argonne National Laboratory, presented
    at IAEA Symposium.

"Thermal Effects Studies in New York State," by Thomas W. Philbin,
    the S.M. Stoller Corporation, and Howard D. Philip, Niagara
    Mohawk Power Corporation, presented at IAEA Symposium.

"Thermal Pollution in the Marine Environment," by Albert C. Jensen,
    The Conservationist, October-November, 1970.

"A Thermal Profile of the Waters of New York State," report of
    the New York State Atomic and Space Development Authority,
    September, 1970.

3. Nuclear Facilities

    a. General

"AEC Authorizing Legislation Fiscal Year 1972," Hearings before
    the Joint Committee on Atomic Energy, Congress of the
    United States, 92d Cong., 1st Sess. (March, 1971).

"AEC Authorizing Legislation Fiscal Year 1971," Hearings before
    the Joint Committee on Atomic Energy, Congress of the
    United States, 91st Cong., 2d. Sess., Pt. 3 (Civilian Pow-
    er Reactors) (March 11, 1970).

"Atomic Energy Legislation Through 91st Congress., 1st Sess.,"
    prepared for the Use of the Joint Congressional Committee
    on Atomic Energy (December, 1969).

"A Citizen's Guide to Nuclear Power," Ralph E. Lapp, (The New
    Republic, Washington, D.C., 1971).

"The Hazardous Industrial Atom," Inglis, David, Bull. of the
    Atomic Scientists, p. 50 (February, 1970).

Hearings before the Joint Committee on Atomic Energy, Congress
    of the United States, 91st Cong., 2d Sess., on Physical Re-
    search, Biology and Medicine, and Plowshare, part 2
    (March, 1970).

"An Investigation of Airborne Radioactive Effluent from an Oper-
    ating Nuclear Fuel Reprocessing Plant," U.S. Department
    of Health, Education and Welfare (Doc. No. BRH/NERHL 70-3).

"Licensing and Regulation of Nuclear Reactors," hearings before
    the Joint Committee on Atomic Energy, Congress of the
    United States, 90th Cong., 1st Sess., parts 1 (April-May,
    1967) and 2 (September, 1967).

Northern States Power Company v. The State of Minnesota, et. al.
    2 Environment Reporter - Cases 1101 (U.S.D.C. Minn. 1970).

Nuclear Power and Public Concern, compiled and edited by Mary P.
    Sinclair (Midland, Michigan, 1971).

Perils of the Peaceful Atom, Richard Curtis and Elizabeth Hogan
    (Ballantine Books, New York 1969).

"Radiation: The Invisible Casualties,"Gofman, John W. and Tamplin,
    Arthur, R., 12 Environment No. 3, p. 12 (April, 1970).

"Radioactive Wastes," Charles H. Fox (United States Atomic Energy
    Commission, Division of Technical Information, 1969).

"Radioactive Wastes from Reactors," Joel A. Snow, Scientist and
    Citizen (Scientists' Institute for Public Information, May
    1967).

"Review of U.S. Power Reactor Operating Experience,"by Professor
    Merril Eisenbud, presented at IAEA Symposium.

"Should We Back, or Sack, the Breeder?" remarks of United States
    Senator Mike Gravel, Alaska, to the National Newspaper As-
    sociation (March 25, 1971).

"Status of Investigations of Salt Formations for Disposal of Highly
    Radioactive Power-Reactor Wastes,"W. C. McClain and R.C.
    Bradshaw, Nuclear Safety, Vol. 11, No. 2 (Mar.-Apr. 1970).

"Status of Solidification and Disposal of Highly Radioactive
    Liquid Wastes from Nuclear Power in the U.S.A.," Schneider,
    Bradshaw, et. al., presented at IAEA Symposium.

The Careless Atom, Sheldon Novick, (Houghton-Mifflin, Boston
    1969).

"Underground Uses of Nuclear Energy," Hearings before the Sub-
    committee on Air and Water Pollution of the Commiteee on
    Public Works, U.S. Senate, 91st Cong., 1st Sess., on
    S. 3042 (November, 1969, August 5, 1970).

"U.S. Regulations for the Control of Releases of Radicactivity
    to the Environment in Effluents from Nuclear Facilities,"by
    Lester Rogers and Carl C. Gamertsfeldar, Division of Radia-
    tion Protection Standards, Atomic Energy Commission, pre-
    sented at IAEA Symposium.

"What We Do Know About Low-Level Radiation," Lauriston S. Taylor,
    President, National Council on Radiation Protection and
    Measurements, (1970).

b. New York State

"Agreement between the State of New York and the United States
    Atomic Energy Commission,"dated October 15, 1962.

Governor Nelson A. Rockefeller's"1959 Special Message to the
    Legislature Initiating the New York State Atomic Energy
    Program."

Governor Nelson A. Rockefeller's "1962 Special Message to the
     Legislature Recommending the Creation of the New York
     State Atomic Research and Development Authority."

Governor Nelson A. Rockefeller's "1968 Special Message to the
     Legislature on Electric Power."

"Life with the Atom in New York State," New York State Depart-
     ment of Commerce, (1968).

"Memorandum of Understanding between the State of New York and
     the United States Atomic Energy Commission," dated May 7,
     1965.

"Nuclear Power Siting Program: Phase I State-wide Survey," New
     York State Atomic and Space Development Authority (April,
     1971).

"Power - A Program Paper," by Governor Nelson A. Rockefeller
     (October 24, 1970).

"Seventh Annual Report," (April 1, 1968 through March 31, 1969),
     and "Eighth Annual Report" (April 1, 1969 through March 31,
     1970), New York Atomic and Space Development Authority.

D. Energy Policy and Siting Issues

"Considerations Affecting Power Plant Site Selection," a report
     sponsored by the Energy Policy Staff, Office of Science and
     Technology of the Executive Office of the President (Jan-
     uary, 1969).

Consolidated Edison Co. of New York, Inc., Project No. 2338,
     FPC Opinion No. 584, August 19, 1970.

"Delays and Bottlenecks in the Licensing Process Affecting Utili-
     ties," James T. Ramey, James P. Murray, Jr., New York Law
     Journal, September 24, 1970.

Department of Water and Power of the City of Los Angeles v.
     Hearing Board of the Air Pollution Control District of
     the County of Los Angeles," 1 Environment Reporter - Cases
     1580 (Cal. Sup. Ct., Sept. 18, 1970).

"Ecological Considerations in Reactor Power Plant Siting," by
     S.I. Auerbach, D. J. Nelson, S. V. Kaye, D. E. Reichle,
     and C. C. Coutant, Ecological Sciences Division, Oak Ridge
     National Laboratory, presented at IAEA Symposium.

"The Economy; Energy and the Environment," A Background Study
     prepared for the Joint Economic Committee, Congress of
     the United States, by the Environmental Policy Division,
     Legislative Reference Service, Library of Congress,

September 1, 1970.

"Electric Power and the Environment," a report sponsored by the
Energy Policy Staff, Office of Science and Technology,
Executive Office of the President (August, 1970).

"Environmental Considerations in the Regulatory Process for
Plants in the U.S. - The Role of the Public and Public Under-
standing," by James T. Ramey, Commissioner, Atomic Energy
Commission, presented at IAEA Symposium.

"Final Report," Temporary New York State Commission on the Environmental Impact of Major Public Utility Facilities
(March 31, 1971).

"Implementation of the National Environmental Policy Act,"
Hearings before the Subcommittee on Fisheries and Wildlife
Conservation of the Committee on Merchant Marine and
Fisheries, U.S. House of Representatives 91st Cong., 1st
Sess. (December 1970).

"Intergovernmental Coordination of Power Development and Environmental Protection Act (S. 2752)," Hearings before the Subcommittee on Intergovernmental Relations of the Committee on
Government Operations, U.S. Senate, 91st Cong. 2d Sess. (1970).

"Metropolitan Siting of Nuclear Power Plants," by Louis H. Roddis,
Jr., President, Consolidated Edison Company of New York,
Inc., presented at the IAEA Symposium.

"National Fuels and Energy Policy (S. Res. 45)," Hearings before
the Committee on Interior and Insular Affairs, U.S. Senate,
92nd Cong., 1st Sess.(February 25, 1971)

"Nuclear Energy and the Malthusian Dilemma," David Inglis, Bull.
of Atomic Scientists (February, 1971).

"Policy Alternatives for Resolving the Power Plant Siting Problem,"
presented by S. David Freeman, Director, Energy Policy Staff
and J. Frederick Weinhold, Technical Assistant, Office of
Science and Technology, Executive Office of the President,
at IAEA Symposium.

Scenic Hudson Preservation Conf. et. al. v. FPC, 354 F. 2d 608
(2d Cir. 1965), cert. denied 384 U.S. 941 (1966).

"Siting Thermal Power Plants in California," a report prepared
by the Resources Agency for Joint Committee on Atomic
Development and Space, California Legislature (February
15, 1970).

"The Total Environment Concept: Balancing Competing Public Inter-
ests," remarks of Charles F. Luce, Chairman, Consolidated
Edison Company of New York, Inc. before FPC 50th Anniversary
Ceremony (June 3, 1970).